AN INTRODUCTION TO COMPUTER STUDIES

AN INTRODUCTION TO COMPUTER STUDIES

P. CRADDOCK and A. R. HASKINS
Birmingham Educational Computing Centre

Wheaton
A Division of Pergamon Press

A. Wheaton & Company Limited
A Division of Pergamon Press
Hennock Road, Exeter EX2 8RP

Pergamon Press Ltd
Headington Hill Hall, Oxford OX3 0BW

Pergamon Press Inc.
Maxwell House, Fairview Park, Elmsford, New York 10523

Pergamon Press Canada Ltd
Suite 104, 150 Consumers Road, Willowdale, Ontario M2J 1P9

Pergamon Press (Australia) Pty Ltd
P.O. Box 544, Potts Point, N.S.W. 2011

Pergamon Press GmbH
Hammerweg 6, D-6242 Kronberg, Federal Republic of Germany

First published 1982

Reprinted 1982

Printed in Great Britain by A. Wheaton & Co. Ltd, Exeter

ISBN 0 08–025002–5

Contents

Acknowledgements

Thanks are due to the following for permission to reproduce photographs:

Birmingham Post Studios (pp. 69, 77, 78, 79, 80)
John Blomfield and Associates (pp. 2, 3, 5, 6, 14)
British Telecom (p. 52)
Computer & Data Machines Ltd (pp. 70, 147)
Crown Copyright. Science Museum, London (pp. 10, 11, 12, 85, 86, 87, 125)
Historical Service Division Dept of the Army Office of the Chief of Military History, Washington D.C. (p. 124)
Honeywell Information Systems Ltd (p. 74)
Hoover Ltd (p. 98)
IBM United Kingdom Ltd (pp. 46, 47, 49, 50, 77, 111, 126, 140)
International Business Machines Corporation, U.S.A. (p. 57)
Lloyds Bank Ltd (p. 47)
Midwest Scientific Instruments (p. 148)
National Physical Laboratory (Crown Copyright) (p. 7) lent to Science Museum, London (p. 125)
Science Museum, London (pp. 32, 35, 36, 37, 82, 84, 85, 88, 124)
Geoffrey Sturdy Photography (pp. 40, 42, 50, 70, 72, 76, 117)
Tesco Stores Ltd (pp. 71, 139)
Peter Waugh (p. 42)

Thanks are also due to the University of Exeter for allowing us to take photographs:
the Computer Unit (pp. 142, 143, 144); the Department of Mathematical Statistics and Operational Research (front cover). Taken by Focus Photography, Exeter.

The authors would like to acknowledge the help and advice given by:

Birmingham Post and Mail
City Treasurer's Department, Birmingham
ICL Publicity Department
Lloyds Bank Ltd, Lichfield
Norman Longworth, Schools and Colleges Liaison Officer, IBM
Tesco Stores Ltd, Wellingborough

Computers boost Braille

Car computer puts you streets ahead

Shopgirls to have computers

By KEN WELSBY

COMPUTERS will take over from tills in many High Street stores, a supermarket boss forecast today.

The super-swift super-market could be appearing in Birmingham shopping centres within two years says Tesco chairman, Mr. Martin Porter.

A big new store at Wellingborough, is being used for trials — to find out how much efficiency is improved and what the customers think.

Tesco is also proposing to abolish price tickets on goods.

Goods will have a code put on when they are packed — and the price label will appear only on the shelves.

Check-out girls will key the code direct into a mini-computer.

A £6 million contract has been placed with IBM for a new generation of computers.

Computer eye on water

Computer will watch civic power bills

Town Hall takeover— by computer

1 Introduction

Fact and fiction

Computers play an important part in our everyday lives, as can be seen from the newspaper headlines shown here, yet very few people understand them. In this book we intend to open up this mysterious box of secrets.

Here are some of the questions we have been asked by students starting out on a study of computers.

1. How does a computer work?
2. How is information stored?
3. How do you get information into it?
4. How do you get information out of it?
5. How do I make it work for me?
6. What do people do with computers?
7. How do computers affect my life?
8. Where did computers come from and what did we do before we had them?

This book attempts to answer these and other questions.

For many years computers have been portrayed in comics, in films and on television as superhuman machines, capable of retaining vast amounts of information, and possessing incredible intelligence. The fictional computer can often speak and indeed hold a normal conversation; it can communicate with other computers over huge distances. In appearance it is very impressive, with numerous banks of flashing lights and switches. Let us look at each of these ideas in turn and see which are fact, fantasy or a possibility for the future.

Vast storage

In the past storage of data was both expensive and space consuming, so stores inside computers were limited. Extra storage, where necessary, was provided by separate backing stores. Recently, however, new means of storage have been developed which are much smaller, cheaper and capable of supplying information far more quickly.

Intelligence

Computers are machines; the only 'thinking' power they possess is that which humans give them. Some computer systems have been developed which *appear* to have intelligence, but they can do only what they have been instructed to do. Computers may be used to play chess and other complex games, but they do this by following plans and rules previously thought out by man. There is much research into machine (or artificial) intelligence but we are far from real success.

Speech

Finding ways of telling computers what to do and of receiving replies from them has been a big problem for computer scientists. Computer systems are available today which can understand human speech and reply, but they can usually deal only with single words or short sentences. However, this is one area in which development can be expected.

Long-distance communication

For some years computers have been connected via telephone and telegraph lines. Airline offices scattered throughout the world are linked together to provide world-wide flight information at any centre. Communications satellites are also used to link computers using radio waves, and in flights to deep space, on-board computers transmit to earth stations. Communication between computer systems over great distances is already a reality.

Appearance

Most modern computer systems are very dull to look at, despite the fact that manufacturers give their colour schemes exciting names like 'hot tango'. Only a very few switches and flashing lights are to be seen. Advances in technology mean that components can be made in much smaller sizes, so that the trend is for new computers to be much smaller than their predecessors.

2 A User's Viewpoint

Computers were first designed for solving complex mathematical and scientific problems, as we shall later discover. However, it is very difficult to find any part of our lives that is not affected by computers today. Look at the photographs below. There seems, at first glance, to be no connection between them.

Above Seating at Villa Park football ground
Top right A doctor's surgery
Lower right The Penta Hotel, London

It is highly unlikely that you would find a computer expert in the back four of the Aston Villa team, attending to guests at the Penta Hotel or listening sympathetically to patients in a doctor's surgery.

Yet all these establishments may use computers. The computer is now an everyday tool to help lots of people do their jobs more quickly and efficiently.

Let us examine the use of the computer in these three places in more detail. In each case, ordinary employees (not computer experts) use the computer to do routine jobs. These systems are designed so that people can operate them with very little training.

Clerk in the booking-office at Villa Park

Receptionist at the Penta Hotel

Ticket booking at Villa Park

Organizing the booking for season or match tickets at a large football club can be a very complicated business. Such questions as: 'How many seats are available?' 'Where are these seats?' 'How many seats have been sold?' and 'How much money has been paid in?' could involve a lot of people in a lot of work.

As soon as someone telephones or visits the booking office to book a seat, such information must be readily available. Then, as soon as the ticket has been sold, all the records need to be updated. The same seat must not be sold twice, but returned tickets should be made immediately available for resale.

The clerk in the office can easily do all these jobs very quickly and have all his paper work complete – if he uses a computer. To gain an understanding of the system let us see what happens when a customer calls.

The clerk is using the machine shown below, called a visual display unit (VDU). **He can obtain a variety of information by typing in a code on the keyboard. He can, for example, get a list of all the league matches to be played during the season.**

The fixture list on the screen of the visual display unit

Suppose our customer wants to buy a season ticket. He must first decide in what section of the ground he wants to sit. The clerk can then get a display of the seats in that block of the ground. The letter 'A' indicates that a seat is available.

The clerk enters the number of the seat chosen and presses the key marked SELL. Immediately that seat will be shown as no longer available.

There are a number of other operations that the clerk can ask the computer to do. The computer will record the sale, reservation or the alteration of a ticket. The clerk does this by pressing a key marked with one of the words SELL, RESERVE or RETURN (he does not have to type in the whole word). Thus the entry of instructions is made easier by the design of the keyboard.

When the customer is satisfied with his booking the ACTION key will cause the tickets for the season to be printed. The printer is a separate machine: you can see it above with a season ticket which the clerk has placed in a wallet.

Also available on the VDU are lists of cup and friendly matches, details of which may be obtained immediately when the clerk types in the correct instruction.

In the pre-season period the computer system is used for the provision of season tickets, and once the season has started tickets can be sold for individual matches held within the following fortnight.

There is no longer a need to spend a lot of time getting the paper work up to date, working out the day's takings or updating the records of seats sold. The computer automatically keeps all the records required.

The most impressive thing from the point of view of the user is that all this can be achieved by very simple entries made on the keyboard.

Left Screen showing the seats available in the area chosen by the customer

Right The ticket printer

Below Season ticket

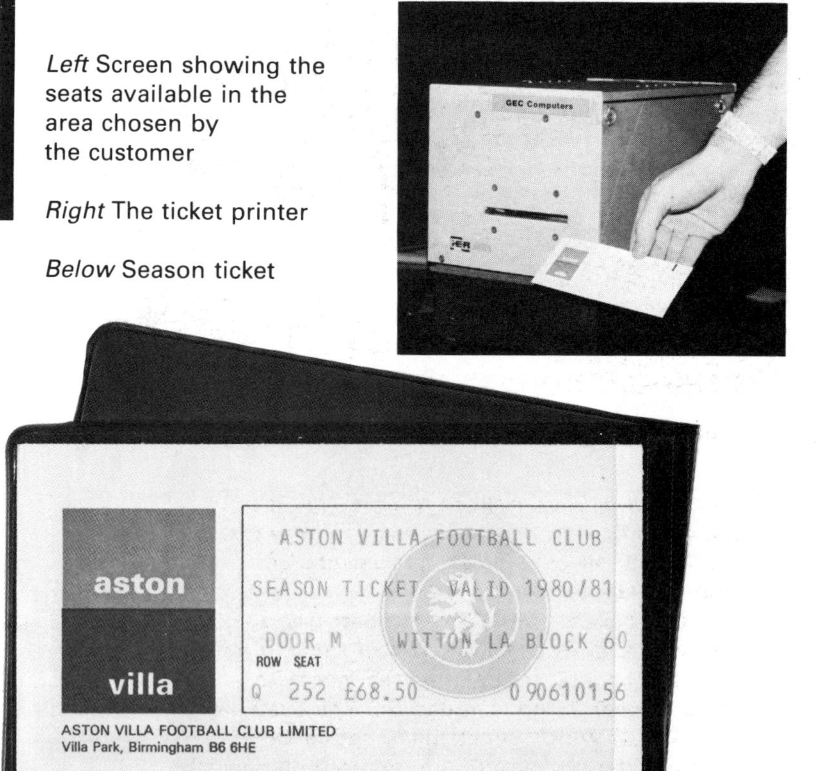

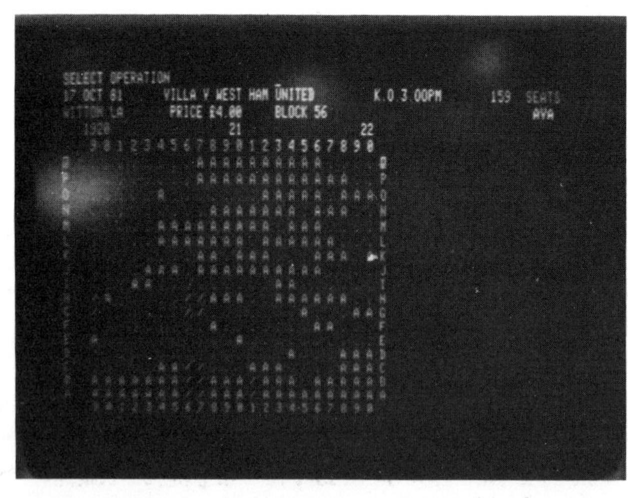

Accounts at the London Penta Hotel

Part of the work at this hotel is similar to that at Villa Park because the computer is used for room bookings. Again by using a visual display unit the receptionist can very simply 'key in' information about a new guest and the computer will immediately find and allocate an available room.

However, this computer system is more complex and is designed to perform several other tasks. Residents at the hotel have the use of bars and restaurants, and in their rooms there are telephones and automatic drinks dispensers. All these facilities need to be accounted for, and guests' bills must be amended with the cost of these services as they are used.

'Bell Captain' automatic drinks dispenser

A few years ago a number of clerks would have spent a great deal of time calculating and preparing accounts. Now all the bills are produced automatically by computer.

Telephone calls are monitored separately and the exact cost is added to the bill held in the computer. Similarly the cost of drinks obtained from the dispenser in each room is added on. The costs of drinks or meals which guests have had in the various bars and restaurants are entered on special point-of-sale terminals. These terminals are linked to the computer so that these charges too may be accounted for.

Terminals

You may be wondering at this stage what is meant by a terminal. The word terminus comes from the Latin word for a boundary. (A bus terminus is at the end, or boundary, of a journey.) A computer terminal is a device found at the end, or boundary, of a computer system. The VDU, the printer, the drinks machines and point-of-sale terminals are not themselves computers. They are parts of a computer system, terminals connected to a central unit which may be in another room or even in another building.

Point-of-sale terminals like this are situated in the bars and restaurants of the hotel

So far we have examined two computer applications where clerks or receptionists have entered details into a computer using a visual display unit (sometimes called a visual display terminal), and have obtained information back from the computer on the same device. The VDU is therefore both an input and an output device.

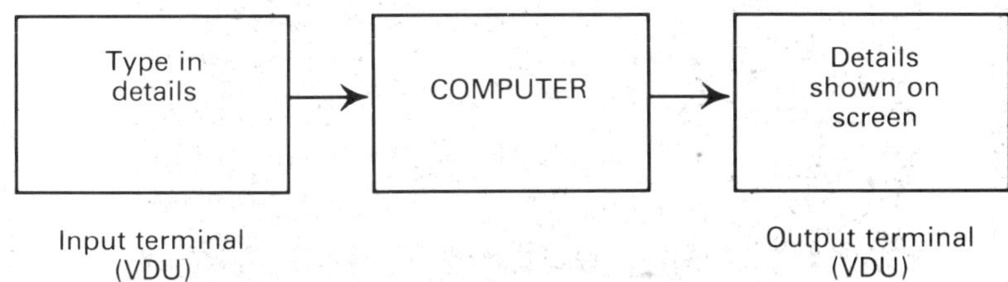

Another word for boundary is 'periphery'. These machines which are connected to the central computer are also called peripherals.

The reception desk

Output devices

Both Aston Villa Football Club and the Penta Hotel make use of other peripherals. They need to print out things for their customers. What was the output peripheral used at Villa Park?

Bills for guests at the Penta Hotel are produced on a printing terminal. You can see in the photograph two terminals used by the receptionist. The printer is in the foreground.

A copy of a bill produced on the printer is shown below. Notice the items we have mentioned.

1. **Automatic telephone charges £0.07, £0.14, £8.61, £0.07, £0.07 and £0.07.**
2. **Bell Captain drinks dispenser charge £3.06**
3. **Beefeater Restaurant charge £8.25**
4. **Apartment charge £19.98**

London
Penta Hotel

Cromwell Road London SW7 4ON
Telephone 01 370 5757 Telex 919663
Cables Pentotel London SW7

Operated by Grand Metropolitan Hotels

STEUER;MS.A

UNITED STATES OF AMERICA

ROOM 1715
CONTINENTAL BREAKFAST (IN ROOM)
PAYMENT - CASH
ARRIVAL DATE - 01/08/81
DEPARTURE DATE - 04/08/81

02/08/81 15:55

TIME	DATE AND DETAILS	VAT %	CHARGES	CREDITS	BALANCE
16.46	01 AUG PAYMENT ON ACCOUNT			20.00	20.00CR
17.06	TELEPHONES - AUTO 51168	8.0	0.07		19.93CR
17.28	TELEPHONES - AUTO 61179	8.0	0.14		19.79CR
20.15	TELEPHONES - AUTO 73464	8.0	8.61		11.18CR
00.27	BEEFEATER REST. DINNER FOOD	8.0	8.25		2.93CR
00.50	APARTMENTS-AUTO	8.0	19.98		17.05
01.05	BELL CAPTAIN - AUTO	8.0	3.06		20.11
11.33	02 AUG TELEPHONES - AUTO 63111	8.0	0.07		20.18
12.13	TELEPHONES - AUTO 61168	8.0	0.07		20.25
12.16	TELEPHONES - AUTO 24140	8.0	0.07		20.32
	AMOUNT TO BE SETTLED BY GUEST £20.32				

Printers are only used for outputting information and are called output devices.

Why is it necessary to use both the VDU and the printer for output?

The VDU shows material on its screen, but it does not give a permanent record which a customer could take away. Only a printer can give a hard copy **(printed on paper).**

There is a peripheral that has a keyboard for input and a printer for output. Such a device is called a teletypewriter **and on it a copy of all the input and output is typed on a continuous roll of paper. However, it is not suitable for all needs: hard copy is not necessary for every operation.**

Teletypewriter

If all the transactions at Villa Park and the Penta Hotel had to be typed out then it would cost a great deal of money for all the paper. More important, a VDU can output information much faster than a teletypewriter. The image on the screen is available almost immediately.

The doctor's surgery

Let us look now at our third example, in the area of medicine. Normally when you visit your doctor it is because you are feeling unwell. If the doctor is to help you he needs some information from you first. What sort of questions is he likely to ask you?

You may be able to tell him how you feel, but the cause of your symptoms may well depend on other facts like your age, sex or previous illness.

Obviously the doctor has to spend a lot of his time making notes on what you say. It is with the aid of these notes that he may be able to discover what is wrong with you. In a very few surgeries, to save time and to provide the doctor with important facts about you, his patient, you may be asked to use a computer.

The terminal shown below is part of a system called 'Mickie'. Instead of idling away your time in the waiting-room reading out-of-date magazines, you can provide the information the doctor wants by answering questions that are given to you on the VDU.

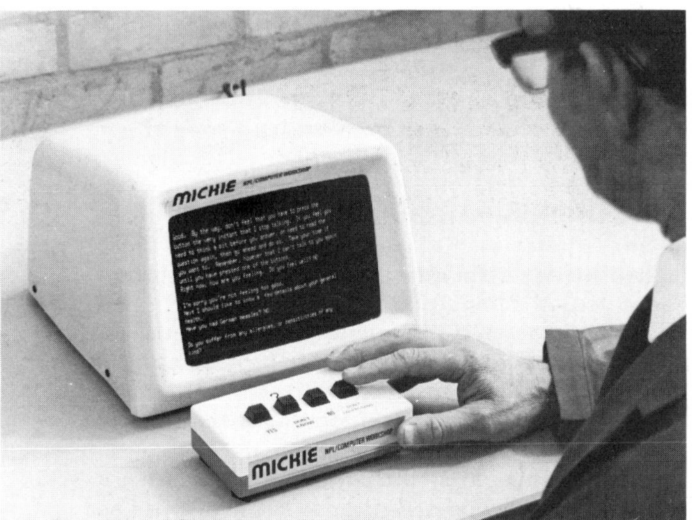

'Mickie' VDU

It is very important that this computer system is easy to use. Many patients have never even seen a computer system before. Therefore the questions have to be very simple (not many patients will be

able to use a keyboard to type in long replies). The responses to the questions will be 'yes', 'no' or 'don't know'. Instead of typing these answers in, all the patient has to do is to press a button marked with one of the three statements.

Here are some of the questions which are asked.

Are you male?	**YES**
Are you younger than 25?	**NO**
Are you younger than 35?	**YES**
Do you feel unwell?	**YES**
Do you smoke?	**NO**
Do you cough a lot?	**NO**
Have you any allergies?	**NO**
Have you had jaundice?	**NO**
Have you had German Measles?	**YES**
Do you suffer from any heart disease?	**YES**
Have you had a blood test recently?	**YES**
Have you had any headaches in the last week?	**NO**
Has your hearing deteriorated lately?	**NO**
Have you had a sore throat recently?	**NO**
Are there any other symptoms that I have not asked you about?	**YES**

When you have answered the questions, the VDU instructs you to report to the nurse or doctor. At this stage the nurse may obtain a hard copy of your responses to give to the doctor.

This simple system provides the information the doctor requires so that when you go and see him he has already been informed of some basic facts about you. It is important to realize that the computer is not a replacement for the doctor's interview with you. It is to provide both you and him with a better service.

We have seen that certain terminals (the VDU, the printers and point-of-sale terminals) enable ordinary people to use the computer without knowing how it works. But these are only input and output devices. Clearly, before information can be printed out – whether it is your medical history or the number of seats in a football ground – it must have been *stored* somehow in the computer.

So this adds another requirement necessary to operate the kind of system that we have just examined. The complete list is thus as follows:

1. **The system must be easy to use.**
2. **Information must be made quickly available on the VDU screen.**
3. **Hard copy must be available for certain purposes.**
4. **An input device is needed to allow existing information to be updated.**
5. **Somehow the information gained must be stored.**

Typical printout from the 'Mickie' system

```
                MEDICAL SUMMARY
                ---------------

SERIES 3

MALE
LESS THAN 35
        FEELS UNWELL
GENERAL MEDICAL HISTORY
        NO ALLERGIES
        NO JAUNDICE
        RUBELLA
        HEART DISEASE
        BLOOD TEST
PRESENT CONDITION
        NON-SMOKER
        NO COUGHING
        NO HEADACHES
        HEARING NORMAL
        NO SORE THROAT
MORE SYMPTOMS TO BE INVESTIGATED
```

Questions

1. Which is more correct?
   A VDU is
   (a) an input device,
   (b) an output device,
   (c) an input and output device.
2. Which is more correct?
   A printer is
   (a) an input device,
   (b) an output device,
   (c) an input and output device.
3. Villa Park uses two VDUs and two printers. The Penta Hotel uses 31 terminals in all. Why do you think the hotel requires more terminals?
4. Why is it necessary to make computerized booking systems easy to use?
5. Explain why VDUs are the main peripherals used in booking systems.
6. Why are separate bills for telephone usage, dispensed drinks and meals not given to guests at the hotel?
7. The output on a VDU can be described as immediate and 'clean' – what do you think is meant by 'clean'?
8. The 'Mickie' system may be used in surgeries because
   (a) it provides a copy of important information for a busy doctor,
   (b) the patients are made to feel important,
   (c) the patients like using the system,
   (d) the doctor can get more information from the computer than he can from the patients.
9. The 'Mickie' system must be easy to use because
   (a) doctors may know little about computers,
   (b) patients may know little about computers,
   (c) the surgery can't afford to pay a computer expert,
   (d) the questions asked by the system are simple.
10. What are the advantages for
   (a) the doctor
   (b) the patient
   in using the 'Mickie' system?

Vocabulary

hard copy
input device
output device
peripheral
point-of-sale terminal
teletypewriter
terminal
visual display unit (VDU)

3 Early History

Computers carry out two tasks that man has done for many thousands of years: the storage and handling of information. In early civilizations men learned to count on their fingers or use small stones for the same purpose. (The word calculate comes from the Latin word *calculus*, which means a small stone.)

The earliest records kept by man were in the form of pictures. Events like tribal clashes were depicted in cave drawings which may still be seen today.

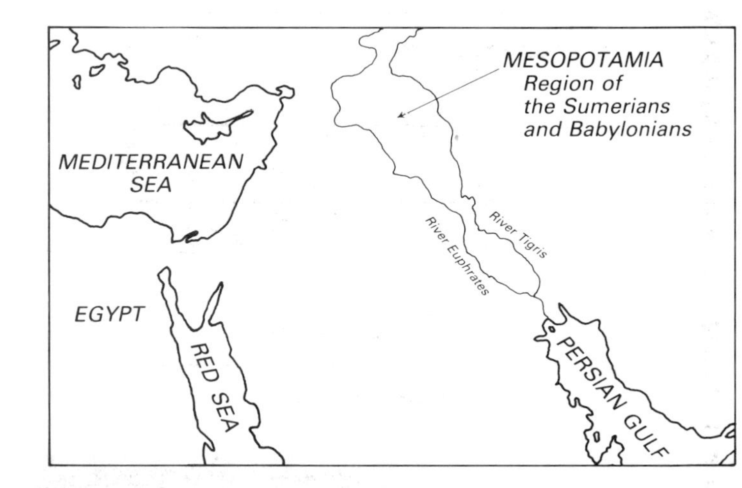

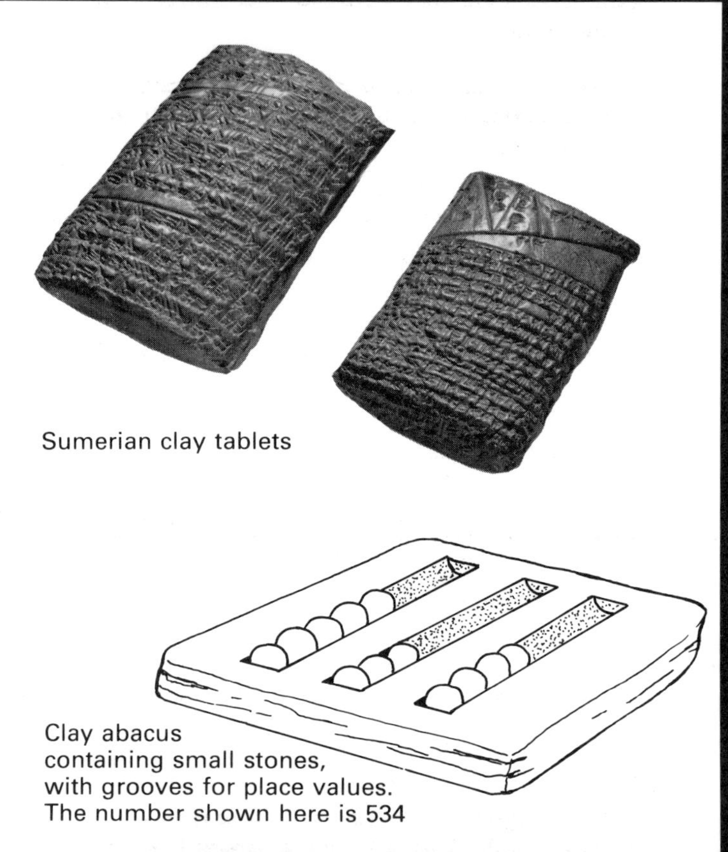

Sumerian clay tablets

Clay abacus
containing small stones,
with grooves for place values.
The number shown here is 534

Some of the clearest evidence of early records being kept in ancient Mesopotamia is the half-million clay tablets which have been unearthed in what is now Iraq.

These tablets date from as early as 2100 BC and as late as AD 300. Many of them contain information in the form of mathematical tables, while others show business records, accounts, bills and other documents. Exactly the same kind of information is often stored in our modern computers. The Sumerians and later the Babylonians who lived in Mesopotamia are also known to have used a simple form of abacus, made from clay.

An abacus is an aid to calculation that makes use of either stones or beads to represent numbers.

Egypt was another civilization that kept vast records. The Egyptians wrote on papyrus, a form of paper made from reeds growing on the banks of the Nile. The earliest papyrus found dates from

2000 BC and contains largely mathematical information. The best example of business records is to be found on the Harris papyrus, dating from 1167 BC. It contains accounts of the temple wealth of Pharaoh Rameses IV.

Early civilizations also used parchment (animal skin) to write on, but because this was so expensive it was used only for more important documents.

Early number systems made calculations very cumbersome, as the illustrations below show.

1	2	3	4	5	6	7	8	9	10	60	100

Babylonian numerals

I	II	III	IIII	III II	III III	IIII III	IIII IIII	III III III	∩	
1	2	3	4	5	6	7	8	9	10	100

Egyptian numerals

•	••	•••	••••	—	• —	•• —	••• —	•••• —	=		
1	2	3	4	5	6	7	8	9	10	20	100

Mayan numerals

I	II	III	IV	V	VI	VII	VIII	IX	X	L	C	D	M
1	2	3	4	5	6	7	8	9	10	50	100	500	1000

Roman numerals

Try doing some calculations using Roman numerals only. You will soon discover how cumbersome this can be.

The abacus was developed by many civilizations to make calculations easier, and to suit the various number systems. Among the countries that used the abacus were Russia, Japan, China, Greece and Rome.

The Aztecs, a tribe of Central American Indians, used rods stuck into a block of wood, on to which beads were threaded. In Russia, Japan and China the beads were threaded on to wires held in a wooden frame.

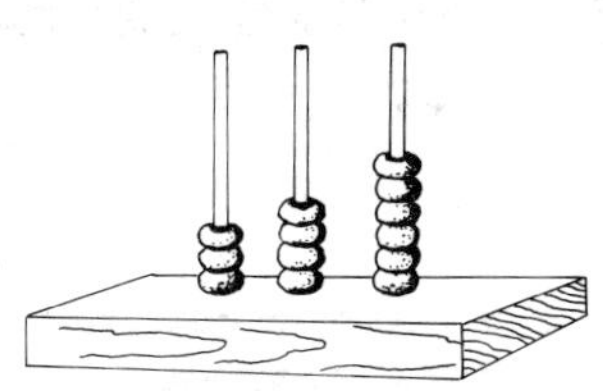

Aztec abacus

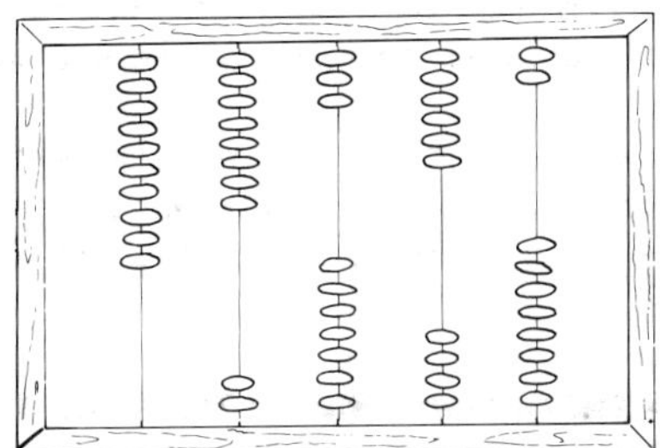

Russian abacus

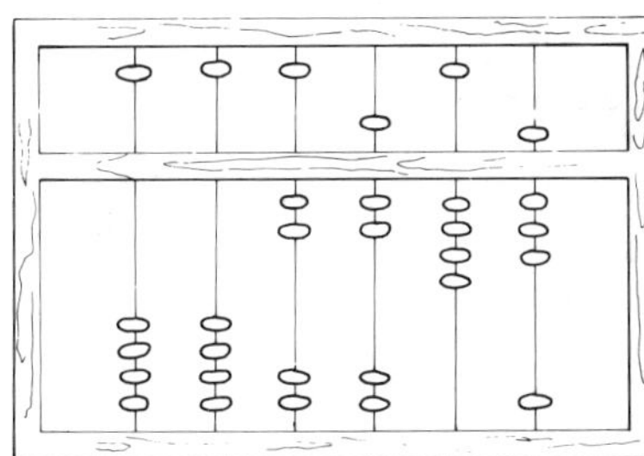

Japanese soroban

Chinese abacus

The Hindu-Arabic number system that we use today was introduced into Europe in the eighth century, but was not widely known until the twelfth century. Because for the first time a symbol for zero was used, this number system allowed written calculations to be performed more easily. From that time the abacus lost its popularity, though it is still used in some Eastern countries. (The Japanese are very skilful in the use of the soroban and in 1946 a competition was held between the U.S. Army's most proficient desk-calculator operator and a bank official from Japan using an abacus. Each man was given five tasks to do, and the abacus operator was quicker in four out of the five.)

Paper was introduced into Europe during the twelfth century although it had been known to the Chinese and Maya (a Central American and Mexican tribe) many centuries before. As the quality of paper improved, so its use as a medium for recording information increased, especially after the invention of the printing press in the fifteenth century.

The form of the Arabic symbols we use today can be seen from the print used on Caxton's press:

1234567890

At the end of the sixteenth century, business and government records were recorded on paper or parchment and calculations were done by hand or by using an abacus. One interesting exception to this was the use of 'exchequer tallies'. These consisted of sticks of wood used to keep records of taxes paid. After notches had been cut into the wood to record numeric information, the stick was split along its length to give identical halves. One half would be retained by the tax collector while the other half was stored in government vaults.

This system was used in this country until 1837: when it was no longer legal, the government ordered that the tally rods should be burnt. However, the rods were disposed of in the cellars of the House of Commons, and the fire got out of hand, so that eventually the Houses of Parliament burnt down. Computing had achieved what Guy Fawkes could not!

Questions

1. Which of these materials was first used for recording information?
   (a) parchment, (b) papyrus, (c) paper, (d) clay.
2. Which of these materials was made popular by the printing press?
   (a) parchment, (b) papyrus, (c) paper, (d) clay.
3. What caused the decline in popularity of the abacus?
4. 'As civilizations became more advanced and their populations grew there developed an increasing need for means of recording information.' Discuss this statement, giving examples of methods of information storage.

Exchequer tallies

4 The Computer System

To look more closely at a computer system, let us return to the Penta Hotel.

Problem solving

One of the services offered at the hotel is currency conversion. This is a tours hotel and therefore a great many of the guests are visitors to this country.

If you have ever been abroad you will know how important it is to be able to change your pound notes or travellers' cheques into the currency of the country you are in. Nowadays the exchange rate, that is, the amount of francs or dollars or marks you get for your pound, varies nearly every day. The computer system at the Penta now allows cashiers to work out the conversion for guests so that they can have exactly the right amount of money.

Every day the cashier checks the various exchange rates and feeds this information into the computer. This is very important: it is this information stored in the computer which is used each time a calculation is performed.

Maybe you have solved similar problems yourself, in mathematics: 'Calculate the amount in pounds an American will get for $100 if the exchange rate is £1 = $1.8642'

When you set about this problem you would probably need a piece of paper to do your working out on and then you would write out the answer neatly in your maths book.

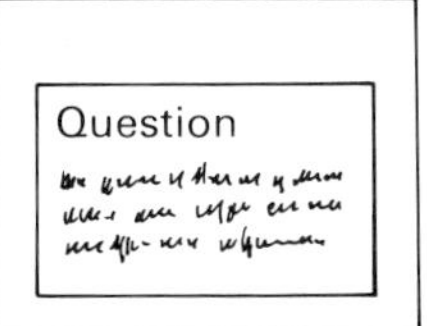

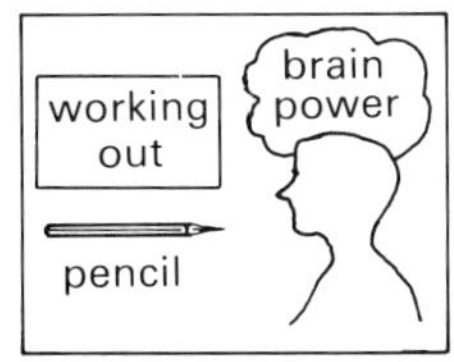

Problem solving by a human

Problem solving can be broken down into three main stages.

1. You must have the necessary instructions to answer the question and the basic information.
2. Using pencil and paper you set about solving the problem with the ideas you have stored away in your head from previous mathematics lessons.
3. Finally you must present your work neatly for your teacher to mark.

These three stages may be called input, process and output.

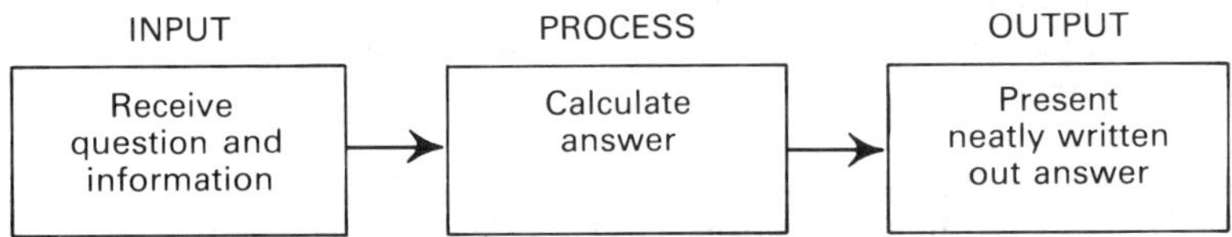

A computer system works in a similar manner.

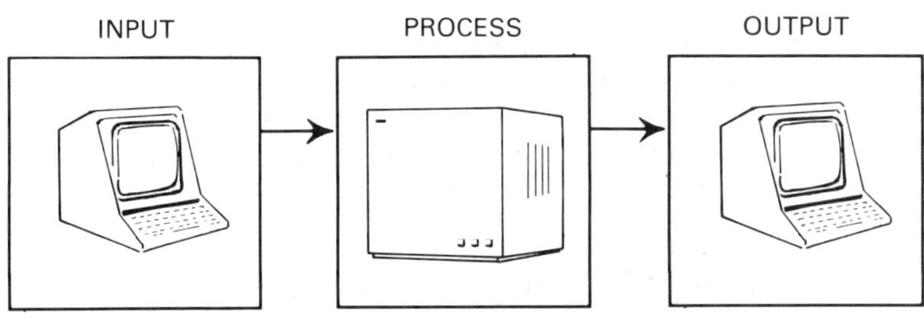

Input: **the computer user (the cashier) needs to call into the computer the correct set of instructions to do the conversion, and also enters through the input terminal the amount of money to be converted.**

Process: **the computer works out the correct answer in the** central processing unit (CPU).

Output: **the correct amount is shown clearly for the cashier and the guest to see.**

Calculation by hand

Consider an example of an American guest wishing to change $72 into pounds. The cashier could of course work out the answer himself. What would he need?

1. **He would need to remember the instructions in order to do the conversion and would require the exchange rate. Let's say the exchange rate is $1.80 to the pound.**
2. **He would now do the conversion:**

$$\text{If } £1 = \$1.8$$

$$\text{then } \frac{£1}{1.8} = \$1$$

$$\text{and } \frac{£72}{1.8} = \$72$$

3. **He would then write down the amount for the guest, which would be £40.**

In this very large hotel, however, the cashier would need to do many such calculations each day and would need to be able to convert most of the world's currencies because the guests come from all over the world. Not only would he get very tired doing this many times a day but he would probably make several errors (the arithmetic will not always be as easy as in the example). The information about exchange rates would probably be on sheets of paper which he would have to refer to constantly.

It therefore makes sense for the cashier to use the computer: all the instructions about the method of conversion, and all the exchange rates can be stored in it.

Calculation by computer

The set of instructions telling the computer how to do any job is called a computer program. **It is written by a person called a** programmer. **As a computer is only a machine it must be 'set up' to do a job. If information is missing or if inaccurate instructions are input, then it cannot produce correct results.**

So for our calculation to be made, three sorts of information are needed:

1. **The instructions about the method of doing the conversion sum (the program).**
2. **The relevant exchange rate (the data).**
3. **The amount of money involved in this particular transaction.**

The first two pieces of information are stored in the computer already: the cashier calls them up from the storage unit. **The third item has to be input specially each time by the cashier. One of the instructions in the program tells him to type in the amount of money, by flashing him a message on the VDU screen.**

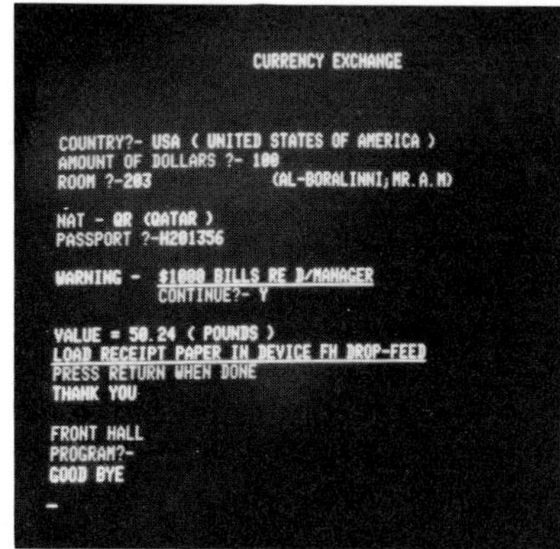

The cashier's VDU is both an input and output device

The calculation can be done very quickly in the central processing unit once all the information is available. Then the result is output on the screen of the VDU. All these activities within the computer are supervised by a control unit **which interprets and carries out the instructions contained in the program.**

We now have the basis of a computer system.

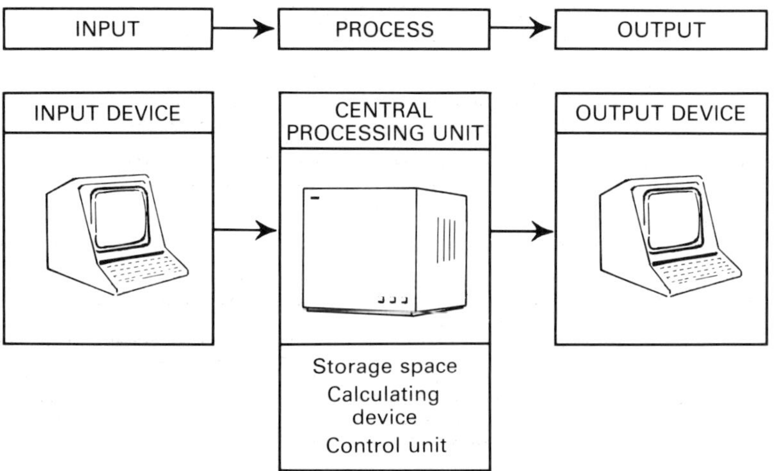

Batch processing

Computers work by electricity so they can calculate very quickly. The CPU is capable of obeying instructions in a few microseconds, that is, in millionths of a second. So it should be easy to see why computers are used to do thousands of routine tasks very quickly.

Here are two more applications. First, local authorities use computers for their payrolls.

All local-authority employees have their wages and salaries processed by computer. For example, all teachers at your school receive, at the end of the month, salary advice slips telling them how much they have earned. Make a list of the information the computer would need in order to do this.

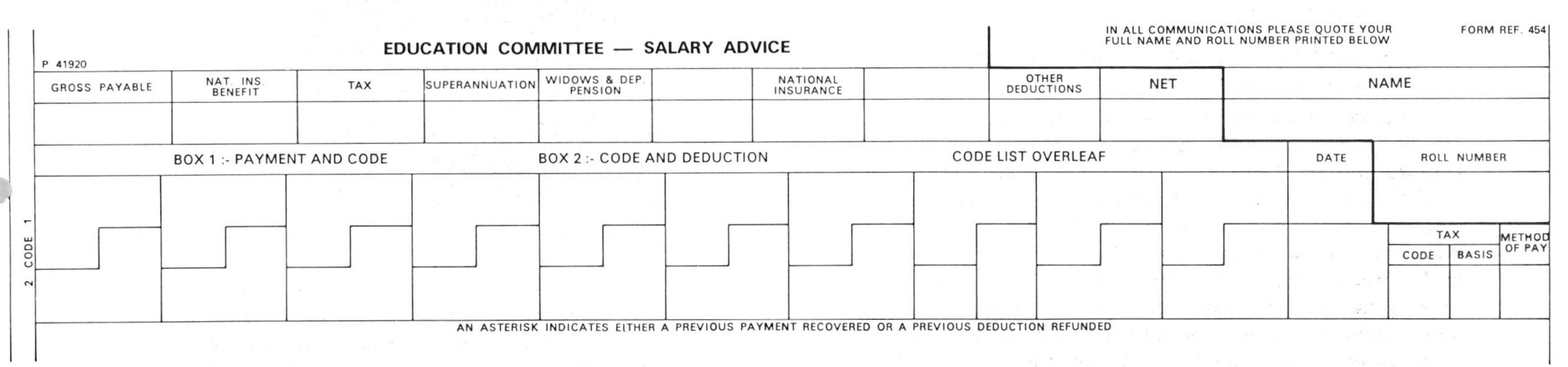

P 41920

EDUCATION COMMITTEE — SALARY ADVICE

IN ALL COMMUNICATIONS PLEASE QUOTE YOUR FULL NAME AND ROLL NUMBER PRINTED BELOW

FORM REF. 454

GROSS PAYABLE	NAT. INS. BENEFIT	TAX	SUPERANNUATION	WIDOWS & DEP. PENSION		NATIONAL INSURANCE		OTHER DEDUCTIONS	NET	NAME

BOX 1 :- PAYMENT AND CODE — BOX 2 :- CODE AND DEDUCTION — CODE LIST OVERLEAF — DATE — ROLL NUMBER

CODE 1 / 2

TAX: CODE, BASIS — METHOD OF PAY

AN ASTERISK INDICATES EITHER A PREVIOUS PAYMENT RECOVERED OR A PREVIOUS DEDUCTION REFUNDED

Pre-printed stationery for a teacher's salary advice slip
The code numbers, which would appear on the salary advice slip, are explained on the reverse side *(below)*

CODE	ALLOWANCE	CODE	ALLOWANCE	CODE	ALLOWANCE	CODE	DEDUCTION	CODE	DEDUCTION	CODE	DEDUCTION	TAX BASIS CODES
200	BASIC SALARY	217	SESSIONAL PAY	234	HONORARIA	292	MUNICIPAL BANK	309	BOARD & LODGING	326		0 SUFFIX CODE (CUM)
201	BASIC SALARY	218	TRAINING	235	EXAMINATION FEES	293	PREMIUM BONDS	310	RENT	327		1
202		219	ARREARS OF PAY	236	SUPPLEMENTAL PENSION	294	NATIONAL SAVINGS	311	RENT-GARAGE	328		2
203	LAB. TECH. QUAL.	220	SPECIAL RESPONSIBILITY	237	SESSIONAL ARREARS	295	M.C.A.P.S.	312	NEW TEACHERS ADVANCES	329		3
204		221	HONORARIA	238	TRAVELLING (TAXABLE)	296	MARTINEAU TEACHERS CLUB	313		330	CHILDRENS FUND	4
205	F.E.SP. RESP	222	SEN. NURSERY ASST	239		297	GUILD CLUB	314		331	OCKENDEN VENTURE	5
	LECTURER GRADE 1	223		240		298		315		332	B.U.P.A.	6 SUFF. CODE (MTH. 1)
206		224		241	UNIFORM	299	MEALS	316		333	LIFE ASSURANCE	7 CODE N.T.
207	SUPPLEMENT	225		242	CYCLE	300	SALARY OVERPAYMENT	317		334	MEDICAL BENEFITS SCHEME	8
208	THRESHOLD	226		243	LAUNDRY	301	REMOVAL EXPENSES	318		335	N.U.P.E.	9 PREF. CODE (MTH. 1)
209	SPECIAL SERVICES	227	S.P.S.	244	TRAVELLING (NON-TAXABLE)	302	F.S.S.N.	319		336	G. & M.W.U.	
210		228	BASIC (NON-SUPER)	245	CREDIT NET ALLOWANCE	303	F.S.S.N.	320	N.U.T.	337		
211	IMMIGRANT	229		246	SUPPLEMENTAL PEN. ARRS.	304	F.S.S.U.	321	N.A.S.	338		
212		230	OVERTIME	247	TAXABLE EXTRAS	305	SCHOOL OF MUSIC SUPER.	322	N.A.L.G.O.	339		METHOD OF PAY
213	"ACTING" IN POST	231	SUBSISTENCE	248		306	SOCIAL WORKERS SUPER.	323	U.W.T.	340	B.H.S.F. 1p.	1 WARRANT
214	SAFEGUARDED	231	LECTURER EXTRA DUTY			307	OTHER DEDUCTION 1	324	A.T.T.I.	341	B.H.S.F. 5p.	2 CREDIT TRANSFER
215	BLIND & DEAF TEACHING	232	EXTRANEOUS DUTY			308	OTHER DEDUCTION 2	325	A.T.C.D.E.	342	ADVANCE NET	
216	CERT. IN CHILD CARE	233	SESSIONAL PAY									

When each teacher's salary has been processed the amounts are printed on a line printer using pre-printed stationery. The computer then prepares figures for each teacher's bank, indicating by how much the bank account should be increased.

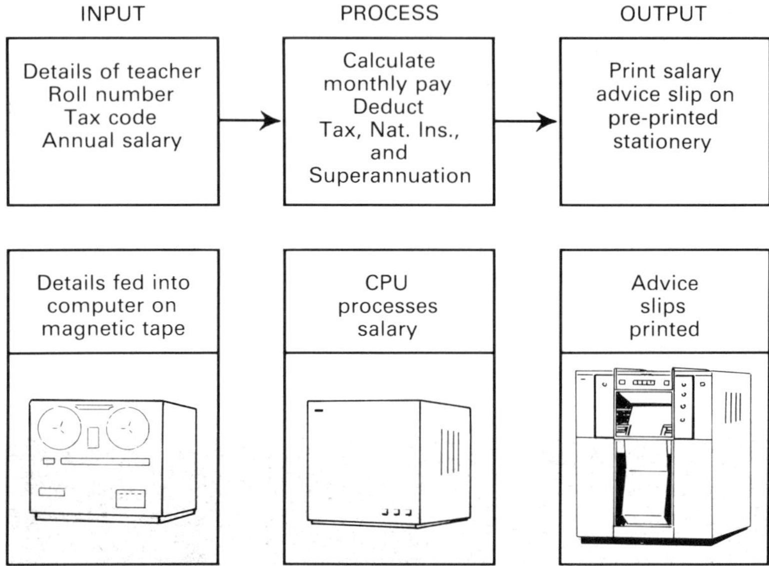

Magnetic tape can be used for input: a reel of tape can hold a vast amount of information. It is specially coded so that it can be read directly into the central processor.

The second example is electricity boards, which need to process figures in order to produce bills for their customers.

INPUT	PROCESS	OUTPUT
Input customers' account numbers with previous and present meter readings, and tariffs for units	Calculate number of units used and the cost of this amount of electricity	Print bills on pre-printed stationery

The two examples given show clearly the input, process and output stages. Notice also that in these applications the computer has been used to process the same *kind* of input information for a large number of cases.

The payroll program allows a local authority to process thousands of wage and salary slips at one time, while the billing system helps to prepare bills for many thousands of customers within a particular electricity-board area.

Such applications are repetitive and thus exceptionally good for computer processing. These systems illustrate large-scale batch processing **and show how a computer's speed enables the job to be done quickly and accurately. In the past a large team of clerks would have been necessary, so the computer is saving the cost of their salaries.**

The speed of the CPU is also a benefit to mathematicians and scientists. They may need to process only a comparatively few calculations, but these may be extremely complicated and by hand would take many days or weeks to finish. Much of our modern technology, including the exploration of space and the landing of man on the moon, would have been impossible without the speed and accuracy of the computer.

Data

So far in this chapter the word 'information' has been used to describe both the facts and figures that we as humans understand, as well as those that the computer processes.

This is rather a loose term. It is more correct to say that information consists of details that only humans can put meaning to. That which is stored in a computer should be referred to as data.

The following example should make this clear.

The figures

49 277 13738 265H 532.50 87.05
31.75 22.70 391.00

are meaningless to us. They are in fact data held in a computer during a payroll run. In order for this data to be made comprehensible to us, the output device should print out the following information:

Roll Number	Tax Code	Gross Salary	Tax
49 277 13738	265H	£532.50	£87.05

Superannuation	National Insurance	Net Salary
£31.75	£22.70	£391.00

Good programmers will produce programs that allow information to be printed out so that anyone reading the output will understand it.

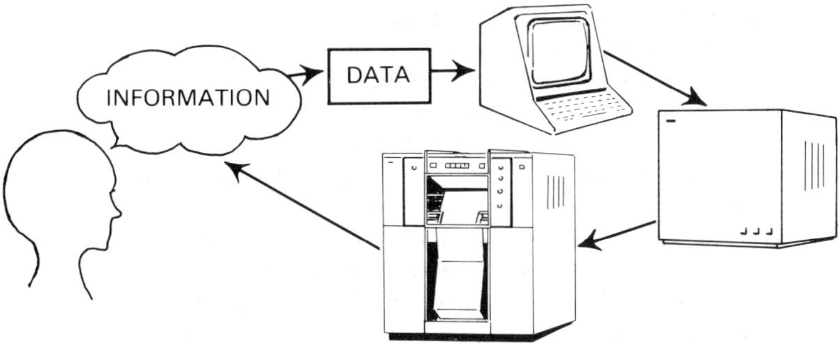

Questions

1. Which of the following applications would *not* require pre-printed stationery for computer output?
   (a) bank statements,
   (b) telephone bills,
   (c) payroll,
   (d) currency conversion.
2. What are the three main parts of the central processing unit?
3. Someone wishes to obtain a driving licence from the Vehicle and Driver Licensing Centre at Swansea. What information would be required about the driver by this centre in order to provide the licence?
4. What information is likely to be held on a payroll file about an employee?
5. What information is likely to be printed on a salary advice slip?
6. Explain the difference between information and data.
7. What is meant by 'batch processing' and what types of application are likely to use this method of processing?

Vocabulary

batch processing
central processing unit (CPU)
control unit
data
payroll
program
programmer
storage unit

5 Flowcharts and Simple Programs

The currency conversion program used at the Penta Hotel is shown below. It may not mean much to you at the moment but you can pick out certain items like 'country', 'pounds', 'maximum limit', 'currency not acceptable' and 'convert to'.

The programmer has written this program to deal with more than one currency, of course, and this makes the program more complex.

From the program listing below see if you can find the answers to the following questions.

1. **At what time and date was the listing taken?**
2. **What is the name of the program?**
3. **Who do you think wrote the program and when?**

In order to understand a little about programming we shall try to build up our own simple program to convert some currencies. But before any program is written, the programmer has to analyse his problem carefully.

Flowcharts

The programmer structures his program by designing a flowchart. **To find out how flowcharts are used, let us have a look at some everyday activities. Suppose that you wanted to clean your shoes. You could write out instructions for this job: 'Fetch your shoes, polish and brushes. First apply shoe polish to each shoe. Then using the other brush take each shoe in turn and rub hard. Put your polish and brushes away and finally put on your shoes.'**

Compare this with the flowchart opposite.

It is much easier to follow the flowchart because it is structured in small, separate sections.

To illustrate this point try writing down instructions to boil an egg and then see if it is easier to draw a flowchart to do the same job. Show your first attempt to someone sitting near you and then show them the flowchart you have drawn. Not only will you find it easier to organize

```
CQA    1278  MARCOL HSD   S3-PENTA  TUE OCT 31, 1978 12:41 PM

CQA    ; CQ - CURRENCY QUERY PROGRAM
       ; D.LEVY 21 FEB 1978 HSDF065PEN (COPYRIGHT MARCOL HSD)
ANN    W £,"CURRENCY ENQUIRY"
GO     W !,*28,!!,"COUNTRY?- ",*29 R COC W *4 G CQAE:'COC,ER1:COC'?1AA,ER1:$L(COC)>3
       I COC="GB" W " ( GREAT BRITAIN )",!,*28,"CONVERT TO?- ",*29 R COC2 G GO:'COC2,ER1:COC2'?1AA,ER1:$L(COC2)>3 S COC=COC2.":".COC
       I $D(↑CUM($P(COC:1)),RES) W " ( ",$P(RES:2)," )",!
       E  G ER4
AMT    W *28,"AMOUNT OF " W:$P(COC:2) "POUNDS" W:'$P(COC:2) $P(RES:5) W " ?- ",*29 R AMT W *4 G GO:'AMT
       I $P(COC:2) G ER2:AMT'?1NN"."2N S AMT=$P(AMT,".",1).$P(AMT,".",2)
       E  I AMT'?1NN G ER3
CONV   C ZZA@XFC[COC,AMT,"RES"] G ER5:'RES
OUT    I AMT=0 W !!,"RATE = ",$P(RES:3):R0.4," ",$P(RES:5)," TO THE POUND" G WARN
       S RS=$P(RES,"\",1) W !!,"VALUE = " I $P(COC:2) W RS," ( ",$P(RES:5)," )"
       E  W RS:R0.2," ( POUNDS )"
WARN   I $P(RES:4) W ?35,*20,"MAXIMUM LIMIT IS ",$P(RES:4):R0.2," POUNDS",*21
       I $P(RES:6) W ?35,*20,$P(RES:6),*21
       G GO
ER1    W *7,*3,*14,?35,"<FORMAT IS UP TO 3 ALPHABETIC CHARACTERS>",*15,! G GO
ER2    W *7,*3,*14,?35,"<FORMAT IS POUNDS.PENCE>",*15,! G AMT
ER3    W *7,*3,*14,?35,"<FORMAT IS WHOLE NUMBER OF ",$P(RES:5),">",*15,! G AMT
ER4    W *7,*3,*14,?35,"<CURRENCY NOT ACCEPTABLE>",*15,! G GO
ER5    W *7,*3,*14,?35,"<LIMITS EXCEEDED>",*15,! G GO
CQAE   O ZXA@XIT
```

your ideas in a flowchart but it should be much easier for someone else to read.

You may like to think of other everyday examples for which you could draw a flowchart: try making a cup of tea or a telephone call.

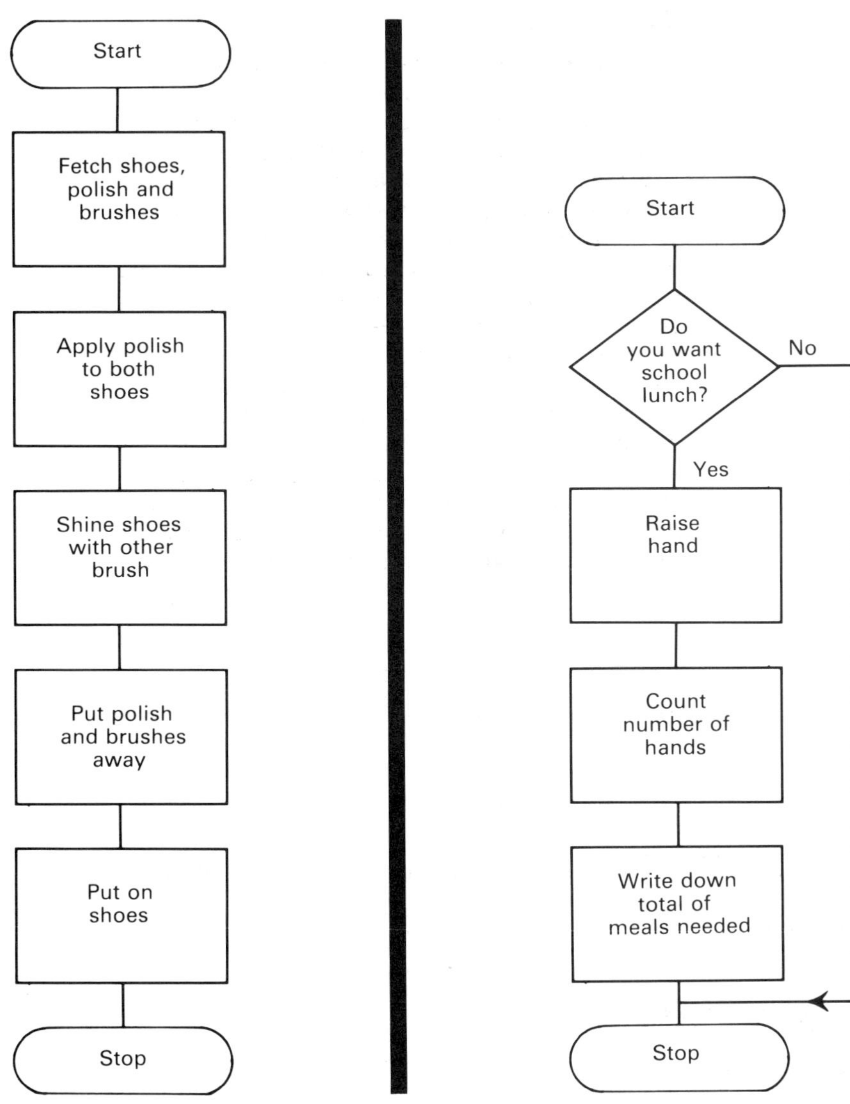

Flowchart symbols

Notice that in the flowchart shown two types of flowchart boxes or symbols have been used.

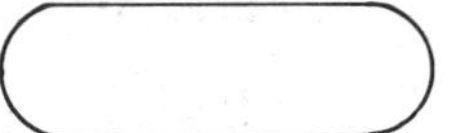

This is a terminal box and has one line either leaving it or entering it.

This is an action box and is used to indicate a particular job to be done. It has one line entering it and one line leaving it in the same direction.

With some activities a decision may have to be made. For example, your teacher may wish to find out how many pupils want to stay for a school lunch. The flowchart is shown on the left.

This time we use a decision box which has one line entering it and two lines leaving it. Responses to questions in the box must be 'yes' or 'no' only and the exit lines must be so labelled.

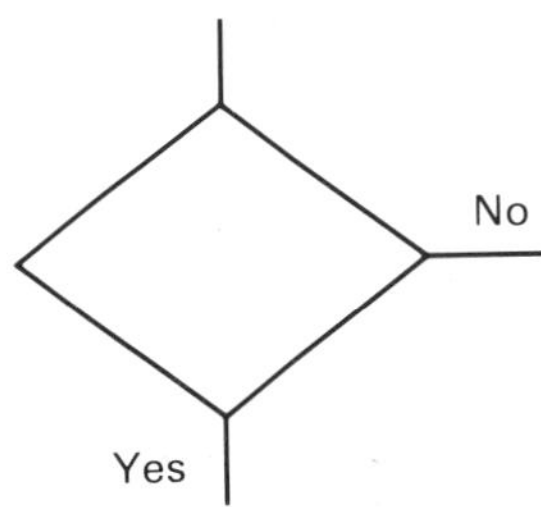

In flowcharts you should use arrows only when the flow is to the left or upwards. The lines without arrows are assumed to flow downwards or to the right.

When a new program is being written, a flowchart enables the programmer to sort out his ideas and make sure that the parts are in the correct order.

Currency conversion flowchart

Now we can try structuring a flowchart for a real program. We shall use a familiar task: the currency conversion we looked at in Chapter 4.

You remember the calculation that the cashier did. This could be summarized as:

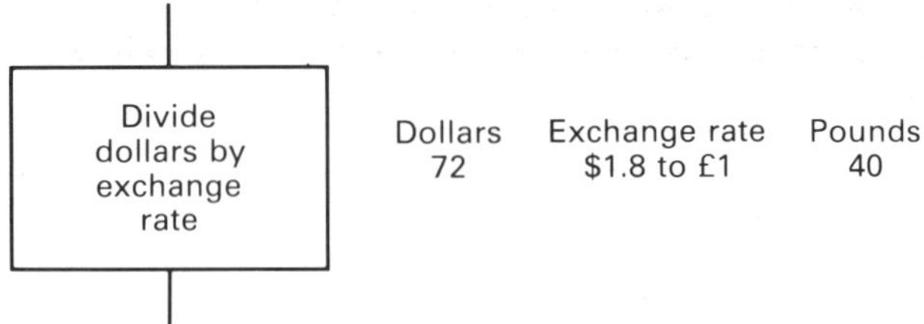

It would be incorrect to say 'convert $72' as the program the cashier used was designed to convert any amount of dollars. We shall do the same.

The number of dollars and the exchange rate must first of all be input. The number of pounds must be output at the end. Another special symbol, a parallelogram, is used as the input/output box.

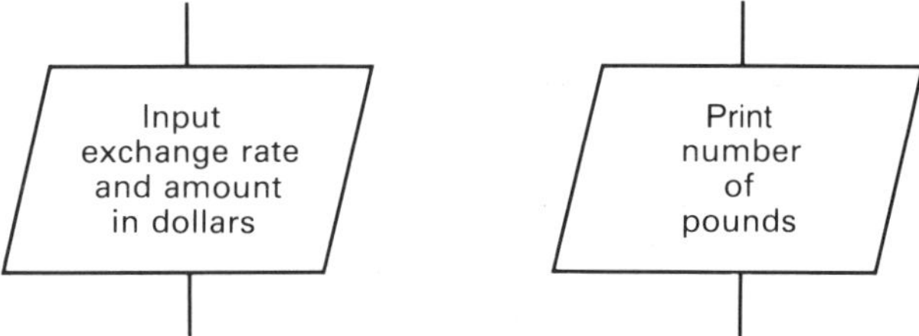

The flowchart so far is given on the right.

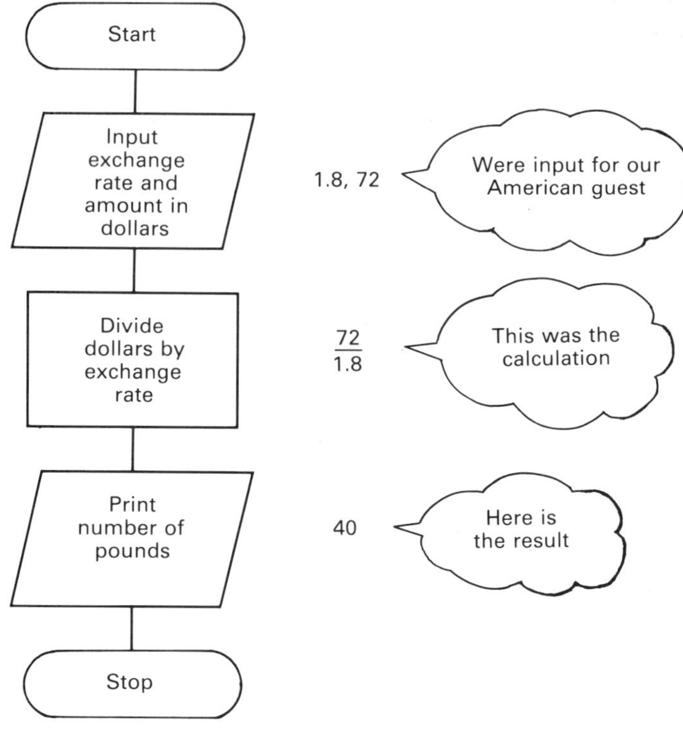

We have mentioned the importance of good information. Anyone running this program at the moment may not know how to enter the data, and would see only a figure printed at the end of the program run with no explanation of what it is.

To improve matters, additional boxes should be given illustrating the title, instructions for use and properly labelled output.

The improved flowchart is on the next page.

Writing a program

When writing programs it is important to remember that others must understand what you have done. When presenting programs (as you will have to for examination course work) you should always bear in mind the needs of three people:

1. **the user, who must know how to run the program and be able to comprehend the output,**
2. **anyone who might want to adapt the program for another use,**
3. **an examiner, who must see very clearly what you are attempting to do.**

If you do this job correctly you will be producing good documentation. **(Examination boards set down their own documentation standards and you must do your best to design your work to meet their requirements.)**

Computer languages

People communicate with each other by writing or talking in their own language. Usually it does not matter if they use language incorrectly – other people can still understand them.

When a man communicates with a computer he has to use a very simple, limited language which has been specially designed for it. It is also important that the language is used in exactly the right way: the computer cannot make allowances for mistakes. There are many computer languages, which will be discussed in detail in Chapter 15.

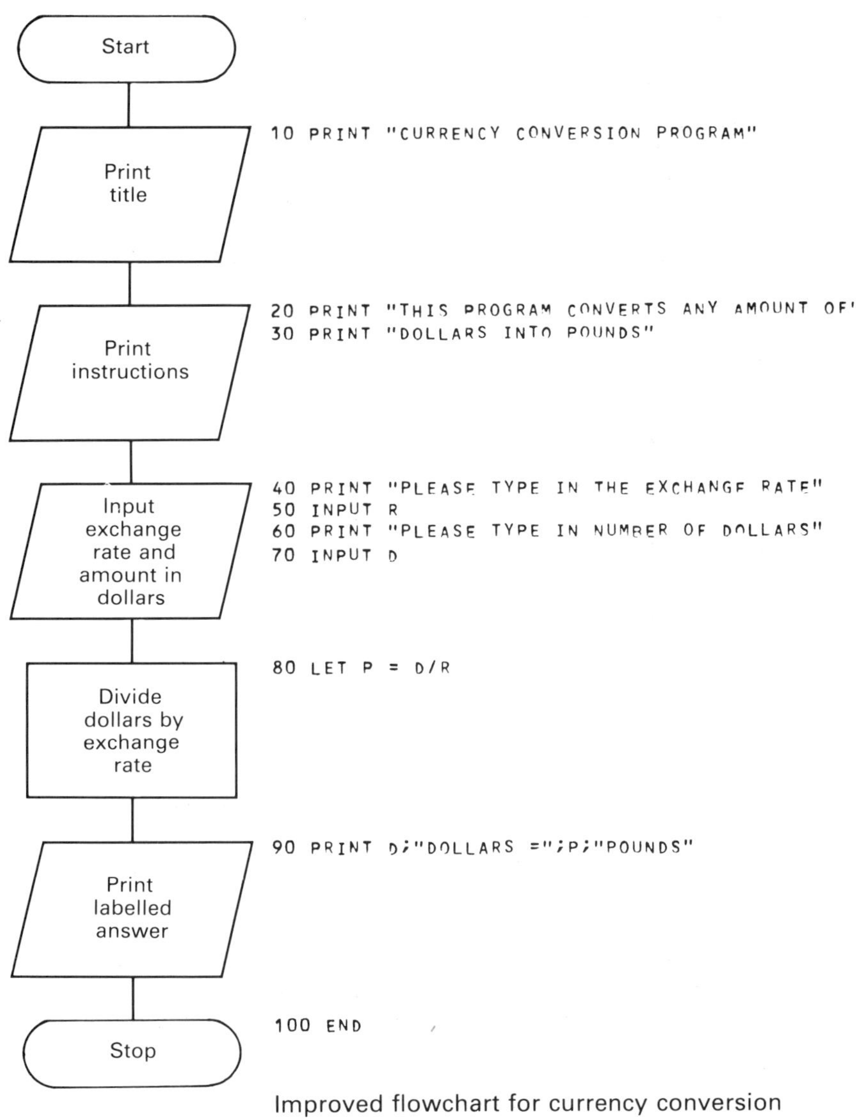

Improved flowchart for currency conversion

Currency conversion programs

We can now look at the extended flowchart (above) for our currency conversion, and see an example of the computer program which would be written from it. The program has been written in BASIC, the language used in most schools. This computer language was designed for people who need not know how a computer works. You should be able to see what the instructions do.

Tourists may, of course, wish to convert their pounds back into dollars when they return to America. The flowchart below shows how a decision can be taken to convert currencies either way.

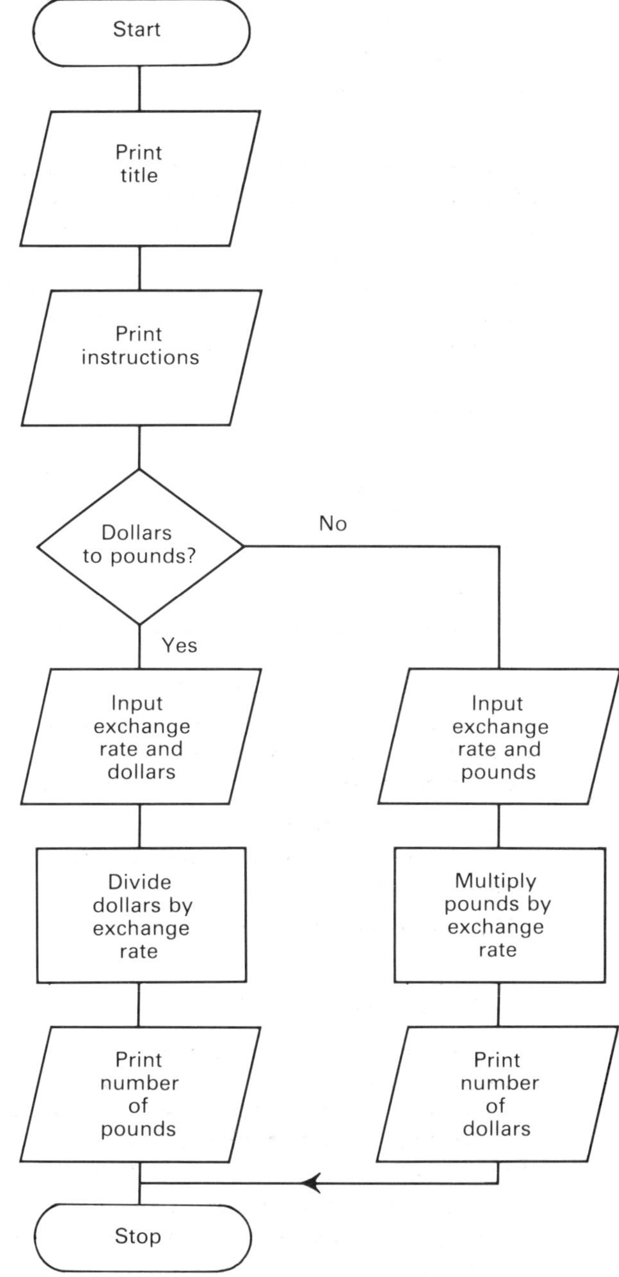

The last flowchart shows clearly the *stages* required to solve this problem. Because flowcharts are written in general terms, computer programs can be written from them in a number of different programming languages.

Here are two programs that have been written from the flowchart. The languages used are BASIC and PASCAL.

BASIC coding

```
10 PRINT "TO CONVERT EITHER DOLLARS TO POUNDS"
20 PRINT "OR POUNDS TO DOLLARS"
30 PRINT "DO YOU WISH TO CONVERT DOLLARS TO POUNDS?"
40 PRINT "PLEASE TYPE 'YES' OR 'NO'"
50 INPUT A£
60 IF A£ = "YES" THEN 140
70 PRINT "PLEASE TYPE IN EXCHANGE RATE"
80 INPUT R
90 PRINT "PLEASE TYPE IN NUMBER OF POUNDS TO BE CHANGED"
100 INPUT P
110 LET D = P*R
120 PRINT P;"POUNDS =";D;"DOLLARS"
130 GOTO 200
140 PRINT "PLEASE TYPE IN EXCHANGE RATE"
150 INPUT R
160 PRINT "PLEASE TYPE IN NUMBER OF DOLLARS TO BE CHANGED"
170 INPUT D
180 LET P = D/R
190 PRINT D;"DOLLARS =";P;"POUNDS"
200 END
```

PASCAL program

```
PROGRAM CONVERT(INPUT,OUTPUT);
VAR POUNDS,DOLLARS:REAL;
BEGIN
        WHILE POUNDS <> -1 DO
        BEGIN
              READ POUNDS;
              DOLLARS = POUNDS * 1.8;
              WRITELN ('£',POUNDS,'=$',DOLLARS);
        END;
END.
```

Questions

1. Rearrange the following flowchart boxes to illustrate the flow of operations when making a cup of instant coffee.

Pour boiled water into cup

Put coffee in cup

Add sugar

Stir milk, coffee and sugar in cup

Start

Boil water

Stop

Add milk

Get cup

2. Rearrange the following flowchart boxes to illustrate the flow of operations when making a telephone call.

Make call

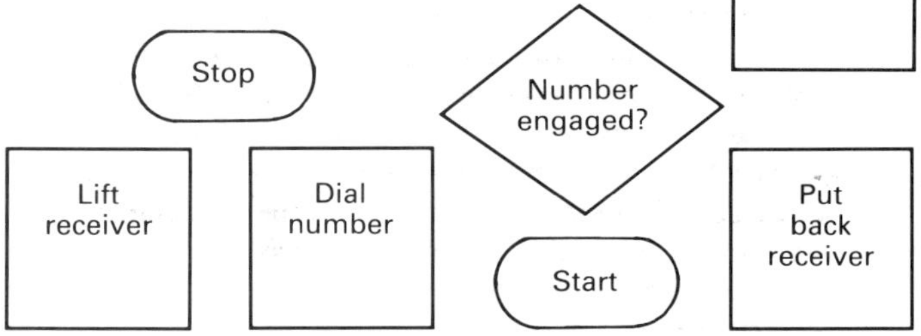

Stop

Number engaged?

Lift receiver

Dial number

Start

Put back receiver

3. Draw a flowchart to show how you would find a book in a library.
4. Draw a flowchart to show a new pupil in your class how he could get from your form room to the headteacher's office.
5. Draw a flowchart to describe how given three sides of a triangle you could determine whether it was equilateral, isosceles or scalene.

Vocabulary

action box
decision box
documentation
flowchart
flowchart symbols
input/output box
terminal box

6 Two-state Arithmetic

Chapter 3 gave examples of how earlier civilizations stored and processed numbers. Some early trading nations like the Babylonians used the number sixty as a base for counting. Later, base-10 (decimal) numbers were used, probably because we have ten fingers. Some African and South American countries used base 20, however.

The Eskimos also used base 20, which could mean that they went backwards as well as forwards on their fingers (or that they got frostbite on their toes!).

In modern computers, fingers have been replaced by electronic circuits. This speeds up operations so much that calculations are done in millionths of a second. In older calculators, calculations were done by moving levers and cogs, rather like those in a typewriter. So the speed at which they worked depended on the speed at which these levers and cogs could move. Modern electronic computers depend only on the speed at which electricity flows in a conductor, which is approximately 300 000 kilometres in a second.

One of the main ways in which we use electricity is in switches. For example, we can switch lights and household appliances *on* and *off*. This involves only two actions and provides us with what we call a two-state system:

Here are some other two-state systems:

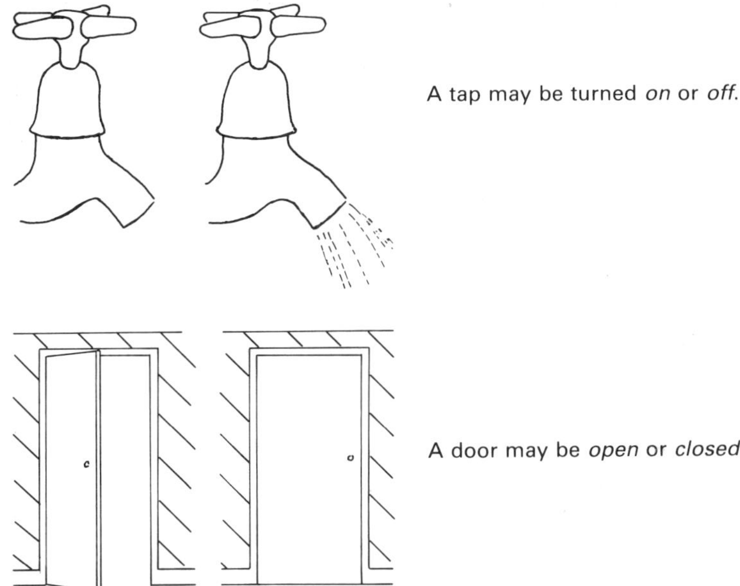

A tap may be turned *on* or *off*.

A door may be *open* or *closed*.

Now list three more two-state systems. Remember that you must choose examples which give two situations only (the door above must be either open or closed; it cannot be half open).

If base-10 (decimal) numbers were used inside the CPU of a computer there would be ten different states to deal with (corresponding to the digits 0, 1, 2, 3, 4, 5, 6, 7, 8, 9). This would complicate matters, although early computers did use a decimal system.

If switches were used in computer circuitry, then the digit 0 could be represented by *off* and the digit 1 by *on*. However, before we can use this two-state system to do calculations, we must find a way of counting with the digits 0 and 1 only.

Our normal counting system is a base-10 (decimal) system and has ten symbols: 0, 1, 2, 3, 4, 5, 6, 7, 8, 9. As soon as we go above 9 we have to use two of these symbols:

$$\begin{array}{r} 9 \\ +1 \\ \hline 10 \\ \hline \end{array}$$

Here the zero is in the *units* column and the one is in the *tens* column. For larger numbers more columns are needed:

Column Headings				
10 000	**1000**	**100**	**10**	**1**

← × 10 ← × 10 ← × 10 ← × 10
(Multiply by the base)

Thus, for example, the number 5978 means

1000	**100**	**10**	**1**
5	9	7	8

or

$(5 \times 1000) + (9 \times 100) + (7 \times 10) + (8 \times 1)$

The highest single digit that can be used is 9 (one less than the base).

If base 8 were used for counting we would have the digits 0, 1, 2, 3, 4, 5, 6, 7 only, and the column headings would be:

. . . 512	**64**	**8**	**1**

← × 8 ← × 8 ← × 8 (Multiply by the base)

This system is called octal.

If base 12 were used we would need twelve symbols, to represent the decimal numbers 0, 1, 2, 3, 4, 5, 6, 7, 8, 9, 10, 11, and the column headings would be:

. . . 1728	**144**	**12**	**1**

← × 12 ← × 12 ← × 12 (Multiply by the base)

Can you suggest a suitable symbol for the decimal number 10 and the decimal number 11?

To find the column headings for any base, start with 1 and multiply successively by the base number.

Example Base 6
$1 \times 6 = 6$, $6 \times 6 = 36$, $36 \times 6 = 216$, $216 \times 6 = 1296$, . . .
So the column headings are

. . . 1296	**216**	**36**	**6**	**1**

Thus 55 in base 6 means

. . . 6	**1**
5	5

or $(5 \times 6) + (5 \times 1) = 35$ in base 10

Now let us consider a further problem. If the highest digit used in any base is one less than the base, what is the lowest base that could be used for counting?

For base 1 the highest digit is $1 - 1 = 0$ and this is plainly no use. For base 2, the highest digit is $2 - 1 = 1$; therefore the digits 1 and 0 can both be used. Base-2 numbers are called binary numbers **and are the numbers used in the CPU of a computer.**

Remember that we can represent the numbers 0 and 1 by using switches. Later we shall see how electronic circuitry can be used to process base-2 numbers. In this chapter we shall study base-2 (binary) arithmetic.

Information to be used by a computer is normally presented in decimal numbers (base 10) whereas data in a CPU is handled in binary (base 2) form. So the computer must be able to convert numbers from one system to the other.

Converting decimal numbers to binary numbers

First check that these column headings for binary numbers are correct:

. . .128	**64**	**32**	**16**	**8**	**4**	**2**	**1**

Example Change 79_{10} to binary (79_{10} is a shorthand way of writing '79 in base 10').

The highest base-2 column heading that may be subtracted from 79 is 64:

$79 - \mathbf{64} = 15$

The highest column heading that may be subtracted from the remainder is 8:

$15 - \mathbf{8} = 7$

Continue this process until the remainder is zero:

7 − **4** = 3
3 − **2** = 1
1 − **1** = 0

The binary number can be formed by writing 1 under the column headings that were subtracted and 0 under those that were not:

64	**32**	**16**	**8**	**4**	**2**	**1**
1	0	0	1	1	1	1

This system can be tedious so we shall look at a simpler way.

In this method we divide the decimal number repeatedly by two until zero is reached, putting each remainder on the right-hand side:

2) 79
2) 39 remainder 1
2) 19 remainder 1
2) 9 remainder 1
2) 4 remainder 1
2) 2 remainder 0
2) 1 remainder 0
0 remainder 1

The binary number can be formed by writing down the remainders in reverse order, i.e. starting with the last. This gives 1001111_2, as before.

Example Change 105_{10} to binary.

2) 105
2) 52 remainder 1
2) 26 remainder 0
2) 13 remainder 0
2) 6 remainder 1
2) 3 remainder 0
2) 1 remainder 1
0 remainder 1

Answer: $105_{10} = 1101001_2$

Converting binary numbers to decimal

Example Change 101011_2 to decimal.
There are six binary digits in this number so write down the first six binary headings. Then write the corresponding digits in the binary number underneath. The decimal number is found by adding the headings of the columns containing 1:

. . . 32	**16**	**8**	**4**	**2**	**1**
1	0	1	0	1	1

32 + 8 + 2 + 1 = 43_{10}

Answer: $101011_2 = 43_{10}$

Example Change 11101010_2 to decimal.

. . . 128	**64**	**32**	**16**	**8**	**4**	**2**	**1**
1	1	1	0	1	0	1	0

128 + 64 + 32 + 8 + 2 = 234_{10}

Answer: $11101010_2 = 234_{10}$

Addition in binary

This table shows the binary form of some decimal numbers.

Decimal	Binary	Decimal	Binary	Decimal	Binary
1	1	7	111	13	1101
2	10	8	1000	14	1110
3	11	9	1001	15	1111
4	100	10	1010	16	10000
5	101	11	1011	17	10001
6	110	12	1100	18	10010

When adding decimal numbers, we start by adding the units, then add the tens, then the hundreds, etc. If the numbers in any column add up to ten or more, the number of tens is carried to the next column to the left, i.e. tens of units are carried to the tens column, tens of tens to the hundreds column, and so on.

The process is similar for binary numbers. We first add the numbers in the units column, then the numbers in the twos column, then those in the fours column, etc. This time, if the numbers in any column add up to *two* or more, the number of twos is carried to the next column to the left, i.e. twos of units are carried to the twos column, twos of twos are carried to the fours column, and so on.

Base ten	Base two
9	1
+1	+1
10	10
1	1

The following sums show the result of adding two binary digits:

0	0	1	1
+0	+1	+0	+1
0	1	1	10
			1

Binary addition is much simpler than decimal addition since it involves the addition of 1s and 0s only. Because of this the electronic circuitry handling it in a computer is relatively simple too.

Example Add the binary numbers 11010 and 10111

32	16	8	4	2	1	
	1	1	0	1	0	
	1	0	1	1	1	
1	1	0	0	0	1	Sum
1	1	1	1	0		Carry

The digits written down as part of the answer are called sum digits. When *two* binary numbers are added either 1 is carried or nothing is carried, so the carry digit is either 1 or 0.

Computers are designed to add only two binary numbers at a time so if three or more binary numbers are to be added together this is done as in the example below.

Example Calculate 1011 + 111 + 1010 + 111

1011	
+111	Add the first two numbers
10010	
+1010	Add the third number to the total
11100	
+111	Add the fourth number to the total
100011	Answer

Subtraction of binary numbers

Binary numbers can be subtracted in exactly the same way as decimal numbers.

Example Subtract 101 from 1110

```
     10
1 1 ~~1~~ ~~0~~
 −1 0 1
1 0 0 1
```

When subtracting binary numbers by this method we often have to do a lot of exchanging of numbers from left to right.

Example Subtract 1101 from 11000

```
  0 1  1 10
1 ~~1~~ ~~0~~ ~~0~~ ~~0~~
 −1 1 0 1
  1 0 1 1
```

Thus subtracting binary numbers directly is more difficult than adding them.

Computers subtract binary numbers by a clever form of addition.

Subtraction using complements in binary

This clever method is called complement arithmetic. Let's see how it works by looking at the binary subtraction $1110_2 - 101_2$.

Since the two numbers do not have the same number of digits we must add a nought to the left of 101:

1110 − 101 → 1110 − 0101

Then we find the one's complement **of the second number (0101) by subtracting 0101 from 1111 (since both numbers in the sum have four digits):**

	1111
	−0101
one's complement of 0101 =	1010

Next we add the one's complement to 1110:

```
 1110
+1010
11000
```

Finally we knock off the 1 at the left and add it to the units digit:

11000 → 1000 + 1 = 1001

If you look at the foot of the first column on this page you will see that this is the same answer as we got by subtracting directly.

Subtraction in decimal can be done by a similar method using nine's complements: this is described in the Appendix (pp. 154–5).

One's complements

We form the one's complement of a binary number by subtracting it from 11, 111, 1111, . . ., according to the number of digits.

Example Find the one's complements of 101, 1110, 10101

	111	1111	11111
	−101	−1110	−10101
one's complements =	10	1	1010

Since
1 − 1 = 0, 1 − 0 = 1

we can also find the one's complement of a binary number by 'flipping over' 1 to 0 and 0 to 1. To check this, flip over the 1s and 0s in 101, 1110 and 10101, then check the one's complements against the answers in the example above.

We can now summarize *subtraction by means of one's complements* as follows:

Step 1 **Make the number of digits in the numbers in the sum the same by adding noughts if necessary.**

Step 2 **Find the one's complement of the number which is to be subtracted by flipping over 1s to 0s and 0s to 1s.**

Step 3 **Add the one's complement to the other number in the sum.**

Step 4 **Knock off the 1 at the left and add it to the units digit to get the answer.**

Example Solve 11000 − 1101 using one's complements.

Step 1 Make the number of digits the same:
11000 − 1101 → 11000 − 01101

Step 2 Find the one's complement of 01101 by flipping over:
one's complement of 01101 = 10010

Step 3 Add to 11000:

```
 11000
+10010
101010
```

Step 4 Knock off the 1 at the left and add it to the units digit:
101010 → 01010 + 1 = 01011 = 1011

Two's complements

Step 4 of the method outlined above can be simplified if we add 1 to the one's complement in Step 2. The binary number formed by adding 1 to the one's complement is called the two's complement**. We can thus summarize *subtraction by means of two's complements* as follows:**

Step 1 **Make the number of digits in the numbers in the sum the same by adding noughts if necessary.**

Step 2 **Find the two's complement of the number which is to be subtracted by flipping over 1s to 0s and 0s to 1s and adding 1 to the units digit.**

Step 3 **Add the two's complement to the other number in the sum.**

Step 4 **Knock off the 1 at the left to get the answer.**

Example Solve 11000 − 1101 using two's complements.

Step 1 Make the number of digits the same:
11000 − 1101 → 11000 − 01101

Step 2 Find the two's complement of 01101 by flipping over and adding 1:
two's complement of 01101 = 10010 + 1 = 10011

Step 3 Add to 11000:

```
 11000
+10011
101011
```

Step 4 Knock off the 1 at the left:
101011 → 01011 = 1011

Thus using two's complements gives us the same answer as before.

Negative numbers

People who sell secondhand cars sometimes (illegally) wind the milometer backwards. A car whose milometer should read

6	8	4	9	6

may then read

2	5	6	2	4

instead. However, if the person who does the job is not careful, the milometer may end up reading

9	9	8	7	3

What do you think has happened?

If we wind back a milometer which reads 00005, we shall get

00005
00004
00003
00002
00001

Each number is one less than the number before so winding back is the same as repeatedly subtracting one.

Now let's see what happens when we wind back a 'milometer' which shows binary numbers with five digits. A 'milometer' which has a fixed number of digits is called a fixed-length register.

If we start with 00101 (= 5_{10}), we get

00101	(5_{10})
00100	(4_{10})
00011	(3_{10})
00010	(2_{10})
00001	(1)
00000	(0)

The numbers in brackets, which are the decimal equivalents of the binary numbers, decrease in steps of one as before. Therefore, if we go on winding back from 00000, we should get binary numbers whose decimal equivalents are *negative numbers:*

00000	(0)
11111	(−1)
11110	(-2_{10})
11101	(-3_{10})
11100	(-4_{10})
11011	(-5_{10})

Therefore these binary numbers represent the negatives of the binary numbers 00101, 00100, 00011, 00010, 00001 in this fixed-length register:

Number	Negative
00101	11011
00100	11100
00011	11101
00010	11110
00001	11111

Calculate the two's complements of the numbers in the left-hand column of the table. What do you notice about the answers?

If you have found the complements correctly, you will see that *in a fixed-length register* the negative of a binary number can be represented by its two's complement.

Multiplication of binary numbers

With binary digits, called bits (binary digits), multiplication is also simple:

$$\begin{array}{r}0\\ \times 0\\ \hline 0\end{array}\qquad \begin{array}{r}0\\ \times 1\\ \hline 0\end{array}\qquad \begin{array}{r}1\\ \times 0\\ \hline 0\end{array}\qquad \begin{array}{r}1\\ \times 1\\ \hline 1\end{array}$$

If we want to multiply a decimal number by 10, we shift each digit one column to the left and add a zero in the units column. Similarly, if we want to multiply by 100 we shift the digits two columns to the left and add a zero in the units column and the tens column:

$15 \times 10 = 150, \quad 76 \times 100 = 7600$

To multiply a *binary number* by the *binary number* 10_2 (= 2), we must move the digits one column to the left and add a zero in the units column. Likewise, to multiply a binary number by the binary number 100_2 (= 4), we must shift the digits two columns to the left and add a zero in the units and the twos column:

$11_2 \times 10_2 = 110_2, \quad 11_2 \times 100_2 = 1100_2$
$(3_{10} \times 2_{10} = 6_{10}) \quad (3_{10} \times 4_{10} = 12_{10})$

Long multiplication in binary is done in exactly the same way as ordinary long multiplication.

Example Multiply 101_2 by 111_2

101	
×111	
101	Multiply by 1
1010	Multiply by 10_2 (or shift left one column)
10100	Multiply by 100_2 (or shift left two columns)
100011	Add to get the answer

Thus $101_2 \times 111_2 = 100011_2$

Check $101_2 = 5_{10}, \quad 111_2 = 7_{10},$
$5 \times 7 = 35_{10} = 100011_2$

Since binary numbers consist of the digits 1 and 0 only, binary multiplication can be done by shifting and adding only. Thus binary multiplication can also be done by a series of very simple operations. (Remember that the adding can be broken up into simple steps.) Here is another example:

Example Multiply 7 by 9 in binary notation.

$7 = 111_2$, $9 = 1001_2$

```
   111
 ×1001
   111
111000
111111  (= 63₁₀)
```

Division of binary numbers

Division of binary numbers can be done by the same method as long division of decimal numbers.

Example Divide 100011_2 by 111_2

```
        101
   111)100011
       111
         111
         111
           0
```

Check that 101 is the correct answer by multiplying 111 by 101.

Here is another example:

Example Divide 110110 by 110

```
        1001
   110)110110
       110
         0110
          110
            0
```

Check that 1001 is the right answer by multiplying.

If you look at the examples above, you will see that division of binary numbers can be done by repeated subtraction and shifting to the right. A computer will do the subtractions by adding complements. Thus binary division can be done by adding and shifting only.

Summary

We have now shown that addition, subtraction, multiplication and division of binary numbers can be done by the simple operations of adding and shifting only:

Subtraction can be done by adding complements.
Multiplication can be done by adding and shifting left.
Division can be done by adding (complements) and shifting right.

Therefore the electronic circuitry in the CPU of a computer required to handle these operations can be very simple.

We have also shown that the negatives of binary numbers can be represented by two's complements.

Questions

1. Give the column headings for base 4 and find the value in base 10 of 1223 in base 4.
2. Give the column headings for base 8 and find the value in base 10 of 143 in base 8.
3. Change the following decimal numbers to binary.
   (a) 25,
   (b) 63,
   (c) 165.
4. Change the following binary numbers to base 10, then convert them back to binary to check your answers.
   (a) 10110,
   (b) 11011011,
   (c) 1111111.
5. Give the two's complements of the following binary numbers.
   (a) 10110,
   (b) 0110111,
   (c) 1000101.

6. Do the following calculations by using two's complements.
   (a) 11011 − 10110,
   (b) 111001 − 1101,
   (c) 10111011 − 1001011.
7. Multiply the following pairs of binary numbers.
   (a) 101 × 110,
   (b) 1101 × 1011,
   (c) 11011 × 11001.
8. Change the following pairs of decimal numbers into binary and then perform the multiplication.
   (a) 7 × 6,
   (b) 12 × 9,
   (c) 61 × 19.
9. Divide the following pairs of binary numbers.
   (a) 1100 ÷ 100,
   (b) 101010 ÷ 110,
   (c) 100011 ÷ 1011.
10. Convert the following decimal numbers to binary and then perform the divisions in binary notation.
    (a) 54 ÷ 9,
    (b) 169 ÷ 13,
    (c) 144 ÷ 12.

Vocabulary

binary number
bit
fixed-length register
octal
one's complement
two's complement
two-state system

7 The Punch-card Era

The American Census Bureau was an organization that needed a solution to the problem of handling large amounts of information.

In 1880 the information received from the census was hand-written on to census forms. It was then sorted and counted by hand. The process took seven years.

The next census was due in 1890, and because of the rapid increase in the American population it was estimated that the processing of this information would not be completed before the next census in 1900.

Dr Herman Hollerith worked for the American Census Bureau at that time. He produced a solution by inventing the first punched-card machinery. This consisted of a keyboard punch, an electrical tabulating machine and a sorting box.

The keyboard punch was used to punch holes in the card, representing information from the census forms, which were still filled in by hand. The information held on each card included details such as age, sex, trade and type of education. One card was used for each member of the population: there were sixty-two million.

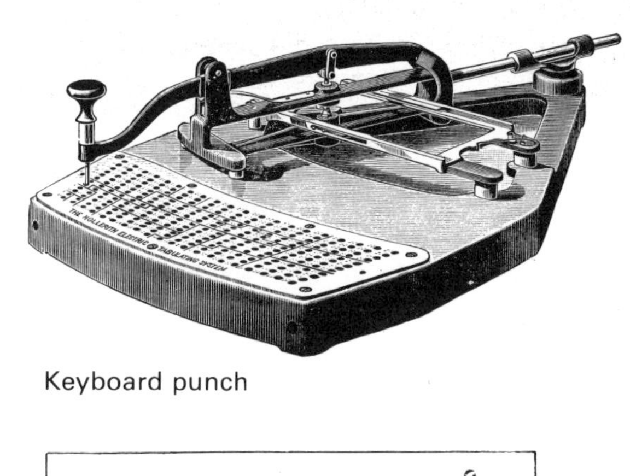

Keyboard punch

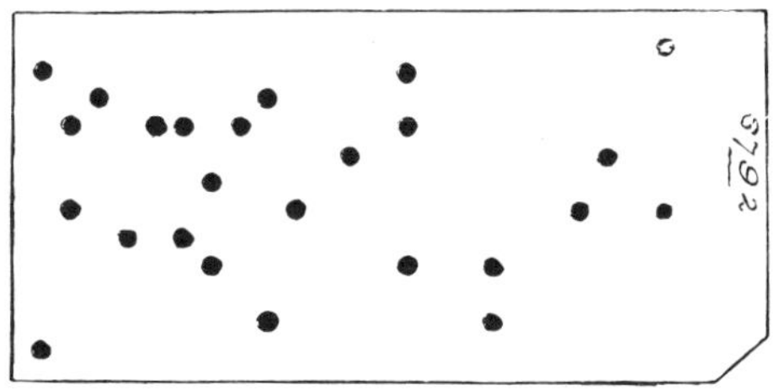

Completed card for one person

HOLLERITH'S PUNCHED-CARD MACHINERY

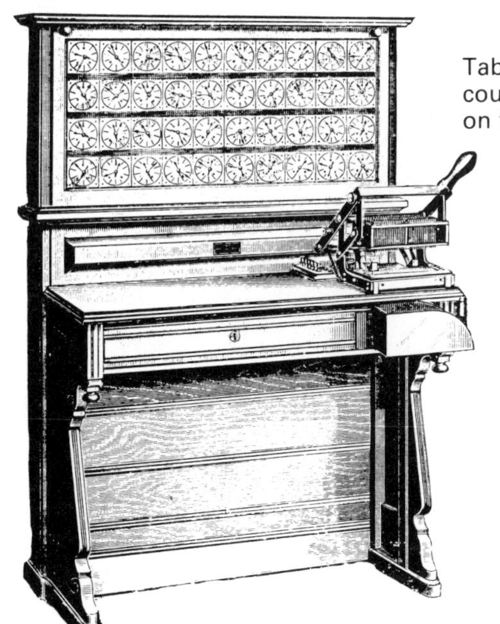

Tabulating machine which counted all the information on the cards

Sorting box in which the cards were placed

SCIENTIFIC AMERICAN

[Entered at the Post Office of New York, N. Y., as Second Class Matter. Copyrighted, 1890, by Munn & Co.]

A WEEKLY JOURNAL OF PRACTICAL INFORMATION, ART, SCIENCE, MECHANICS, CHEMISTRY, AND MANUFACTURES.

Vol. LXIII. No. 9. Established 1845. | NEW YORK, AUGUST 30, 1890. | $3.00 A YEAR. Weekly.

Scientific American showing Hollerith's tabulator in use for the census

Each card was put in the press on the tabulating machine. An electrical connection was made by a rod passing through a hole in the card into a cup of mercury below. When a hole was sensed, the appropriate dial was turned to increase its record by one, and the correct flap was opened in the sorting box. The operator placed the card in the box and then closed the flap manually.

The cards and machines were used in the census of 1890 and all the information from it was processed in three years. In spite of many people's misgivings about the tabulator, the results it produced proved to be most accurate.

Hollerith improved his design and in 1896 formed a company called the 'Tabulator Machine Company' of New York, which was later to become part of what is today the world's largest computer company, International Business Machines (IBM).

The tabulator had a control panel something like a telephone switchboard. The points on this switchboard were connected to ends of wires coming from the card columns and counter positions. The job of the operator was to complete the connections by inserting the right plugs in the appropriate holes on the control panel.

Two companies to use Hollerith's machines in those days were the New York Railroad, who used them to keep track of rolling stock, and the Pennsylvania Steel Company, who used them for costing labour and materials.

Punch-card equipment was first introduced into Britain in 1904 by a small company called The Tabulator Ltd, who assembled Hollerith's machines. They were first tried out in the Woolwich Arsenal to total wages and production costs. However, opposition by employees prevented the machines being used permanently. Why do you think this was so?

Vickers of Sheffield were the first British company to install punched-card equipment, in 1906. In 1907 The Tabulator Ltd was taken over by the British Tabulating Machine Company (BTM).

James Powers, who was an associate of Hollerith at the American Census Bureau, started his own punch-card company, and his machines were used

to process the American census of 1910. In 1914 the Prudential Assurance Company ordered Powers' machines and eventually bought the manufacturing rights and formed the Accounting and Tabulating Corporation of Great Britain, which was later to become the Powers-Samas company. The Prudential were the first company to use this equipment for their own business requirements. Other early users were Cadbury's, the Royal Aircraft Factory and Kalamazoo.

BTM punch-card office of 1910

Much later, BTM merged with the Powers-Samas Accounting Machine Company Limited to become International Computers and Tabulators (ICT), in 1959. In 1968, ICT merged with English Electric Computers Ltd to form International Computers Ltd (ICL).

In 1911 punched-card equipment was used for the first time to process the British census. An early form of the punches used appears in the photograph from *Scientific American* opposite.

The pin-box tabulator shown below could add amounts together (say 76 and 46) and indicate the result (122) on the counters which could be seen through small windows in the front panel.

This showed a marked difference from the 1890 tabulator, which could only add one at a time. This facility to add amounts together changed the type of work that a tabulator could do from simple statistical work (like the census) to accounting.

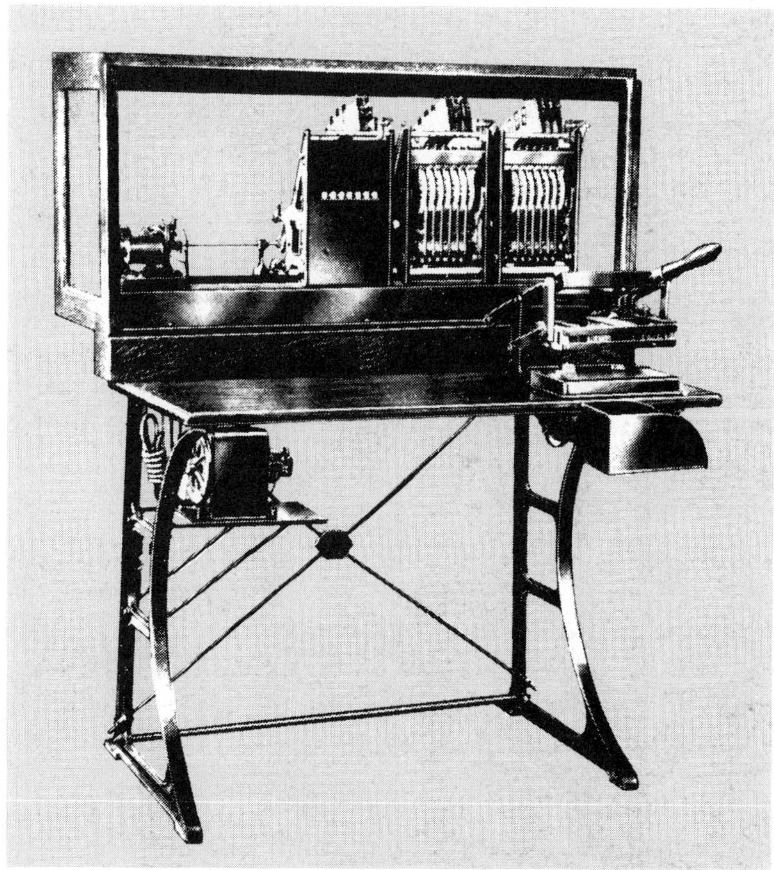

One of the earliest hand-operated pin-box tabulators

Once accounting was a possibility, many more companies became interested in using the machines, and there were new developments in both punching cards and sorting them.

When the cards had been punched and checked it was very likely that they would then have to be sorted into numerical order, perhaps by customer account numbers and then by stock account numbers. The vertical sorter shown below was used for this purpose. It was driven by the electricity available in a normal lamp socket of the time. The cards would then be tabulated into daily, weekly or monthly batches.

Early Hollerith vertical sorter

When a set of cards was to be punched with the same information in the first few columns, or in any particular area of the card, a gang punch was used.

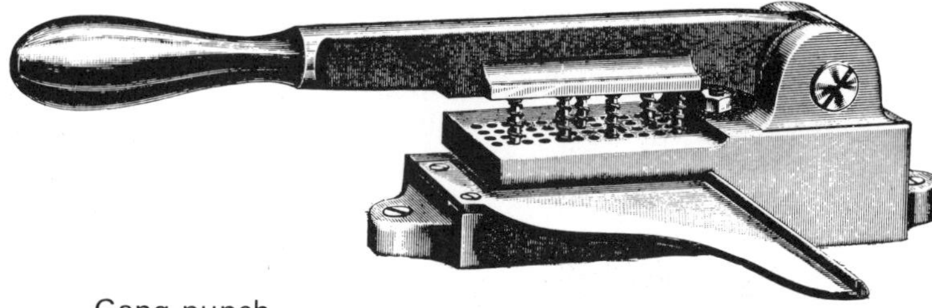

Gang punch

Below we see a later form of card punch. It was used rather like a typewriter (but with fewer keys) and operators could quickly be taught to use one. The speed of operating varied according to the amount of detail on the cards, but generally 250 to 800 cards could be punched in an hour.

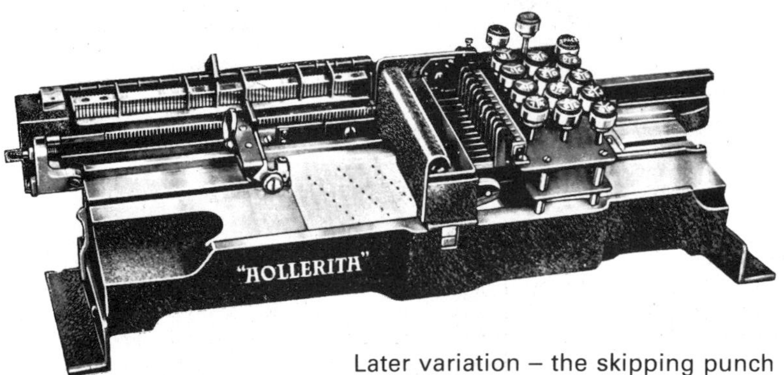

Later variation – the skipping punch

Relatively unskilled people could easily learn to be punch operators, but even so the likelihood of error could not be ignored. Each card was checked against the original document to make sure that it was correct. If a card was in error it had to be punched again.

The particular card shown opposite has 45 columns and 12 rows. Each column on this card is used to represent a single number. Some information needs more than one column, e.g. 'Wages No.' needs three columns.

The column or columns used to represent each item of information are called fields.

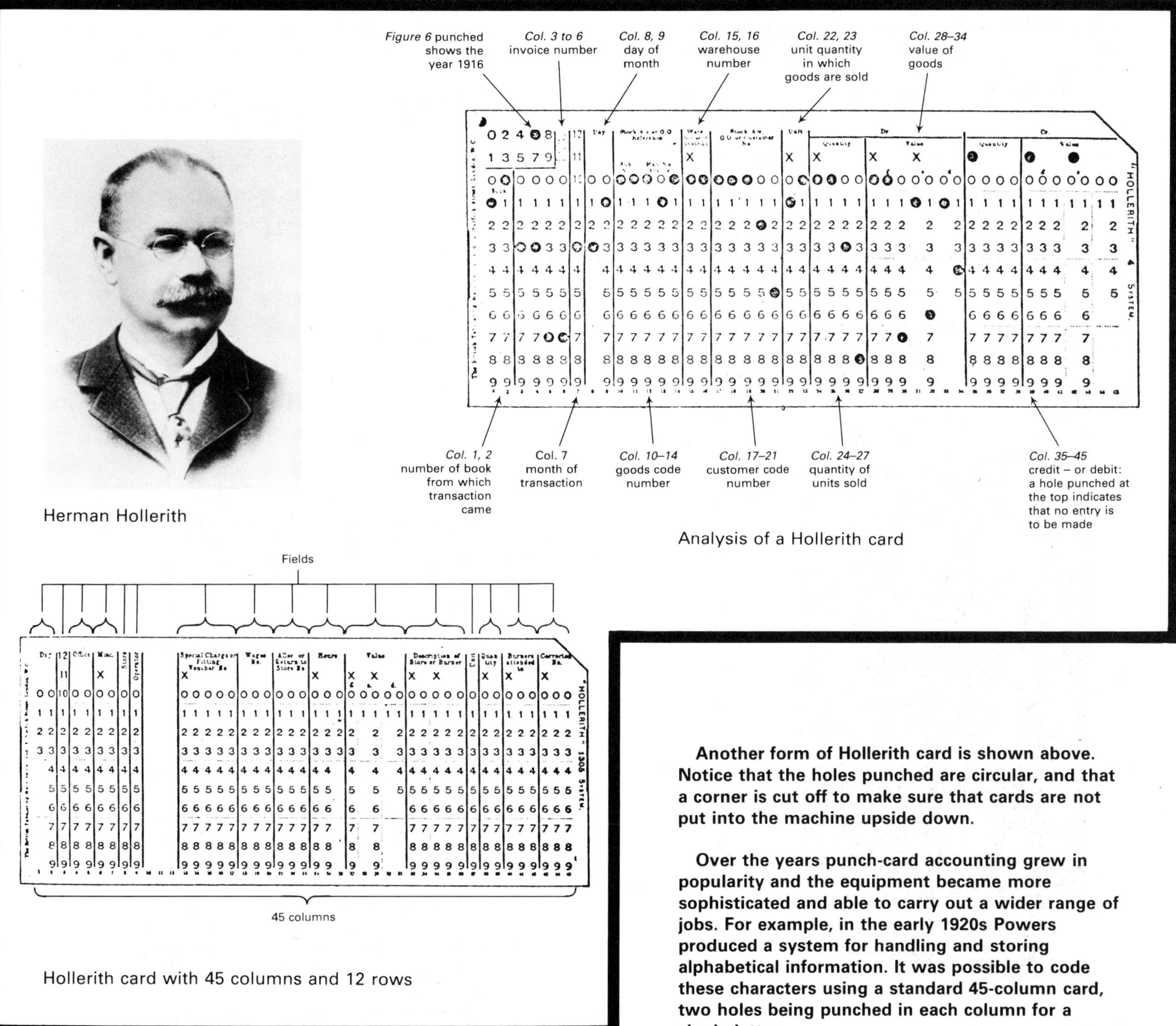

Herman Hollerith

Analysis of a Hollerith card

Hollerith card with 45 columns and 12 rows

Another form of Hollerith card is shown above. Notice that the holes punched are circular, and that a corner is cut off to make sure that cards are not put into the machine upside down.

Over the years punch-card accounting grew in popularity and the equipment became more sophisticated and able to carry out a wider range of jobs. For example, in the early 1920s Powers produced a system for handling and storing alphabetical information. It was possible to code these characters using a standard 45-column card, two holes being punched in each column for a single letter.

I C T 4-353 INTERNATIONAL COMPUTERS AND TABULATORS LIMITED PRINTED IN ENGLAND

Standard 80-column card used by the tabulator industry

A few years later, in 1929, IBM introduced an 80-column card with rectangular holes, which could hold almost twice the amount of information. The code used had been developed by Hollerith using one hole to represent numbers and two for letters. This became the standard format for the tabulator industry, and an example is shown above.

Printing tabulator (1930)

Card sorter (1930)

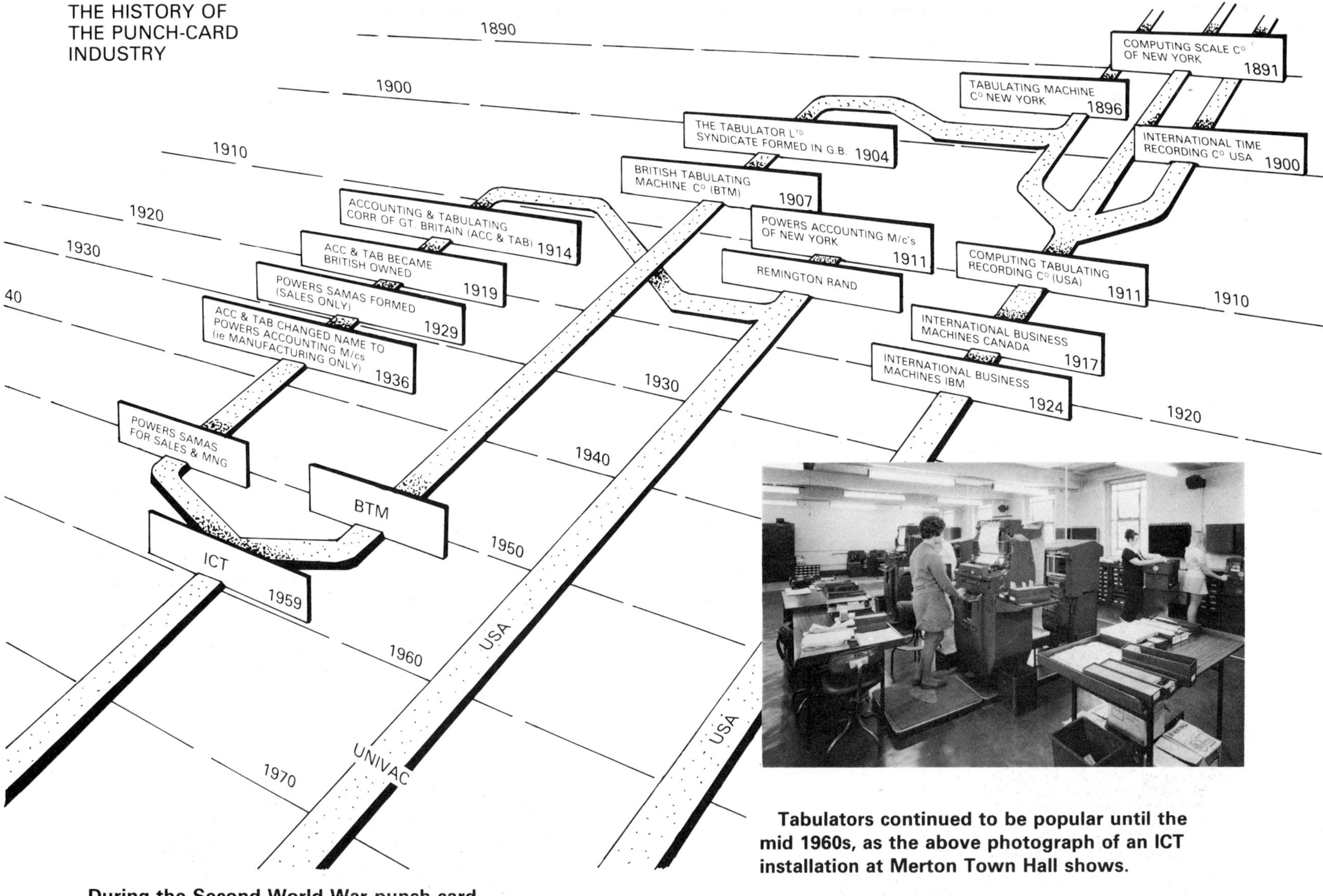

Tabulators continued to be popular until the mid 1960s, as the above photograph of an ICT installation at Merton Town Hall shows.

During the Second World War punch-card machines were widely used by both the armed forces and the government. A mobile unit was used by the army in Europe.

Although the first electronic computers were working by 1946, it was not until the early 1950s that the first commercial computers were used. At this time tabulators were still being designed with the latest electrical circuitry, and some early computers were built with parts originally designed for modern tabulators.

Questions

Look at the punched card on page 35.

1. How many possible rows are there on this card?
2. Give the full date shown on the card.
3. What is the customer code number and the goods code number?
4. How many fields are there on the card?

8 Input Methods and Data Preparation

We have already seen the amount of preparation that is required to process data on cards when using tabulators. In this chapter we shall examine how data is input, paying particular attention to the input media and devices that are used to read this data.

In Chapter 6 we studied two-state arithmetic and in a later chapter we shall see how data is stored inside the CPU. At this stage it is sufficient to know that all data must be stored in some form of binary code. That is, all the characters (letters and numbers) must be represented in the computer's store as 1s and 0s. Therefore all data must leave the input device in some form of two-state system.

Punched cards

Early commercial data processing relied heavily on punched cards as an input medium and indeed cards are still used today. Let us examine again a punched card that uses the Hollerith code.

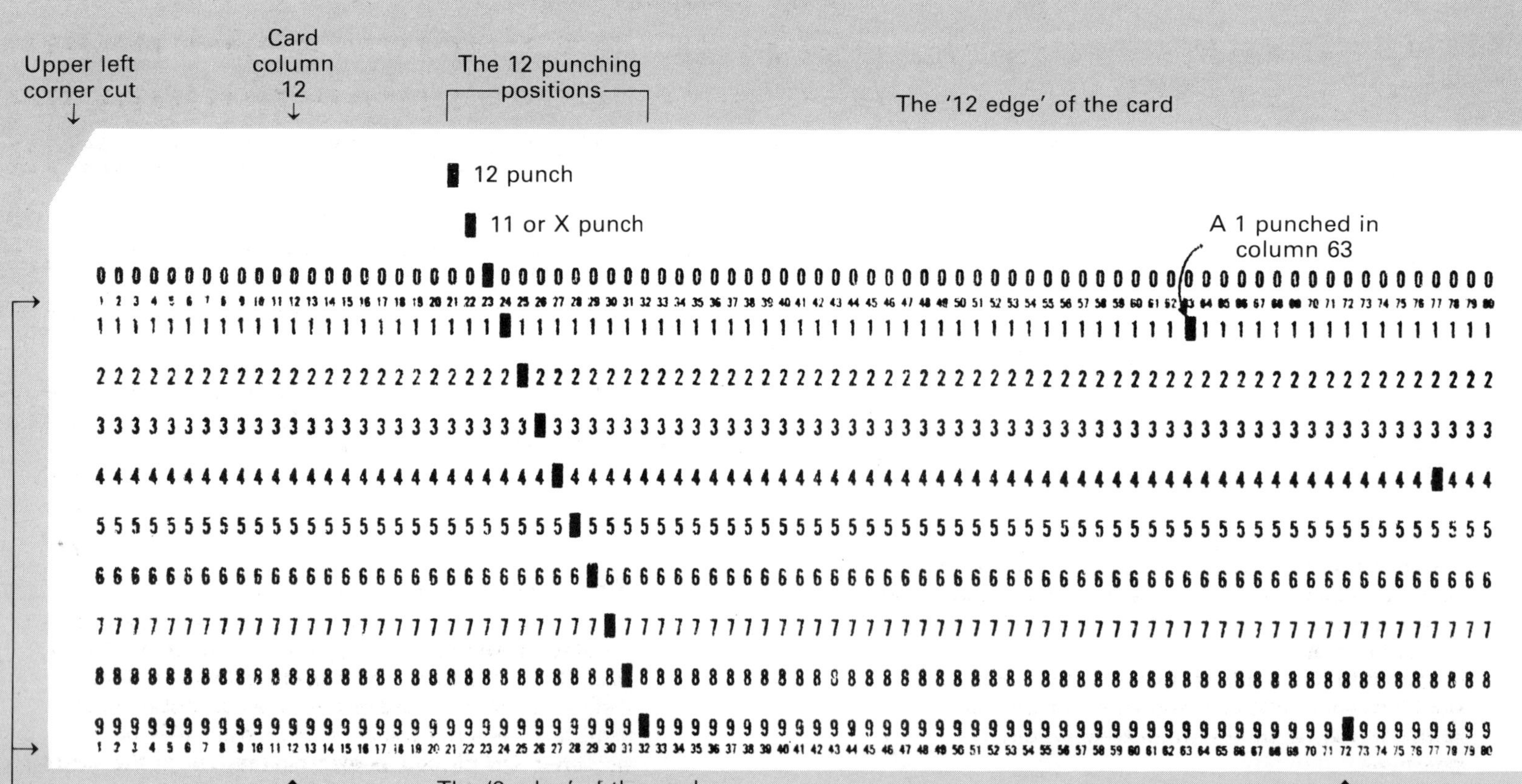

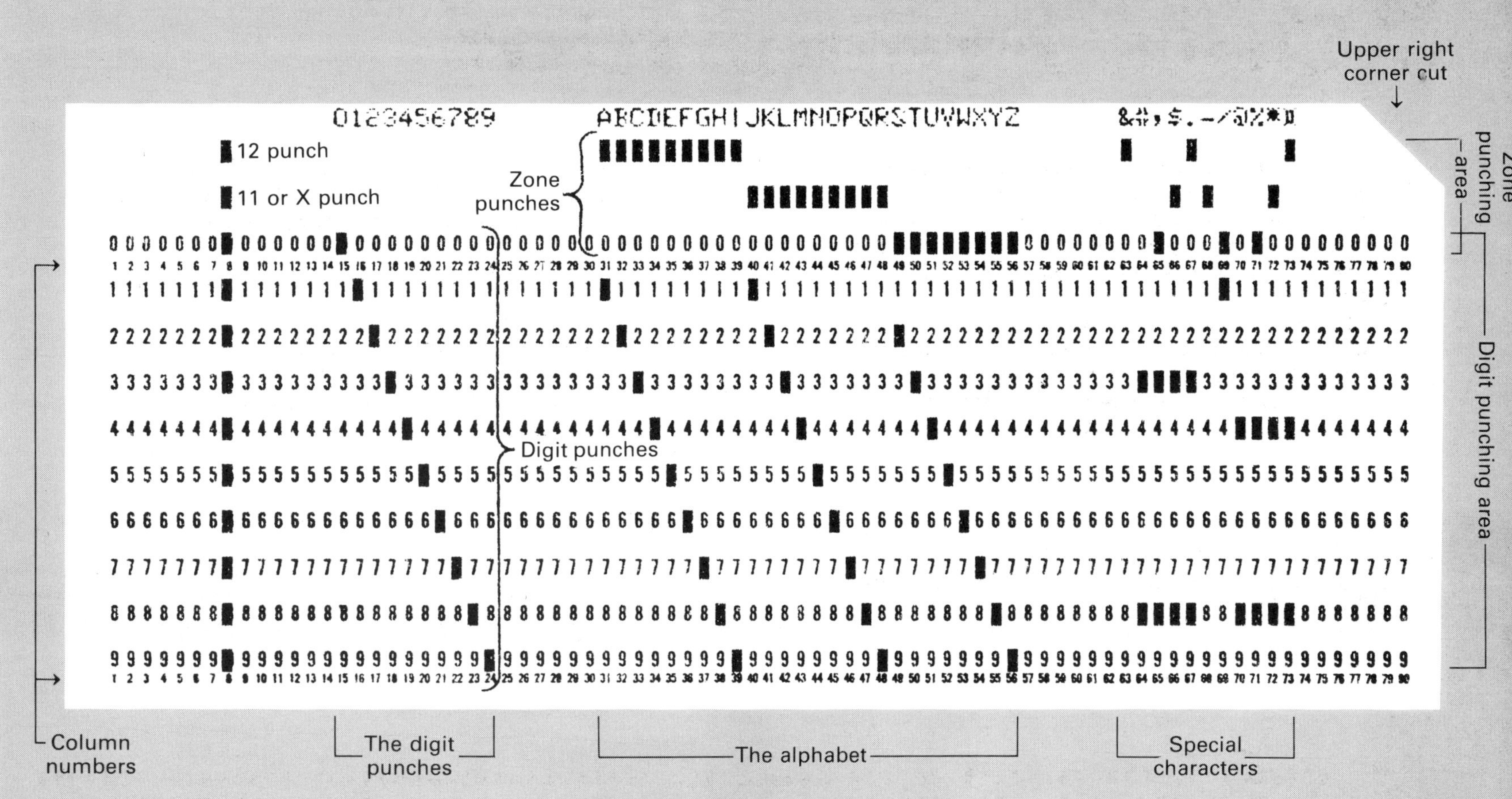

Remember that a hole represents 1 while 'no hole' represents 0. By this method binary codes can be punched into cards. The card above shows the codes for characters.

The code for numbers involves one punch position while letters of the alphabet can be punched with a combination of two punch positions.

Reading punched cards

In Chapter 7 we saw how early cards were read by tabulators: the presence of a hole enabled a wire to pass through and make an electrical connection. Clearly, a modern card reader in a computer must work on the same principle. How can holes be detected and passed as electrical pulses to the CPU?

If a light is placed on one side of the card, the holes will let light through. Light detectors then sense the positions where the light has passed through.

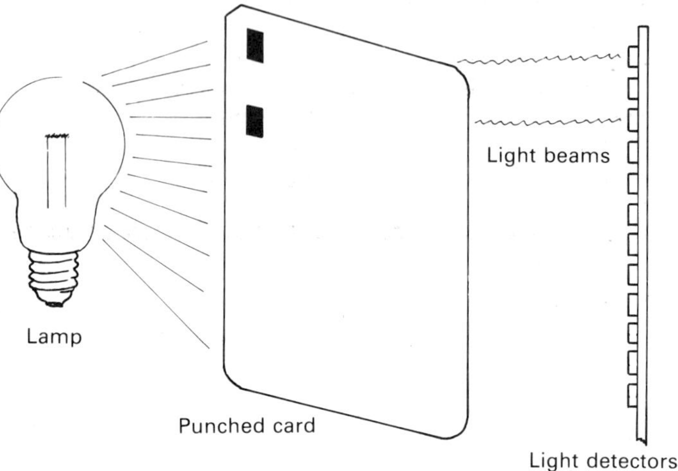

When light falls on photoelectric cells **they emit a current in the form of a pulse. A** pulse train **is formed from the output of 12 photoelectric cells.**

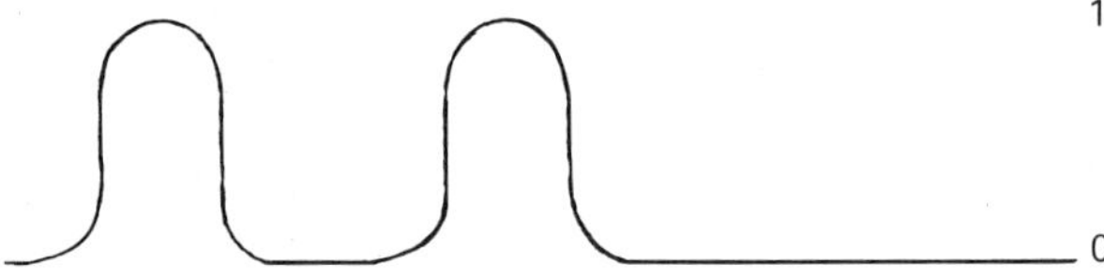

The current at the top of the pulse represents 1 and that at the bottom represents 0. This is the kind of pulse that you may have seen on an oscilloscope. Unfortunately the wave is not always exactly at 1

or 0. Thus it does not give only two states. Such pulses need to be fed through an electronic circuit called a 'square-wave rectifier'. Here only the exact levels at 1 and 0 are registered and intermediate values are ignored.

If the code for 'A' were punched into a card the square-wave pulse would come out as shown below.

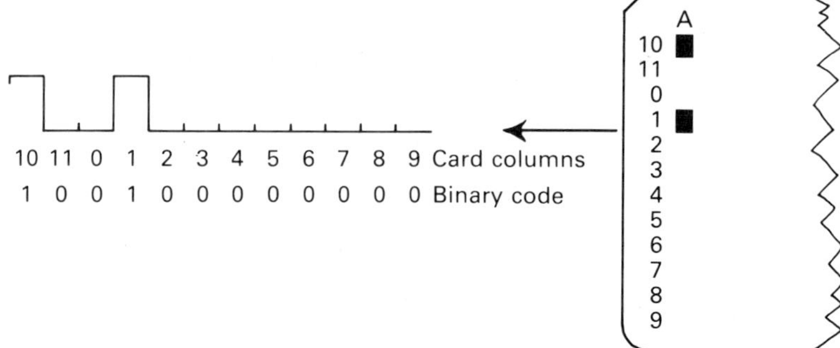

All the machines which make up a computer are known as hardware. **The hardware that produces pulse trains from holes in cards is a** card reader.

Card reader

Card readers generally consist of

1. **A hopper for receiving the cards to be read.**
2. **A transportation system to carry the cards through the reader.**
3. **A reading mechanism.**
4. **A stacker which collects the cards once they have been read.**

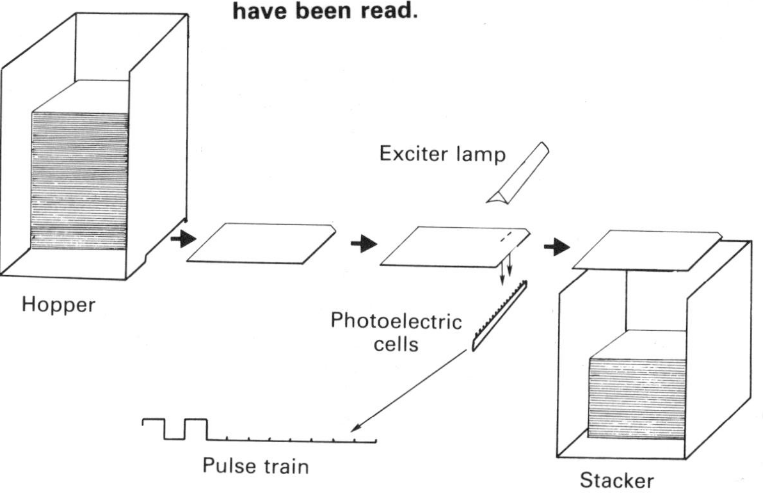

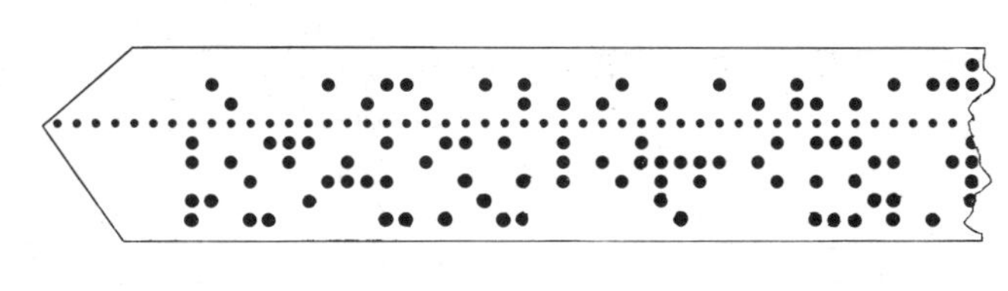

Paper tape

Another input method uses punched paper tape. In the examples you can see that there are 8 tracks or channels across the tape. Each character has its own particular binary code and is punched in a 'frame' across the tape.

Paper tape with 8 tracks is common although 5, 6 or 7 tracks are sometimes used.

The small holes (sprocket holes**) are not part of the coded information. They are there to enable the tape to be moved through the reader. The paper-tape reader operates in a similar way to the card reader.**

If you look carefully at the code you will notice that there is an even number of holes in each frame. This is because the tape has been punched with even parity**. The eighth track has been used for this purpose: a hole is punched there whenever the total of holes in the first seven tracks gives an odd number. (A few systems use** odd parity**, punching an additional hole in track 8 whenever the total would otherwise be an even number.)**

Using this eighth track for a parity check gives a very simple means of testing for mispunching. When using even parity, if an odd number of holes is read, then an error will be registered.

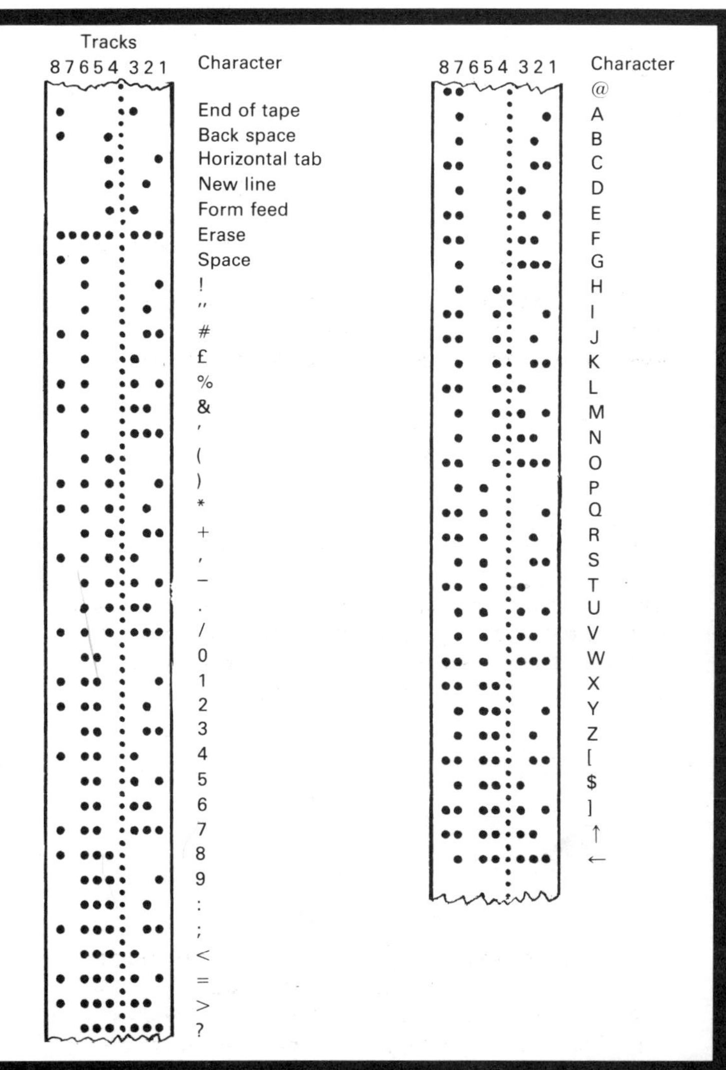

Card and tape punching

Although data held on punched cards or paper tape may be passed to the CPU relatively quickly, a lot of preparation is required beforehand.

The information from handwritten documents and coding sheets is prepared off line. **This means that the devices used for this kind of data preparation are not connected to the computer. The punch machines have keyboards like typewriters and use either knives or needles to punch the holes.**

When data is transcribed from source documents to cards or tape, errors may occur. These may be due to mistakes on the original documents or to errors in punching.

In order to type the information correctly, the operator must read carefully the handwritten document to be transcribed. All characters must be clearly distinguishable, and there are certain characters which often cause problems. Because of this, certain conventions are usually followed.

1, I, and 7 are written as l, I, 7
The numeral 0 and the letter o are written as ø, O
2 and Z are written as 2, Ƶ

Paper-tape reader/punch

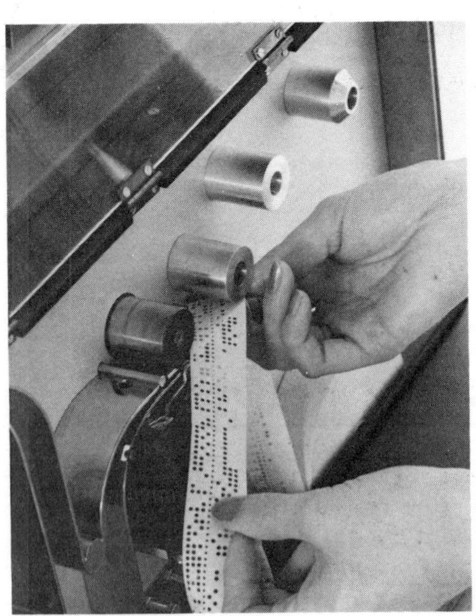

Paper tape being fed into a tape reader

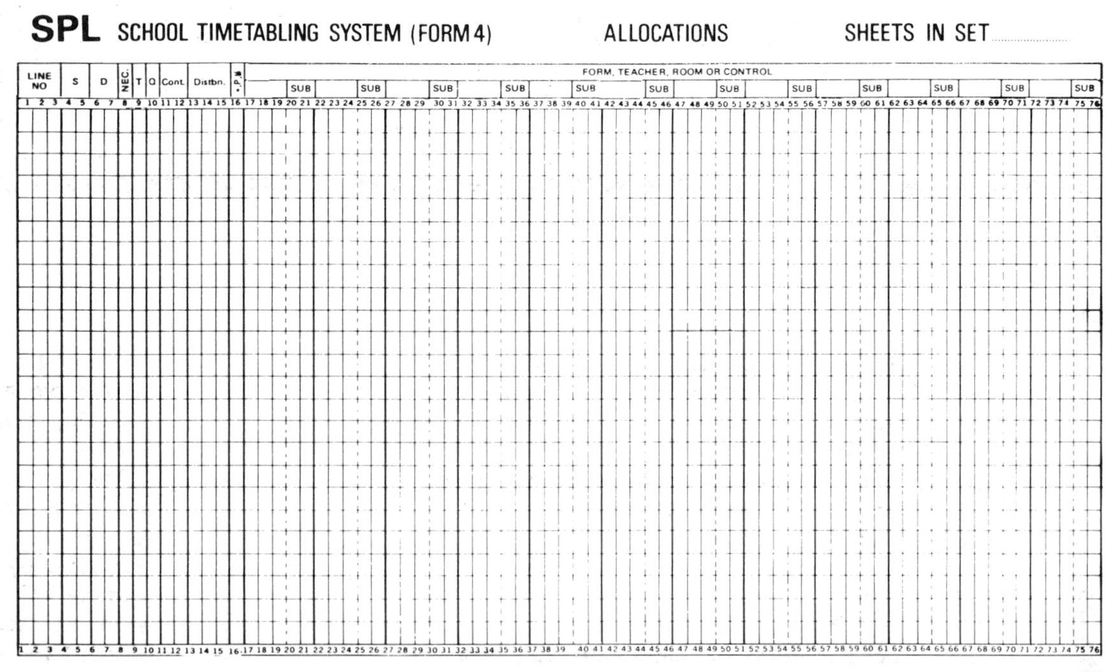

SPL SCHOOL TIMETABLING SYSTEM (FORM 4) ALLOCATIONS SHEETS IN SET

LINE NO | S | D | NEC. | T | Q | Cont. | Distbn. | FORM, TEACHER, ROOM OR CONTROL: SUB | SUB | SUB | SUB | SUB | SUB | SUB | SUB | SUB | SUB | SUB | SUB

COBOL

PROGRAMMING FORM

PROBLEM ____________ PAGE 5 OF ______

PROGRAMMER ____________ DATE ______

PAGE | SERIAL | CONT. | A | B | C

Two typical coding sheets are shown here, one for COBOL programs and the other for school timetabling.

Even when the original document is correct, operators may make mistakes when punching. A common error is to type characters out of order, e.g. 39178 instead of 31978.

Checking for errors

However, various tests may be applied to input data to see if it is valid. (Some of these tests will be shown later in various applications.) There is a special piece of off-line equipment which is used for checking punching errors. This machine is called a verifier.

The process of verification involves punching data a second time. The first copy made on punched tape is fed into the machine and compared character by character with the second tape being punched. If the two tapes are not identical, the verifier locks and allows the operator to check which tape is in error. The correct version is then punched.

Cards may be verified in a similar manner, except that a new card has to be punched only if an error has occurred. Although a second typing of the data is done, a second set of cards is not punched automatically. Marks may be entered on to the cards to show that they have been verified. It is also common practice to 'interpret' the cards at this stage. This means that the actual characters are printed on the top of the cards so that they can be read easily by eye.

Comparison between cards and tape

Cards are bulky and easily damaged, and bent cards may make reading difficult. However, paper tape is easily stored without damage.

Editing cards is relatively easy: you simply take out the offending card or cards and punch others. To correct an error in a paper tape you have to punch the whole tape again, and when verifying a

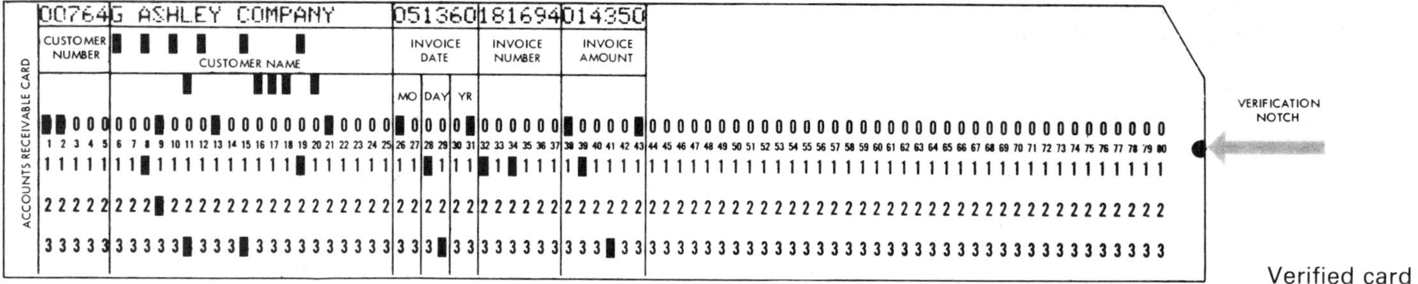

Verified card

Another interpreted card is shown below.

002655 AFTER ADVANCING 2 LINES FINDERLS

IBM SERVICE BUREAU

IBM 866 - 01645

second tape must be punched. In spite of this, tape is still cheaper to use.

Data is held more efficiently on tape: only the necessary amount of tape is used. With cards it is unlikely that the whole of the card would be punched, which means that several columns are left unused at the end.

Other methods of data input

To produce low error rates when entering data from cards or tape it is obvious that a great deal of data preparation is required. Unfortunately this stage of processing is very labour intensive. Lots of punch operators are needed in a large computer department, and the rate of processing depends upon the speed of the operators.

It is for such reasons that other methods of data entry have been developed. Ideally, the source documents themselves should be input, or at least there should be the minimum of data preparation.

The methods we shall examine are

1. **Mark reading.**
2. **Magnetic Ink Character Recognition (MICR).**
3. **Optical Character Recognition (OCR).**
4. **Merchandising tags.**
5. **Key to disc or tape (Direct data entry).**
6. **Remote data entry.**

Mark reading

The following examples are input documents for mark reading. **The first is a meter reading sheet used by a gas board. The second (overleaf) is**

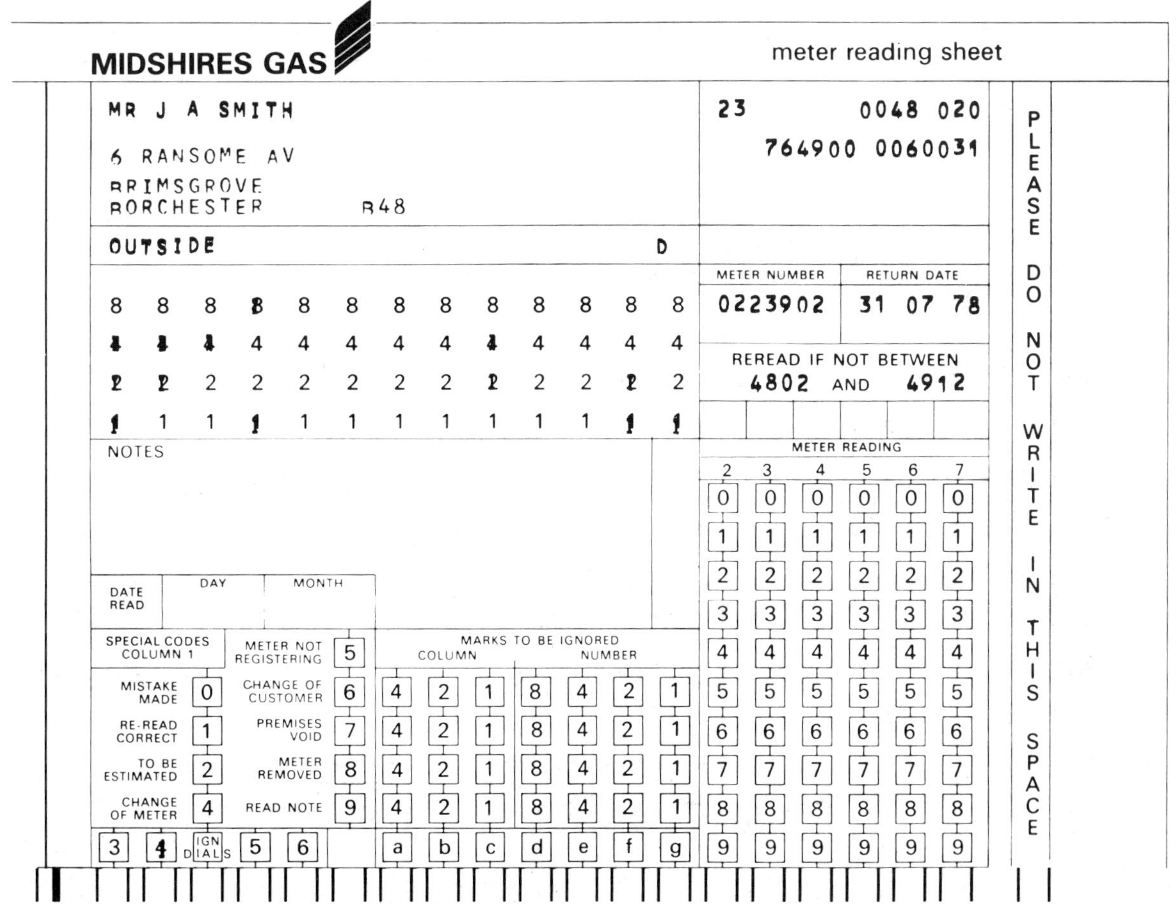
MIDSHIRES GAS
meter reading sheet
MR J A SMITH
6 RANSOME AV
BRIMSGROVE
BORCHESTER B48
OUTSIDE D
23 0048 020
764900 0060031
METER NUMBER 0223902
RETURN DATE 31 07 78
REREAD IF NOT BETWEEN 4802 AND 4912
8 8 8 8 8 8 8 8 8 8 8 8 8
4 4 4 4 4 4 4 4 4 4 4 4 4
2 2 2 2 2 2 2 2 2 2 2 2 2
1 1 1 1 1 1 1 1 1 1 1 1 1
NOTES
DATE READ DAY MONTH
SPECIAL CODES COLUMN 1
MISTAKE MADE 0
RE-READ CORRECT 1
TO BE ESTIMATED 2
CHANGE OF METER 4
METER NOT REGISTERING 5
CHANGE OF CUSTOMER 6
PREMISES VOID 7
METER REMOVED 8
READ NOTE 9
MARKS TO BE IGNORED
COLUMN NUMBER
4 2 1 8 4 2 1
METER READING
2 3 4 5 6 7
0 1 2 3 4 5 6 7 8 9
3 4 IGN DIALS 5 6
a b c d e f g
PLEASE DO NOT WRITE IN THIS SPACE

Meter reading sheet

a card used for the computer marking of pupils' responses to multiple-choice questions.

Pre-printed stationery is required for these documents so that the marks are made in pre-set positions. Light detectors over the mark positions sense the pencil marks as each column of the document is scanned from a light source.

Of course, it is important when using this method to make sure that the impression left by the pencil is dark enough.

The pupil using a multiple-choice test card fills in one of the options A to E for each question. The optical mark reader **sends the corresponding pulse train to the CPU for each character in the pre-set positions.**

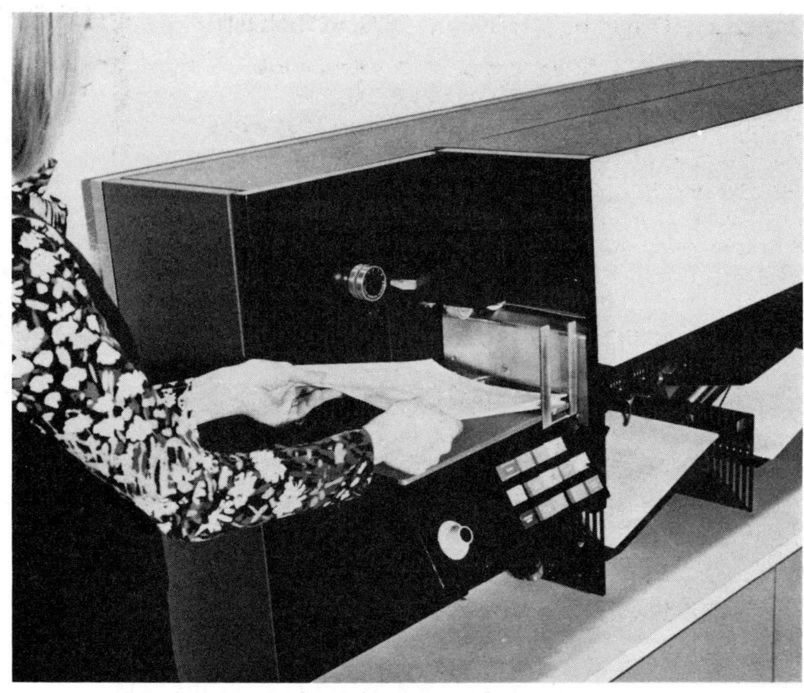

Optical mark reader

Multiple-choice response card

STUDENT NUMBER

EXAM NUMBER

1 2 3 4 5 6 7 8 9 10 11 12 13 14 15 16 17 18 19 20 21 22 23 24 25 26 27 28 29 30 31 32 33 34 35 36 37 38 39 40 41 42 43 44 45 46 47 48 49 50

SECTION

0 1 2 3 4 5 6 7 8 9

A B C D E

1 2 3 4 5 6 7 8 9 10 11 12 13 14 15 16 17 18 19 20 21 22 23 24 25 26 27 28 29 30 31 32 33 34 35 36 37 38 39 40 41 42 43 44 45 46 47 48 49 50

NAME

Dataset Limited 07.11303.001/002 Printed in the U.K.

Magnetic ink character recognition

Magnetic ink characters are printed with an ink containing a substance capable of being magnetized. Documents containing such characters may be read directly by machine, and therefore no data preparation will be required. Magnetic ink character recognition **is used mainly in banks, where characters are printed on cheques using magnetic ink.**

MICR encoder

MICR reader/sorter

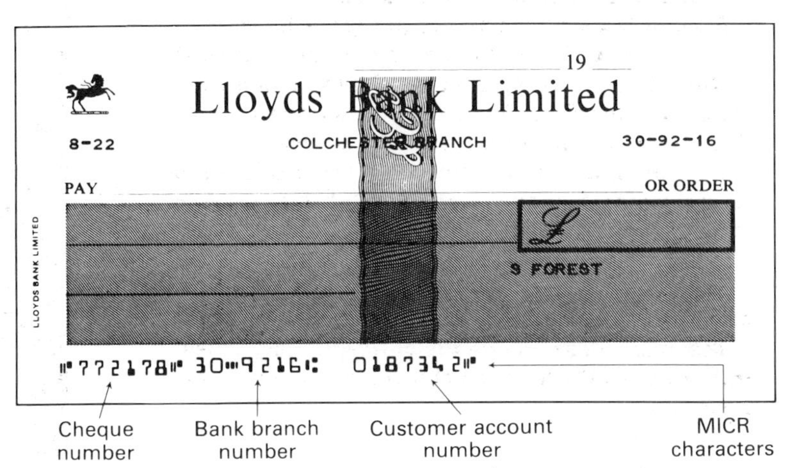
19
Lloyds Bank Limited
8-22
COLCHESTER BRANCH
30-92-16
PAY
OR ORDER
£
S FOREST
LLOYDS BANK LIMITED
⑈772178⑈ 30⑆92161⑆ 0187342⑈

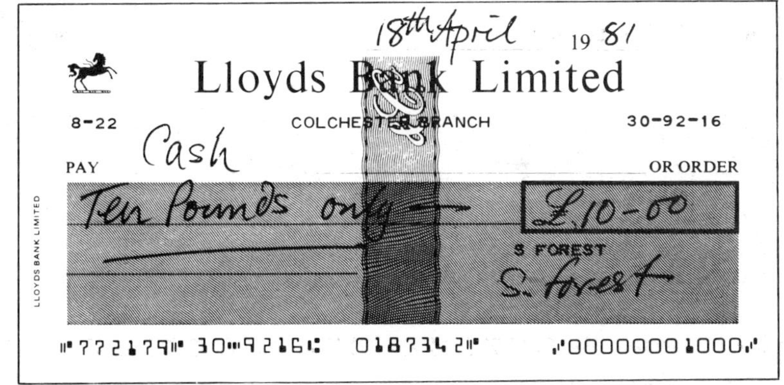
18th April 1981
Lloyds Bank Limited
8-22
COLCHESTER BRANCH
30-92-16
PAY Cash
OR ORDER
Ten Pounds only
£10-00
S FOREST
S. Forest
LLOYDS BANK LIMITED
⑈772179⑈ 30⑆92161⑆ 0187342⑈ ⑇0000001000⑇

When the user has filled in the cheque, the only detail then needed by the bank is the amount. This is encoded (at the bank where the cheque is delivered) by an MICR printer.

Most cheques are then sent to a main clearing house where they form the input to an MICR reader/sorter.

When a character printed in magnetic ink passes under the reading head, the magnetic effect is sensed and a current of electricity is produced. The presence or absence of a current is registered as a bit pattern in a matrix. This matrix can be compared with the stored bit pattern for each of the characters and if the character being read is not valid an error is signalled.

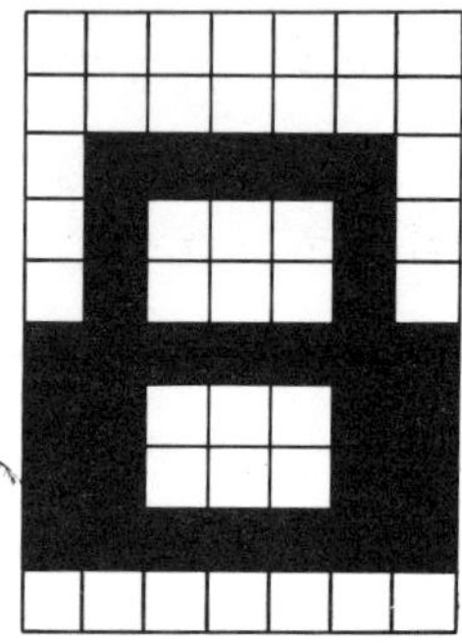

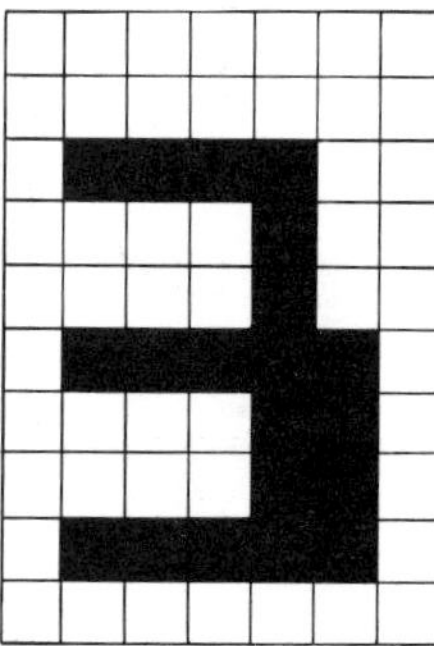

Patterns in a matrix for the E13B characters 8 and 3

The characters printed on cheques obviously need to be typed in a particular style or font. The font used on cheques in this country is called E13B and originated in the United States. There are fourteen characters, ten digits and four special characters, most of which can be seen on the sample cheques given earlier.

MICR allows input to a computer to be read directly by both machine and man. From the bank's point of view there is the added security that if the figures are overwritten in any way they can still be read. Thus any attempted alterations may be detected.

In Europe a different font (CMC7) is used. In this, each character is made up of vertical lines with either narrow or wide spaces between them. A binary code for each character can be produced by representing wide gaps as 1 and narrow gaps as 0.

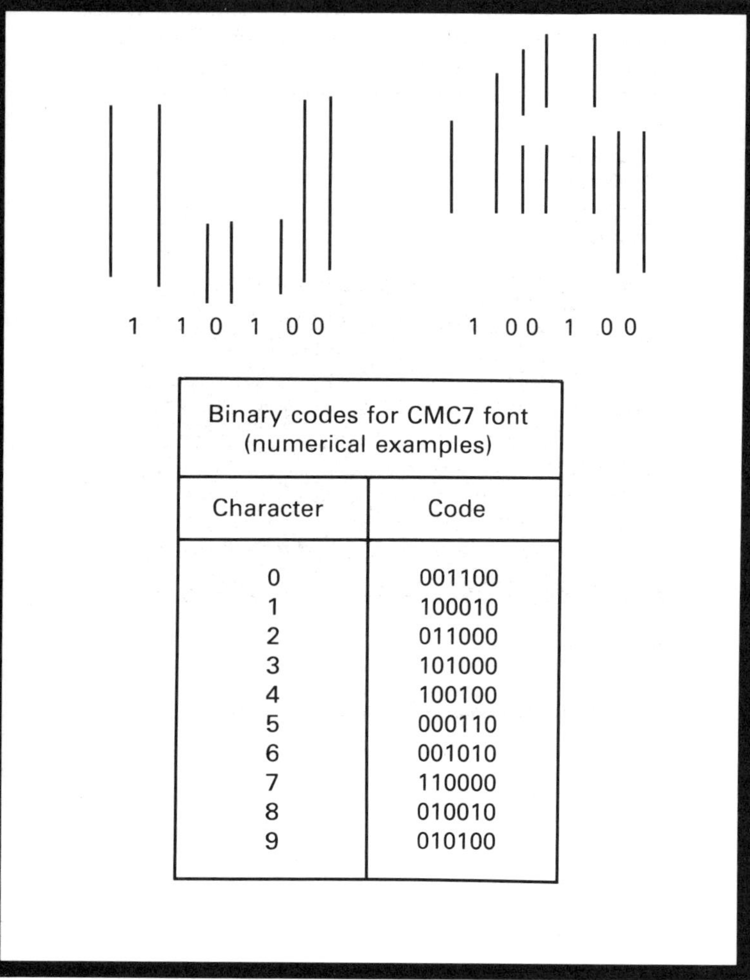

Binary codes for CMC7 font (numerical examples)	
Character	Code
0	001100
1	100010
2	011000
3	101000
4	100100
5	000110
6	001010
7	110000
8	010010
9	010100

Optical character recognition (OCR)

When a light source is passed over a document the written or typed characters reflect less light than the background area. Thus the shape of characters may be determined. Each character is scanned several times and an electronic picture of it is built up. This pattern is compared with patterns stored in the computer; the one which matches with the fewest errors is considered to be the character read. Optical character recognition **involves no verification so error rates are relatively high.**

OCR characters can be printed by simple devices such as cash registers and line printers. Therefore tally rolls (from cash registers) and line-printer paper may be used as input media to OCR readers.

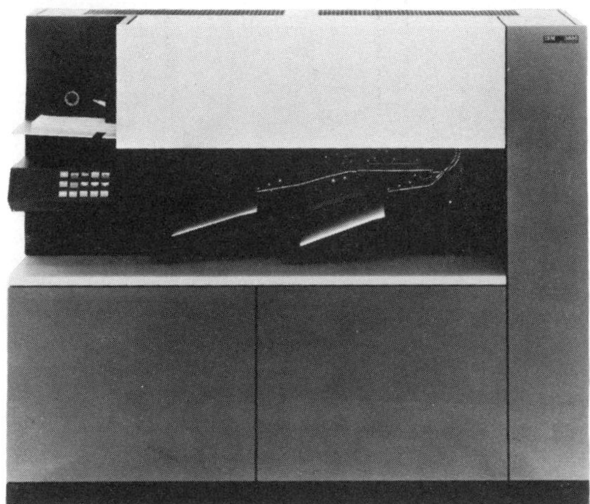

Optical character reader

Some acceptable OCR fonts are shown below.

8 5 2 0
1 6 7 4
3 9 7 5
6 2 4 8

Carefully written handwriting can also be accepted.

1	2	8	0		
	3	5	6	7	
9	0	1	3		

An OCR reader may even accept less tidy writing.

1	2	8	0		
	3	5	6	7	
9	0	1	3		

But even you would have difficulty making sense of this, wouldn't you?

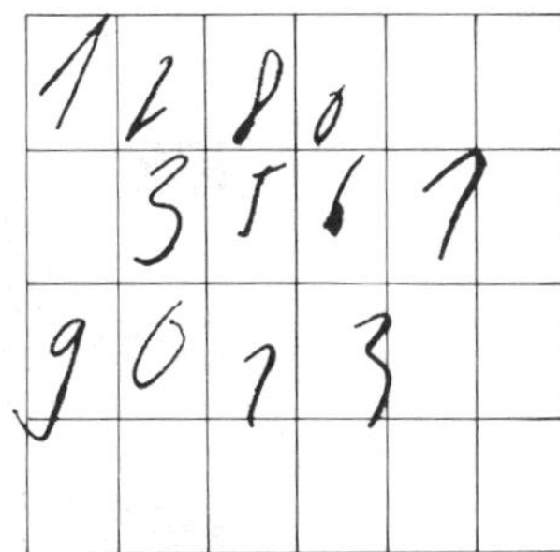

However, characters not accepted by an optical character reader may be input to a video-image processor. **Images of machine printed or handwritten characters are converted into digital form and sent to a display screen. Here the operator can correct the character, verify it and enter the correction.**

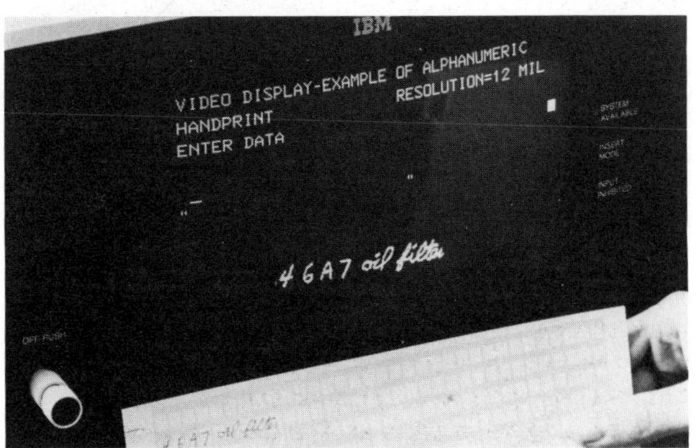

Video-image processor

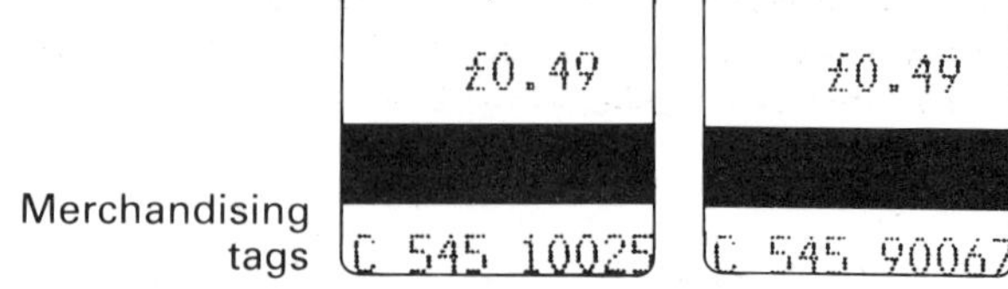

Merchandising tags

Punched-hole tag being read

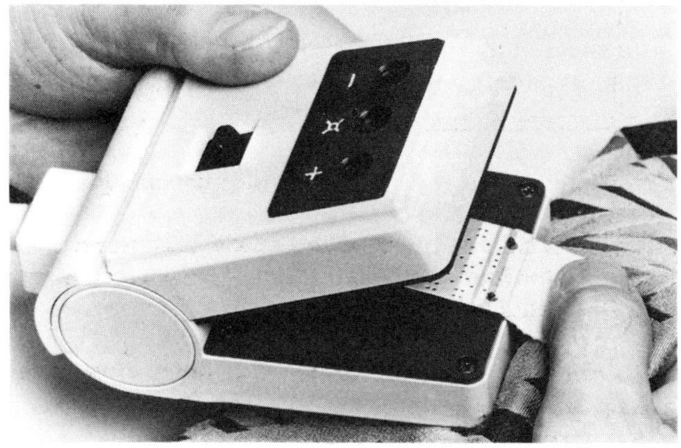

Point-of-sale terminal with a magnetic wand reader

Below Magnetic-strip tag being read

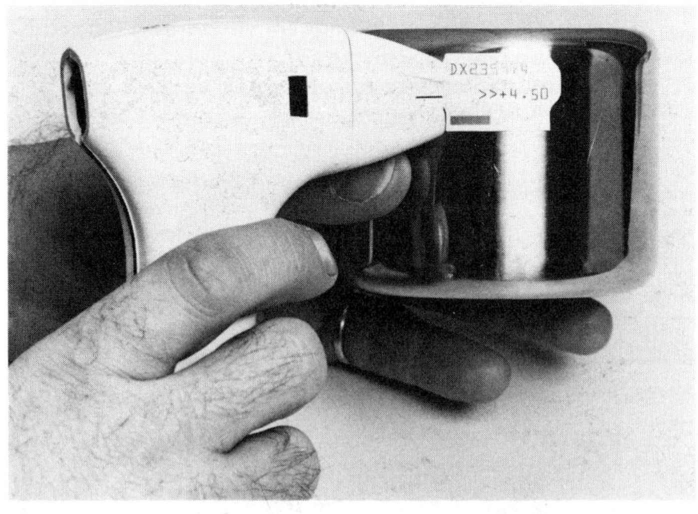

Merchandising tags

Kimball tags are special price tickets attached to goods, especially clothing. These tags come in various shapes and sizes and contain information such as cost, colour and size.

When the goods have been sold the tag is removed to be read by a Kimball tag reader. **The information contained in it is used to update stock levels.**

The Kimball tag may contain information either in the form of punched holes or coded in a strip of magnetic tape (see top left). A magnetic wand reader **can be attached to a point-of-sale terminal to enable the Kimball tag to be read as the goods are paid for. By this method data may be collected accurately and quickly.**

Key to disc or tape (Direct data entry)

Another method of data input involves a storage device known as a disc. **A magnetic disc looks rather like an LP record, and information is stored on both sides as a series of magnetized or non-magnetized spots. A small** discette **(sometimes spelt 'diskette') may also be used. One discette can hold as much data as almost 2000 punched cards.**

The data entry system shown here contains a keyboard, display screen and disc drives. Information is typed out on the keyboard. As it is typed it appears on a display screen so that the operator may detect any errors. Then the corrected information is transferred to the discette.

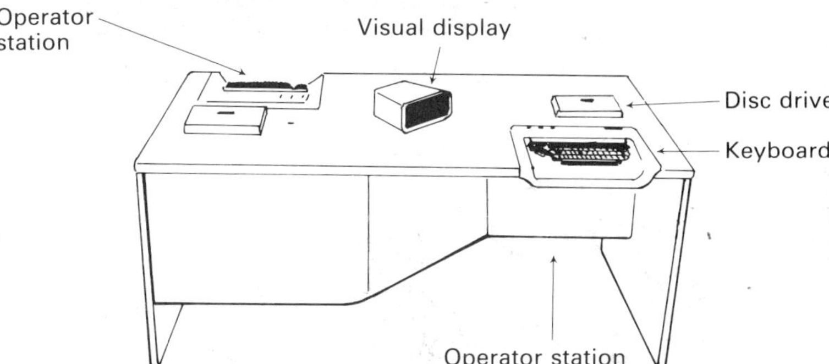

The discette can be removed easily and stored until the next batch of related data is received, or until it is required for processing.

The photograph below shows data entry operators at work at a large local-authority computer centre. Here visual display units are connected to an exchangeable disc system, and the verified input is then dumped on to magnetic tape.

Other systems are available which allow data to be keyed directly on to magnetic tape.

Remote data entry

As we have seen in earlier chapters, data may be keyed in directly to a central processor by the use of teletypewriters or visual display units. When the central processor and the terminals are in the same building, communication is over a very small distance. However, if a terminal is a long way away from the computer then information may have to be transmitted as signals along telephone or telegraph lines.

However, the pulse trains from these terminals are not acceptable for transmission down telephone lines and so they have to be 'modulated'. At the terminal end of the telephone line the pulses are MOdulated, and at the computer end the signals are DEModulated. Hence the British Telecom device which does this is named modem.

British Telecom modem

The photographs on the right were taken at the Birmingham Educational Computing Centre. In the first, input from the terminal is being sent via a telephone line to a computer situated at Newcastle upon Tyne. In the second, multiple-choice test cards are being input to a reader and the data is then being transmitted to a computer about four kilometres away.

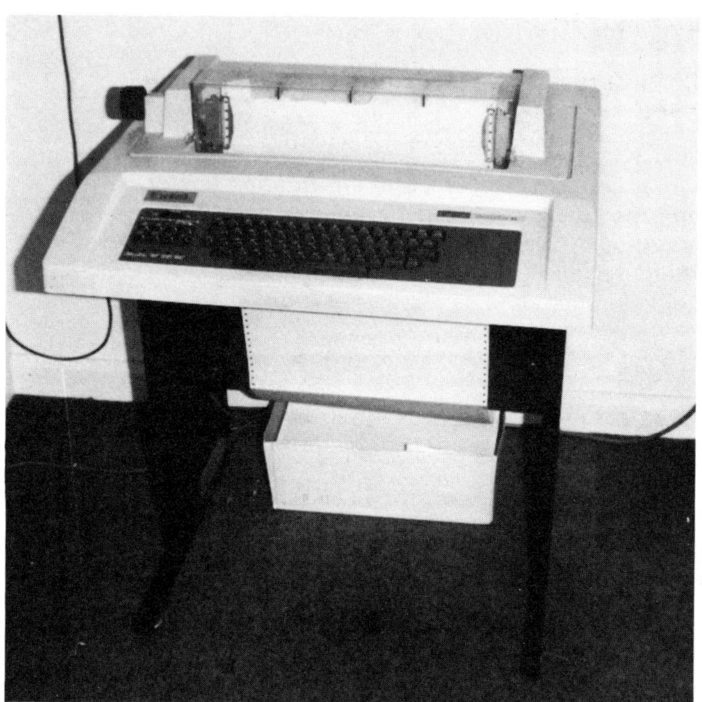

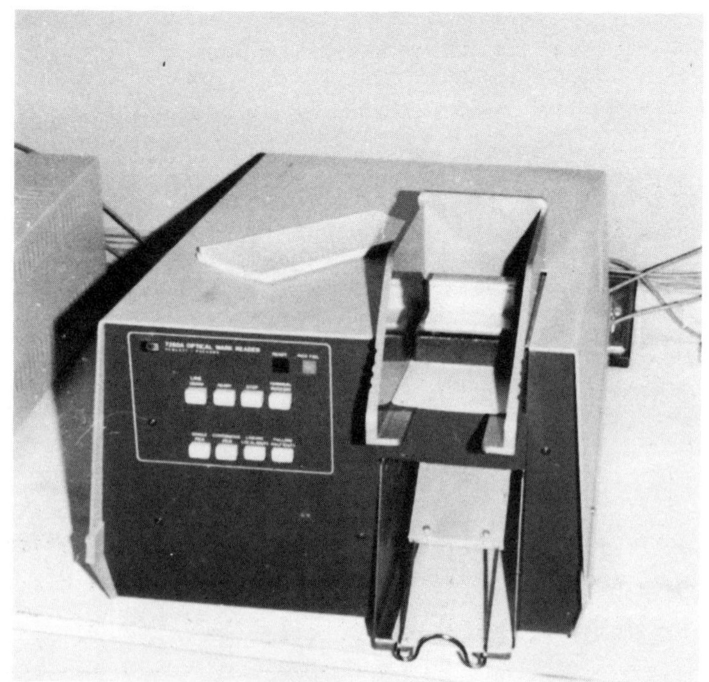

Questions

1. Cards may be divided into fields as the example below shows.
   (a) What date has been punched?
   (b) How many fields are shown?

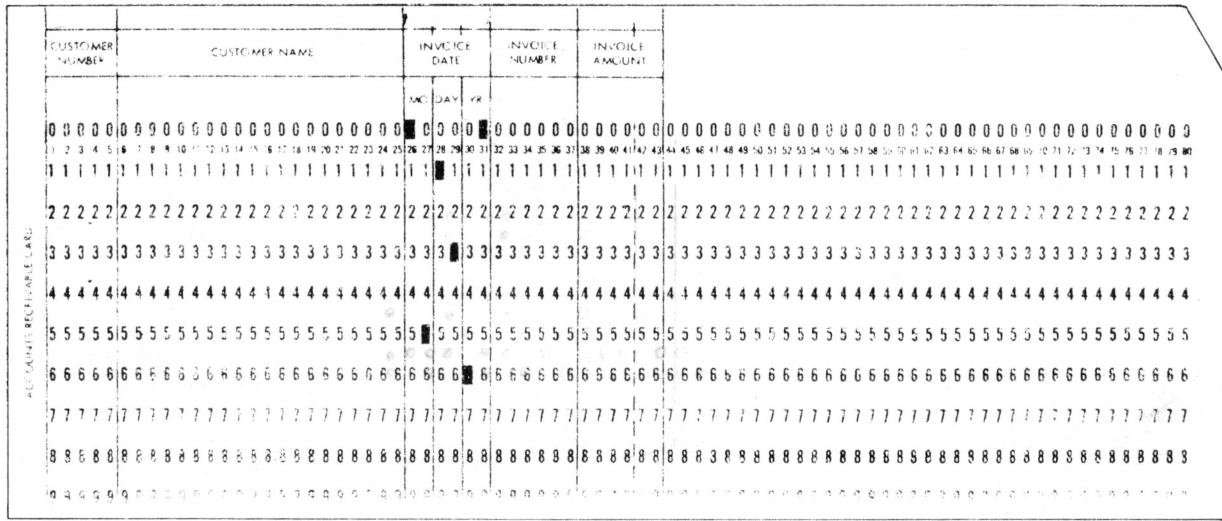

2. Using the punch-card code given on page 39, find out what has been punched on the card below.

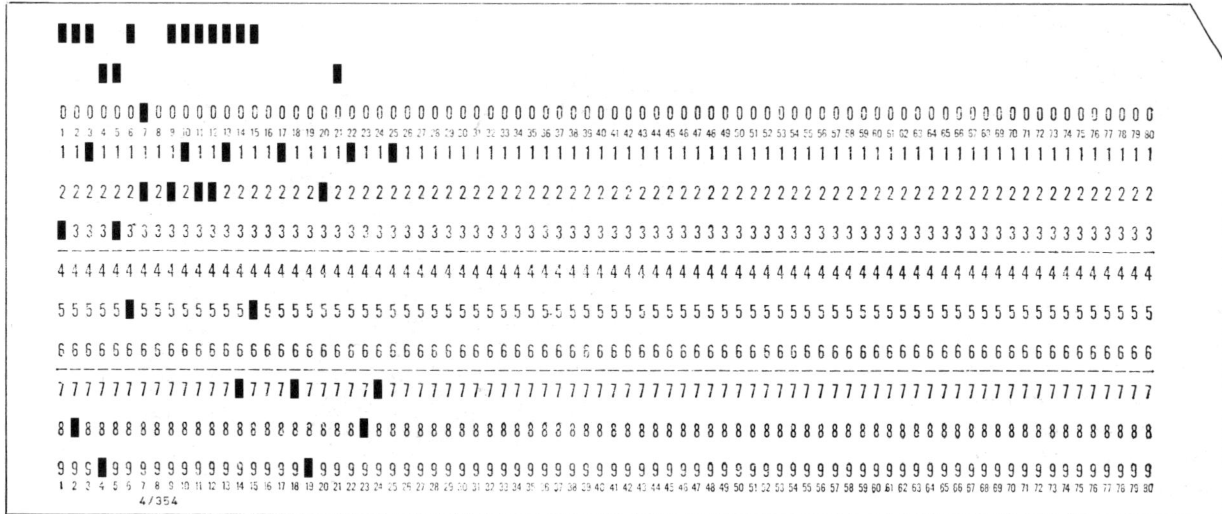

3. What is the message contained on the punched paper tape below?
4. Examine the sections of paper tape below, and state whether they have been punched with odd or even parity.
5. An error was registered when the section of paper tape illustrated below was read. The tape was punched with even parity.
   (a) Which frames have been mispunched?
   (b) What do you think caused the error?
6. What is meant by verification and how is this done?
7. Give advantages and disadvantages of using either punched cards or punched paper tape.
8. On the meter reading sheet opposite, the meter reader has entered the present reading by 'spot marking' the correct numbers in each column.
   (a) What is the reading marked on the sheet?
   (b) How many dials are there on the meter?
   (c) Why has 're-read' been spot marked?

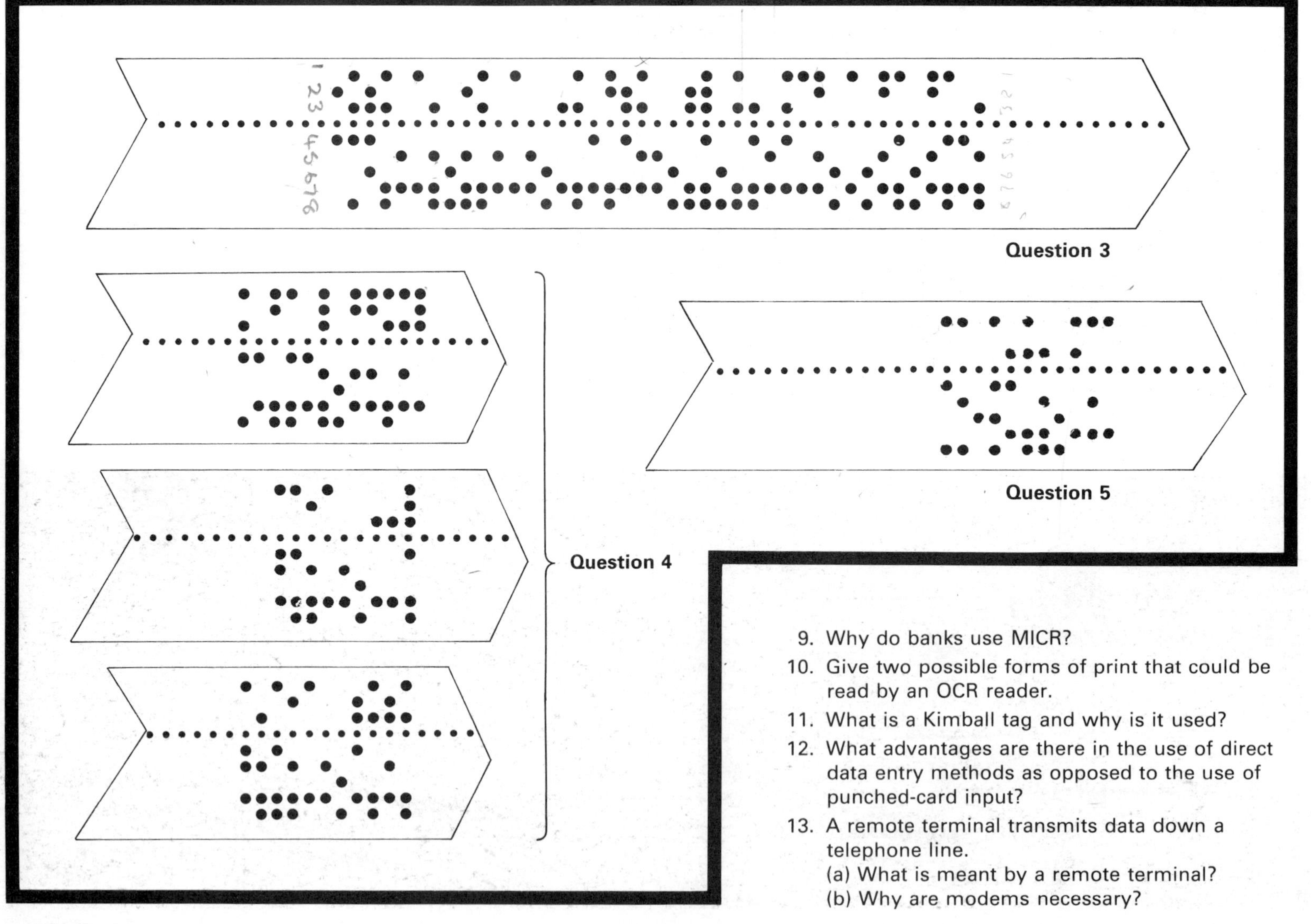

9. Why do banks use MICR?
10. Give two possible forms of print that could be read by an OCR reader.
11. What is a Kimball tag and why is it used?
12. What advantages are there in the use of direct data entry methods as opposed to the use of punched-card input?
13. A remote terminal transmits data down a telephone line.
    (a) What is meant by a remote terminal?
    (b) Why are modems necessary?

MIDSHIRES GAS meter reading sheet

MR A C COLES

28 BLYTHESWOOD
BRIMSGROVE
BORCHESTER B48

23 0050 041
764940 0280016

GARAGE D

METER NUMBER	RETURN DATE
0196701	31 07 78

REREAD IF NOT BETWEEN 1360 AND 1468

1489

METER READING

8 8 8 8 8 8 8 8 8 8 8 8 8
4 4 4 4 4 4 4 4 4 4 4 4 4
2 2 2 2 2 2 2 2 2 2 2 2 2
1 1 1 1 1 1 1 1 1 1 1 1 1

NOTES

DATE READ: DAY 28, MONTH 7

SPECIAL CODES COLUMN 1

MISTAKE MADE	0	METER NOT REGISTERING	5
RE-READ CORRECT	1	CHANGE OF CUSTOMER	6
TO BE ESTIMATED	2	PREMISES VOID	7
CHANGE OF METER	4	METER REMOVED	8
		READ NOTE	9

3 4 IGN DIALS 5 6

MARKS TO BE IGNORED: COLUMN 4 2 1; NUMBER 8 4 2 1

a b c d e f g

PLEASE DO NOT WRITE IN THIS SPACE

Question 8

Vocabulary

card reader
disc
discette
even parity
hardware
key to disc
key to tape
Kimball tag
Kimball tag reader
magnetic ink character recognition (MICR)
MICR printer
MICR reader/sorter
magnetic wand reader
mark reading
modem
odd parity
off line
optical character recognition (OCR)
OCR reader
optical mark reader
photoelectric cell
pulse train
remote data entry
sprocket hole
verifier
video-image processor

9 The CPU – Storing and Processing Data

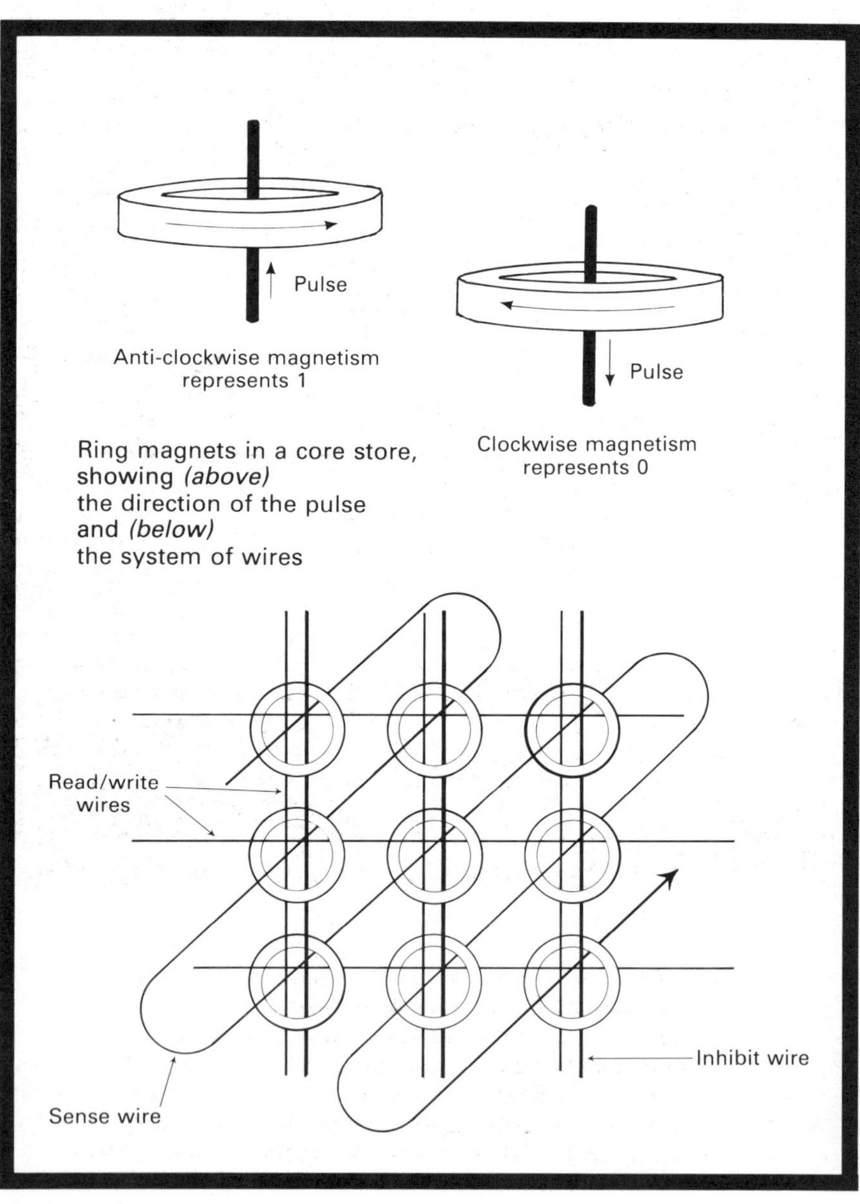

Ring magnets in a core store, showing *(above)* the direction of the pulse and *(below)* the system of wires

Storage

Core stores

Until recently the type of store used in almost all computers was the core store. **This involved magnetizing tiny ring magnets (cores) in one of two directions to represent 1 or 0. This was done by sending an electric pulse along a wire threaded through the core: depending on which way the current flowed, the core would be magnetized in one direction or the other.**

A core store contains many thousands of these tiny magnets each capable of storing a single bit. This type of storage is quite effective, but it has a number of drawbacks. It is difficult and expensive to manufacture. To enable bits to be stored it is necessary to thread four wires through each core, as shown on the left. One core can be accessed by passing currents down corresponding horizontal and vertical wires. The sense wire and inhibit wire are used when data is read from the store.

One advantage of this kind of store is that when the computer is switched off the cores stay magnetized and so retain the data held in them. This property of a store makes it non-volatile.

Semi-conductors

With the advances in micro-electronics, new storage methods have been developed. Today's computers contain an electronic form of store called a semi-conductor memory.

Components have become so miniaturized that circuits no bigger than a postage stamp can store up to 64 000 characters of data. One drawback of this type of store is that data is lost when the computer is switched off, i.e. the store is volatile. **(Designers are, however, finding new ways round this problem.)**

Because large numbers of components are contained in a single integrated circuit or chip they are called large-scale integrated circuits **(LSI).**

Memory chips are made up of a large number of identical circuits each capable of storing a single bit, which is represented as a high or low level of voltage. These storage circuits are called bistables **or** flip-flops. **A flip-flop has two inputs and one output.**

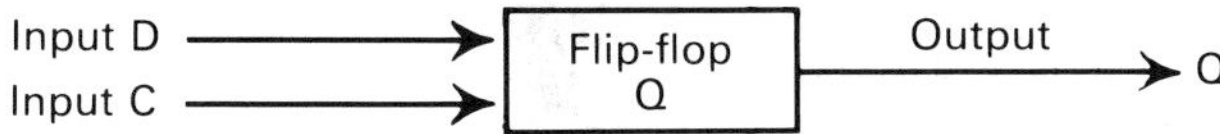

The bit to be stored is input on D (data) but it does not enter the store until a 1 is pulsed on input C (the control input). When a pulse is received on C the value on D is stored in the flip-flop. Input C always reverts to 0 in order to prevent the contents of the store from being changed. The value stored in the flip-flop can easily be obtained by testing the voltage level at output Q.

C	D	Contents of flip-flop (Q) before C pulse	Output on Q after C pulse
0	0	0	0
0	0	1	1
0	1	0	0
0	1	1	1
1	0	0	0
1	0	1	0
1	1	0	1
1	1	1	1

Truth table for the flip-flop

Notice that a change can take place only when C is set to 1. There are a number of different types of flip-flop.

Magnetic bubbles

The latest kind of storage device uses magnetic bubbles. These bubbles are formed within crystals of garnet and can be moved around by magnetized needles. Bits are stored by altering the magnetic structure of the bubble walls. Magnetic bubble memory **may soon be replacing more conventional kinds of storage.**

1K-bit chip

The photograph shows a bubble memory chip. The parallelogram in the middle of the chip contains 1024 bubbles. Gold conductors feed individual bubbles in and out of the memory. Magnetic bubbles are produced in a 'write station', which is the rectangular area below the bubbles. The 'read station' is the smaller rectangle above the bubble lattice.

Word length

When a computer is designed, an important question is how numbers, character codes and instructions are to be stored. The designer must decide such things as how accurate the numbers need to be, how many bits should be used to represent characters and how many bits are required to form an instruction.

A common number of bits to be grouped together is 16, so one hears of 16-bit machines. The group of bits is called a word and so a computer might have a word length of 16. Different machines may be designed with different word lengths such as 12, 18, 24 or 32 bits.

Once the word length is decided (say, 16 bits), the store is divided into words of this size. This is achieved by giving each 16-bit position an address, i.e. a label to identify each storage location.

Most computer manufacturers group data in lengths of 8 bits, therefore a computer with a word length of 16 bits can form two groups of 8. This is convenient because characters are most frequently represented inside the computer by an 8-bit code as seen in Chapter 8 and used on paper tape. When a word is subdivided into smaller groups in this way these divisions are called bytes. Thus we can say that we have a computer word of 16 bits made up of bytes of 8 bits.

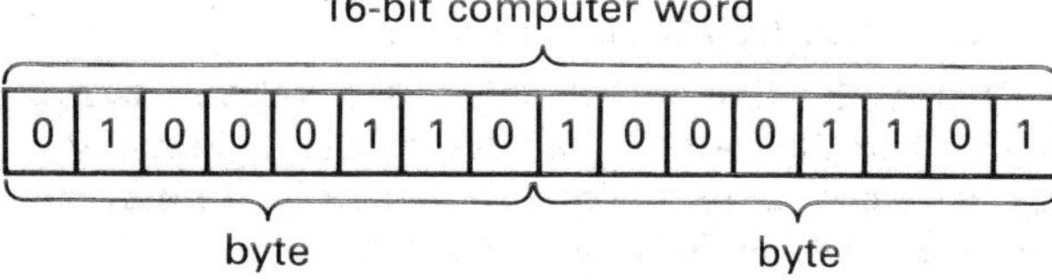

The size of a computer's store is given in terms of K, where K represents 1024 locations. Thus a mini-computer may have a size of 8K, while a large mainframe computer could well have a store size of 392K.

The data stored in the 16-bit word illustrated above could have a number of meanings. It might be representing a number, character, or an instruction. It could also be part of a number or instruction if more than one word was required to represent them. In Chapter 15 there is an example of an instruction from a 12-bit machine.

Registers

When data or instructions are retrieved from store they must be held elsewhere in the computer. To do this special stores called registers are used. Registers are used for such tasks as

1. holding numbers retrieved from store,
2. holding instructions when the computer is working on them,
3. receiving data from an input device,
4. holding one of the numbers being processed during a calculation.

Data representation

Consider storing the decimal number 7 in a 16-bit word.

0	0	0	0	0	0	0	0	0	0	0	0	0	1	1	1

This way of storing data may be very inefficient because most of the bits in the word may not be needed. It is also likely that many instructions stored in such a computer would require far less than 16 bits. Thus in many modern micro-computers data and instructions are held in bytes of 8 bits. The number 7 would then be represented in store as

0	0	0	0	0	1	1	1

If longer instructions or data are required then 2, 3 or 4 bytes may be used to store them. To store the decimal number 1000, for example, 2 bytes would be used.

0	0	0	0	0	0	1	1

1	1	1	0	1	0	0	0

Computers whose storage is organized in this way are said to be byte oriented.

Hexadecimal and octal

Some computer programs have data and instructions that are coded in binary notation. It would be very tedious if the data were entered purely in binary numbers, and it is quite likely that the programmer would make mistakes. To enable the programmer to do his job better, hexadecimal (base-16) and octal (base-8) numbers may be used. Both these number bases can easily be converted into binary notation.

Examine the conversion tables below.

Decimal	Binary	Hexadecimal	Octal
0	00000	00	00
1	00001	01	01
2	00010	02	02
3	00011	03	03
4	00100	04	04
5	00101	05	05
6	00110	06	06
7	00111	07	07
8	01000	08	10
9	01001	09	11
10	01010	0A	12
11	01011	0B	13
12	01100	0C	14
13	01101	0D	15
14	01110	0E	16
15	01111	0F	17
16	10000	10	20

Notice that with the hexadecimal numbers we run out of symbols after 9 and so the letters A to F are used to represent the numbers 10 to 15.

If you look more closely at the binary and hexadecimal tables you may discover a quick way of converting between them. Each hexadecimal (hex) digit consists of 4 binary digits, e.g.

$5_x = 0101_2$, $C_x = 1100_2$ ($_x$ = hexadecimal, $_2$ = binary).

Thus a number stored in a 1-byte location can be represented by two hex numbers, e.g.

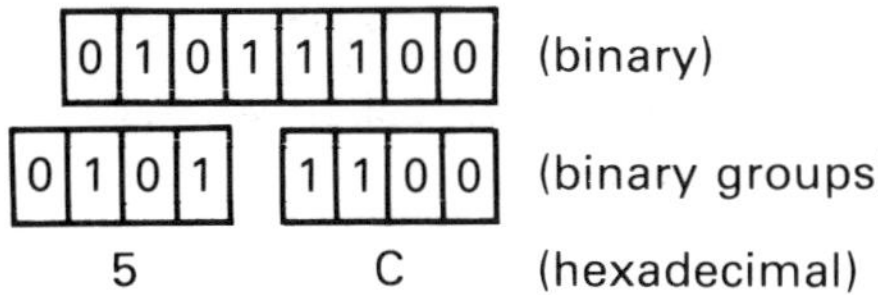

To convert any binary number to hex, separate the binary number into groups of 4 bits from the right to the left, e.g.

1010000010110011				(binary)
1010	0000	1011	0011	(binary groups)
A	0	B	3	(hexadecimal)

On some computers, programs and data may be coded using octal numbers, and here each base-8 number can be represented by 3 bits:

Binary	Octal
000	0
001	1
010	2
011	3
100	4
101	5
110	6
111	7

For instance, to change 010111_2 to octal, the binary number must be separated into groups of three bits, thus:

010111		(binary)
010	111	(binary groups)
2	7	(octal)

The reverse process can be used to change hex or octal numbers to binary notation. For instance, to change $6D_x$ to binary, each hex digit is written as 4 binary digits:

6	D	(hexadecimal)
0110	1101	(binary groups)
1101101		(binary)

Similarly, to change 54_8 to binary, each octal digit must be written as 3 binary digits:

5	4	(octal)
101	100	(binary groups)
101100		(binary)

Positive and negative numbers

In Chapter 6 we saw that negative numbers always have a 1 in the extreme left bit position. Below you can see how some positive and negative numbers have been stored in a byte of 8 bits.

Positive numbers	00001000	+8
	00000111	+7
	00000110	+6
	00000101	+5
	00000100	+4
	00000011	+3
	00000010	+2
	00000001	+1
	00000000	0
Negative numbers	11111111	−1
	11111110	−2
	11111101	−3
	11111100	−4

Number stored in an 8-bit byte

The extreme left bit indicates whether the number is positive or negative and is known as the sign bit. This means that one bit (used to indicate the sign) is not used as part of the number. So the highest positive number that can be stored in 8 bits is 127. (What is the lowest negative number that can be stored in 8 bits?)

If 2-byte numbers are processed, the highest positive number that can be stored will consist of a sign bit of 0 followed by fifteen 1s:

0	1	1	1	1	1	1	1

1	1	1	1	1	1	1	1

while the lowest negative number has a sign bit of 1 and fifteen 0s:

1	0	0	0	0	0	0	0

0	0	0	0	0	0	0	0

This gives a decimal number range of +32 767 to −32 768.

It may seem that because we can now recognize and store positive and negative numbers, they can be manipulated without further difficulty. Remember that the operations of addition, subtraction, multiplication and division can all be achieved by binary addition and shifting (see Chapter 6).

Examine carefully what happens with the following additions.

```
 01010001     Number A
+00101100     Number B
 01111101     Answer
```

Look at the two numbers and the answer: are they positive or negative? The answer in this example is what you might expect – check it by using the equivalent decimal numbers:

```
 01010001      81
+00101100     +44
 01111101     125
```

Thus the addition of two positive numbers gives a positive answer. Will this always be the case?

Now consider a further example.

```
 01010111     Number A
+00110010     Number B
 10001001     Answer
```

Here the sum of the two positive numbers A and B produces an answer that is negative, as you can see from the sign bit. Why should this be so? Again we can check using decimal numbers:

```
 01010111      87
+00110010     +50
 10001001     137
```

We have seen earlier that +127 is the highest positive number that can be stored in 8 bits. In this case the binary number has exceeded this, and it is therefore registered as a negative number. Thus adding two positive numbers may give an answer that is stored as a negative number.

Finally, let us look at a subtraction problem. Remember that to subtract a number, its two's complement is added, as in the following example.

```
  01010101    Number A
 +10110110    Number B
 100001011    Answer
```

Here the sign bit has changed, but there is no room for the last 1 carried to be stored in this byte and we say that overflow has occurred. Nevertheless the 8 bits left give the correct answer – check this using decimal numbers.

```
 01010101        +85
+10110110     +(−74)
 00001011         11
```

Binary coded decimals

Besides using hexadecimal or octal notation, binary coded decimals (BCD) may also be used to represent numbers. Each decimal digit in a base-10 number is represented by 4 bits:

Decimal number	Binary coded decimal
0	0000
1	0001
2	0010
3	0011
4	0100
5	0101
6	0110
7	0111
8	1000
9	1001

This makes long binary numbers easier to read and to convert to their decimal equivalent. The decimal number 3728 would therefore be represented in BCD as:

0011 0111 0010 1000,

whereas in ordinary binary notation it would be 111010010000 and this would take some time to convert back to decimal for us to understand its value.

For example, give the decimal number value of 0110 0101 1000 BCD:

0110	0101	1000	(BCD)
6	5	8	(decimal)

Fixed-point arithmetic

When computers are used in any form of accounting, it is very probable that the output will be in the form of pounds and new pence. This means that all the arithmetic concerning money is done with the decimal point always in the third position from the right. Any calculations like this where the decimal point is always in the same position (whatever that position may be) are known as fixed-point arithmetic.

Floating-point arithmetic

Many scientific and mathematical applications require numbers that are either too large or too small to be fitted into a 2-byte number or a 16-bit word. In those cases two 16-bit words are used, and the 32 bits are separated in the following manner:

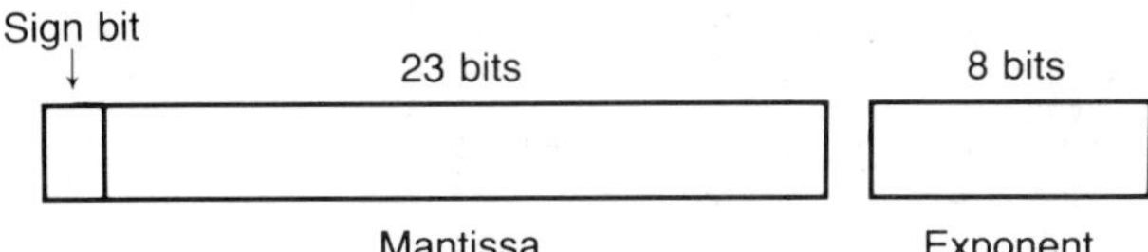

The mantissa holds a 23-bit number with an additional bit on the left for the sign. The exponent indicates where the decimal point is to be placed.

Floating-point numbers are output in the following form.

First, a mantissa with the decimal point in front, e.g.

.245876 or −.3427

Then an exponent which indicates where to put the decimal point, e.g.

E+3 (move the decimal point 3 places to the right)
E−6 (move the decimal point 6 places to the left)

This gives full floating-point numbers as:

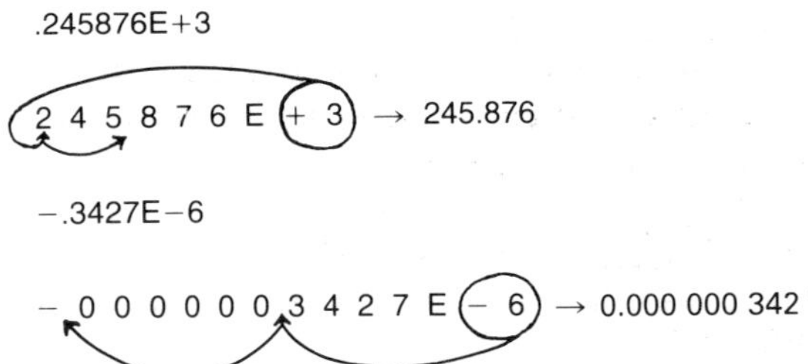

So to find the value of the floating-point number .785E+8, you write down 785 (mantissa), then move the decimal point 8 places to the right (exponent +8). This gives:

.785E+8 = 78 500 000

Clearly, floating-point arithmetic gives greater flexibility than fixed-point arithmetic, since a greater range of numbers can be output.

Questions

1. How many bytes are needed to store the hexadecimal number A0B3?
2. Change the following binary numbers to hexadecimal notation:
   (a) 1010,
   (b) 11000011,
   (c) 10001011,
   (d) 11011001001011,
   (e) 1000001111111.
3. Change the following hexadecimal numbers to binary notation:
   (a) 3C,
   (b) 88,
   (c) D0,
   (d) E1D1,
   (e) C02E.

4. Change the following octal numbers to binary notation:
   (a) 4,
   (b) 45,
   (c) 76,
   (d) 3056,
   (e) 1715.

5. Complete the addition of the following pairs of binary numbers and comment on the answers: state whether the sign bit changes and whether overflow occurs.
   (a) 01010010 + 01001101,
   (b) 00101111 + 10101000,
   (c) 10111000 + 10010101.

6. Give the value of the following floating-point numbers:
   (a) .45E+5,
   (b) −.6532E+9,
   (c) −.3879E−4,
   (d) −.80876E−6.

7. Give the following numbers in floating-point format:
   (a) 12 000 000,
   (b) 0.000 705 6,
   (c) −23.6547,
   (d) −0.000 000 77.

Vocabulary

address
binary coded decimals
bistable
byte
core store
exponent
fixed-point arithmetic
flip-flop
floating-point numbers
hexadecimal numbers
large-scale integrated circuit (LSI)
magnetic bubble memory
mantissa
non-volatile store
octal numbers
overflow
register
semi-conductor memory
volatile store
word

10 The CPU – Fetching and Executing Instructions

The CPU

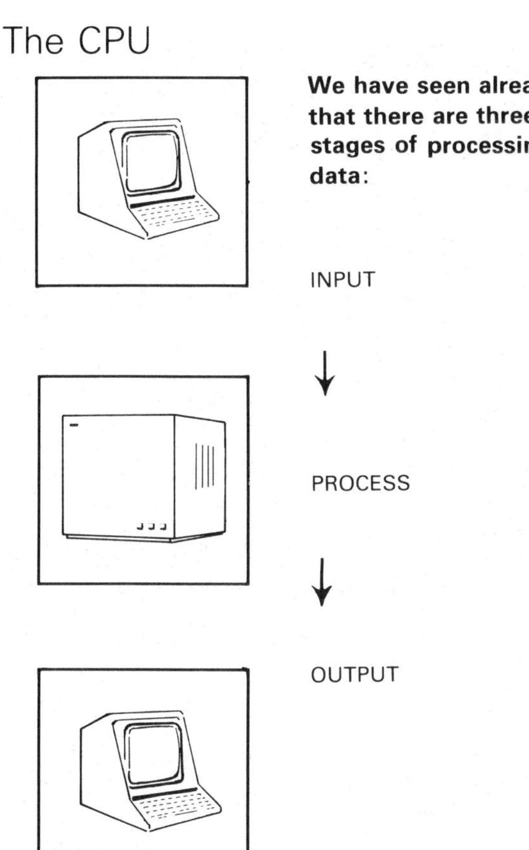

We have seen already that there are three stages of processing data:

INPUT

↓

PROCESS

↓

OUTPUT

Also we have seen that in order to carry out a process a computer must first have been given a list of instructions called a program. The task of processing is carried out in the central processing unit and here there are three main jobs:

1. to understand the instructions,
2. to store data and instructions,
3. to do the calculations.

The CPU consists of three main parts: the immediate access store, the arithmetic/logic unit and the control unit.

Immediate access store

The store of the CPU contains many thousands of locations each of which has its own address. You know already that both the instructions and the addresses of locations in the store are in binary number form. However, to make it easier to understand we shall use ordinary words and decimal numbers.

Address	Contents
1	ADD 54 TO 49
2	ADD 100 TO THE ANSWER
3	PUT THE ANSWER INTO STORE NUMBER 8
4	PRINT OUT THE ANSWER
5	END OF PROGRAM
6	0
7	0
8	0
9	0

Arithmetic/logic unit

Two registers are available in the arithmetic/logic unit (ALU). These hold the two numbers which the computer is capable of dealing with at any one time.

The ALU receives an operation signal, and the

result of the operation on the two numbers is stored in one of a set of registers called the accumulator.

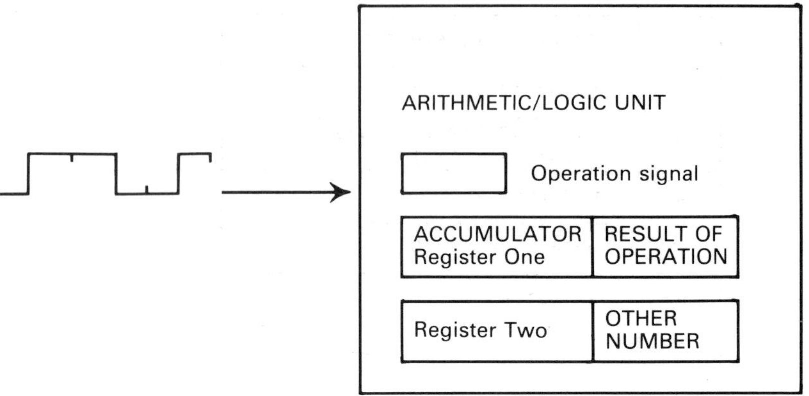

Control unit

The control unit, as its name suggests, controls the activities of all the other parts of the computer system. Its main registers are the sequence control register **and the** instruction register.

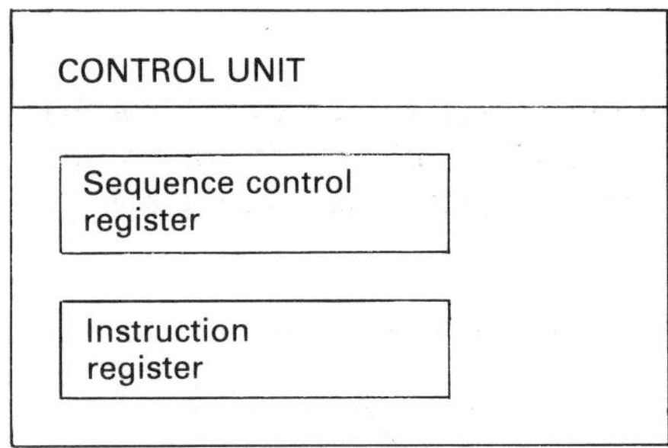

The sequence control register holds the address of the store location where the next instruction is to be found.

The instruction register holds the present instruction, which is decoded to see what must be done.

The fetch/execute cycle

When a computer carries out an instruction it is said to be 'executing' that instruction. The process of getting an instruction from the immediate access store and obeying it is known as the fetch/execute cycle.

The fetch/execute cycle is shown in the following flowchart.

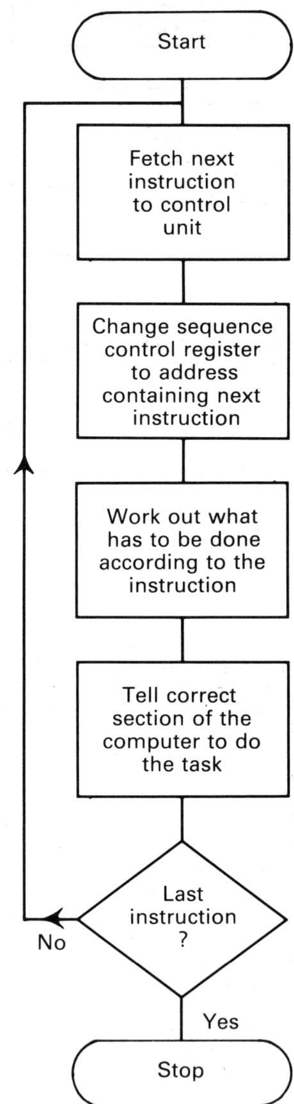

Consider now what happens when the simple program below is executed.

```
INPUT 26 TO STORE 7
INPUT 42 TO STORE 8
ADD CONTENTS OF STORE 7 TO CONTENTS OF STORE 8
PUT ANSWER IN STORE 9
OUTPUT CONTENTS OF STORE 9
END OF PROGRAM
```

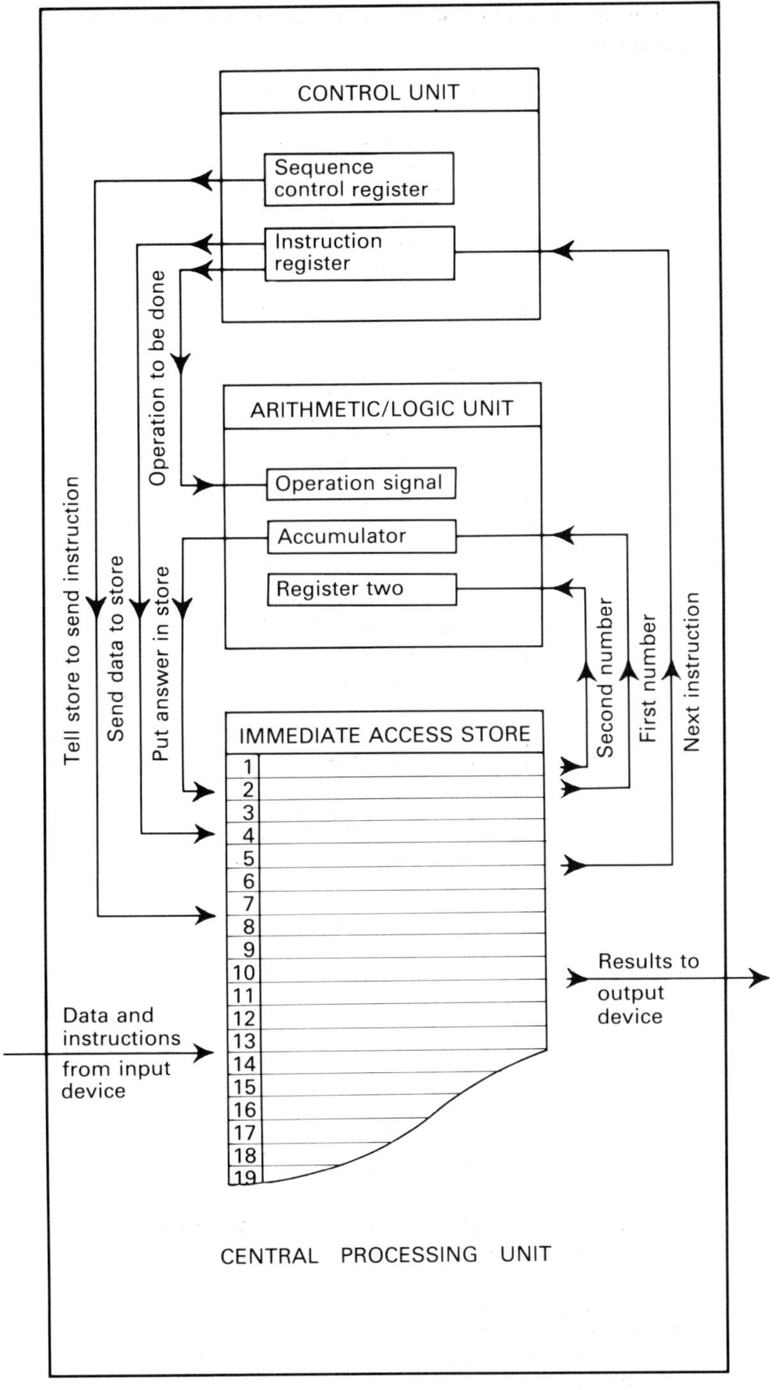

At the beginning the contents of the store are:

	IMMEDIATE ACCESS STORE
1	INPUT 26 TO STORE 7
2	INPUT 42 TO STORE 8
3	ADD CONTENTS OF STORE 7 TO CONTENTS OF STORE 8
4	PUT ANSWER IN STORE 9
5	OUTPUT CONTENTS OF STORE 9
6	END OF PROGRAM
7	
8	

What will the sequence control register show at the beginning of the program? How many fetch/execute cycles will there have been when the program has been run?

Instruction One

The sequence control register is set to 1. Thus the instruction INPUT 26 TO STORE 7 is fetched into the control unit. (The sequence control register is then set to 2.)

CONTROL UNIT	
SCR	2
IR	INPUT 26 TO STORE 7

The first instruction is executed, so now the number 26 is stored in address 7.

6	END OF PROGRAM
7	26
8	

Instruction Two

The sequence control register (SCR) has been set to 2. The instruction INPUT 42 TO STORE 8 is fetched into the control unit. (The SCR is then set to 3.) On execution 42 is stored in address 8.

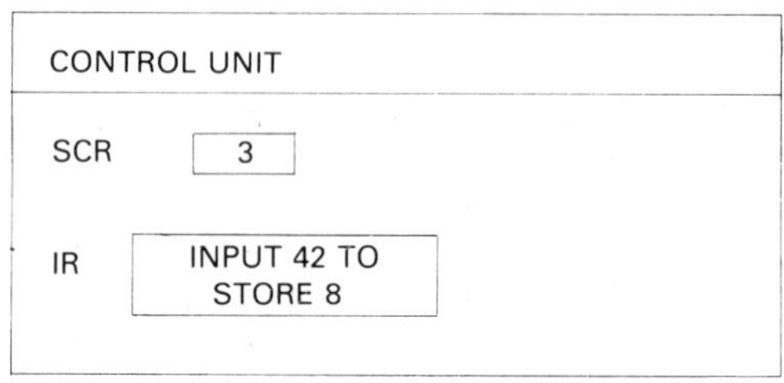

6	END OF PROGRAM
7	26
8	42
9	

Instruction Three

The SCR has been set to 3 so the instruction ADD CONTENTS OF STORE 7 TO CONTENTS OF STORE 8 is fetched to the control unit. (The SCR is then set to 4.) Copies of the numbers in stores 7 and 8 are sent to the arithmetic/logic unit. The control unit sends a signal to the ALU to add the two numbers. After execution the result will have replaced the number previously in the accumulator.

CONTROL UNIT

SCR 4

IR ADD CONTENTS OF STORE 7 TO CONTENTS OF STORE 8

ARITHMETIC/LOGIC UNIT

In Sig ADD

ACC 68

Reg Two 42

Instruction Four

The SCR has been set to 4, thus PUT ANSWER INTO STORE 9 is fetched into the control unit. (The SCR is then set to 5.) The control unit signals the accumulator to send a copy of the number it holds to address 9.

CONTROL UNIT

SCR 5

IR PUT ANSWER IN STORE 9

ALU

I Sig SEND TO STORE 9

ACC 68

R. Two 42

8	42
9	68
10	

Instruction Five

The SCR has been set to 5, and so the instruction OUTPUT CONTENTS OF STORE 9 is fetched into the control unit. (The SCR is then set to 6.)

CONTROL UNIT

SCR 6

IR OUTPUT CONTENTS OF STORE 9

On execution the number 68 which is held in address 9 is sent to the output device.

ARITHMETIC/LOGIC UNIT

IS SEND TO OUTPUT DEVICE

ACC 68

R TWO 42

68 ⟶ OUTPUT DEVICE

Instruction Six

The sequence control register has been set to 6 so the instruction END OF PROGRAM is fetched. The program stops execution.

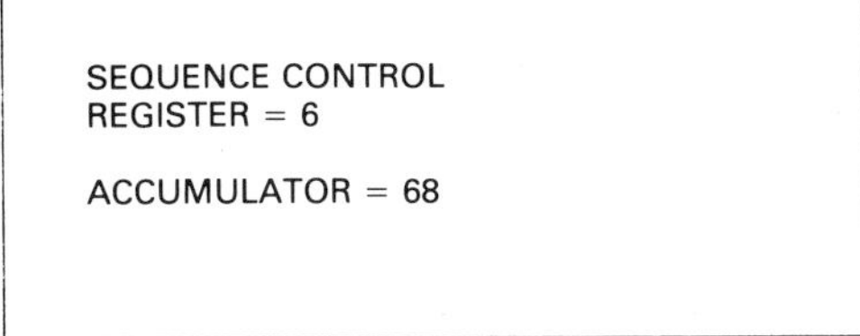

Jump instructions

The sequence control register may not always increase by one. If a jump instruction **is read, control is transferred to an address indicated by the program.**

If, for example, the instruction were GOTO ADDRESS 5, then instead of automatically incrementing by one, the sequence control register would be set to 5. Similarly, the instruction IF NUMBER IN ACCUMULATOR EQUALS 5 THEN GOTO 12 would (when that condition is met) result in the SCR being reset to 12.

Below is a program that uses two jump instructions.

```
 1  PUT THE NUMBER 1 IN THE ACCUMULATOR
 2  STORE THE NUMBER 1 IN ADDRESS 13
 3  MULTIPLY THE NUMBER IN THE ACCUMULATOR BY 6
 4  SEND THE NUMBER IN THE ACCUMULATOR TO THE OUTPUT DEVICE
 5  PUT THE NUMBER HELD IN ADDRESS 13 INTO THE ACCUMULATOR
 6  ADD 1 TO THE NUMBER IN THE ACCUMULATOR
 7  IF THE NUMBER IN THE ACCUMULATOR EQUALS 5 GOTO ADDRESS 12
 8  PUT THE NUMBER HELD IN THE ACCUMULATOR INTO ADDRESS 13
 9  MULTIPLY THE NUMBER IN THE ACCUMULATOR BY 6
10  SEND THE NUMBER IN THE ACCUMULATOR TO THE OUTPUT DEVICE
11  GOTO ADDRESS 5
12  END OF PROGRAM
```

Dry runs

A dry run **may be used to test the program. To do this, a table is drawn up in which headings are given for the sequence control register, the accumulator, store 13, a conditional jump test and output. The dry run involves writing in the contents of stores as the program is executed by hand. Copy and complete the dry run table given at the top of the next column.**

Sequence control register	Accumulator	Store 13	Jump test	Output
1	–	–	–	–
2	1	–	–	–
3	1	1	–	–
4	6	1	–	–
5	6	1 1	–	6
6	1	1	–	–
7	2	1	–	–
8	2	1	ACC≠5	–
9	2	2	–	–
10	12	2	–	–
11	12	2	–	12
12	12	2	–	–
5	12	2	–	–
6	2	2	–	–
	etc.			

Machine instructions

Now let us see what happens when we work with binary codes and numbers, as computers do.

We have noted previously that an instruction consists of an operation code and an address. Imagine the operation codes below:

CODE	OPERATION	MEANING
001	INPUT	Input number from input device to the accumulator
010	STORE	Store number found in accumulator in the address given
011	LOAD	Load accumulator with number in the address given
100	ADD	Add the contents of the accumulator to the number in the store given
101	END	End of program

If the words in a particular computer were 12 bits long, then the instruction

0 1 0 0 0 0 0 1 0 0 1 1

would be examined in the control unit and decoded as:

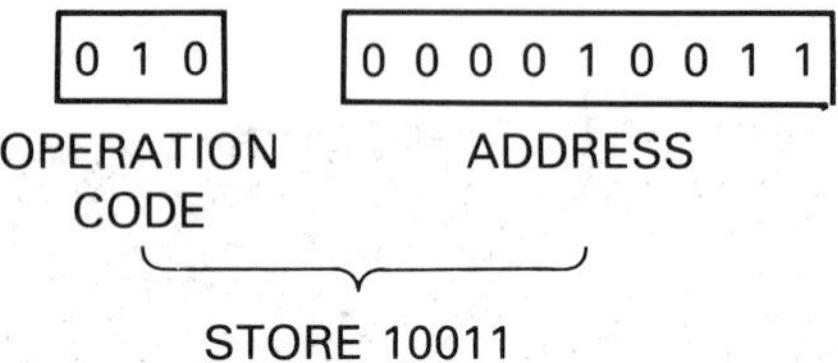

Thus the number in the accumulator would be stored in address 10011.

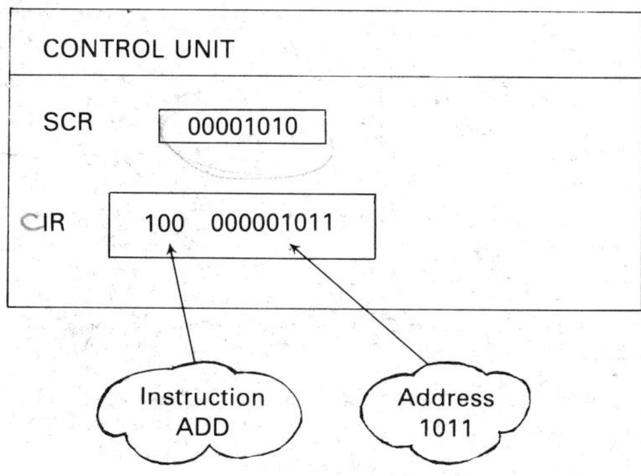

For example, suppose the instruction register holds 100000001011. The operation code is thus 100 (meaning ADD) and the address part is 000001011.

First, the control unit interprets the instruction. Then the control unit sends the contents of the address 1011 to register 2 in the ALU and issues an instruction signal to add.

Finally, the number from the store is added to the contents of the accumulator.

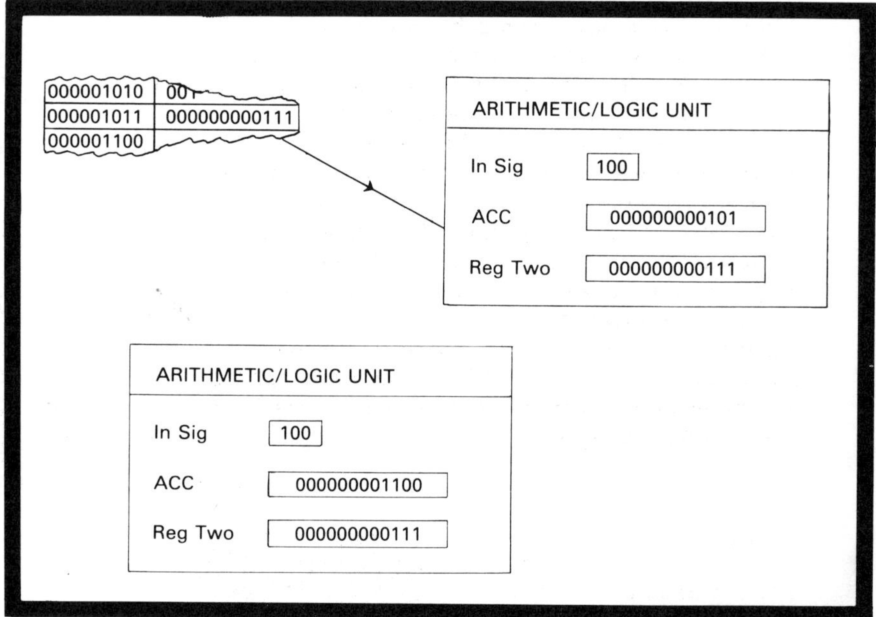

Questions

1. Decode the following instructions and give brief details of what would happen if the instructions were executed.
   (a) 001000000000,
   (b) 010000101101,
   (c) 011001011011,
   (d) 100001011011,
   (e) 101000000000.
2. Explain with the aid of diagrams what happens when the instruction 010000110000 is obeyed. (The sequence register is set at 00001101 before this instruction is read.)

Vocabulary

accumulator
arithmetic/logic unit (ALU)
control unit
dry run
fetch/execute cycle
immediate access store
instruction register
jump instruction
sequence control register

11 Output Devices

Output from a computer can be of two types: either in a form that humans can understand, or in a form that computers or other machines can use.

Output for machines is a fairly straightforward business: results produced by a CPU may be output on to magnetic tape or magnetic disc; they may also be output to a device which is controlling another process. For instance, when a computer is used to control aircraft flight, output signals are sent directly to the flight control mechanisms. Computers used to control industrial machinery output directly to mechanisms operating the machines in a factory.

However, there are many situations where the output must be in a form which is comprehensible to humans, and many different arrangements have been devised for this.

LED

The simplest form of output is by light-emitting diode (LED). **Digital displays like those in pocket calculators or games controlled by microprocessors use this form of output for simple displays. This mathematical game has a display panel at the top which is produced by LED.**

Video

One of the most popular forms of output is on a television or video screen. There are many advantages in this: it is fast, versatile in presentation, quiet in operation and clean to use.

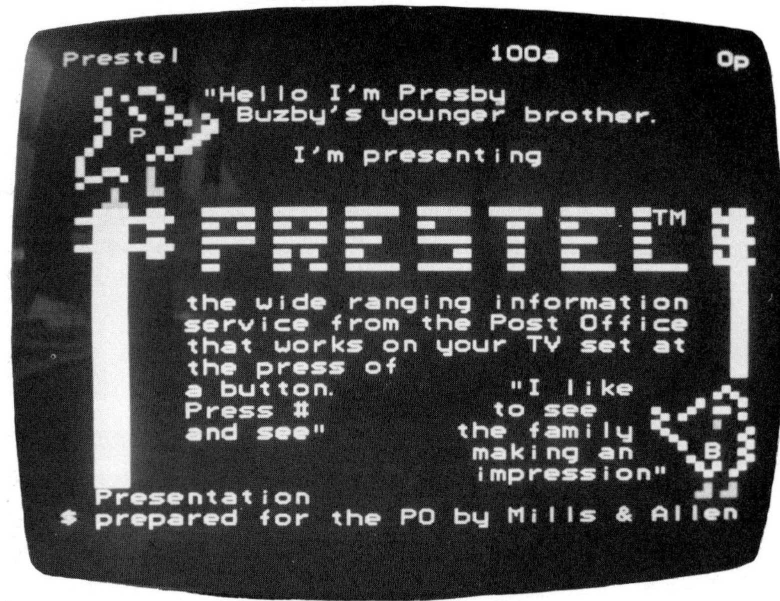

Television screen presentation – Prestel

The one big disadvantage is that previous output may be lost when new output is displayed.

The output is usually displayed on 16, 20 or 24 lines, each containing between 40 and 80 characters. The binary code received from the processor is translated into a pattern of dots representing a character. This pattern is typically formed from a 5 × 7 matrix, as shown below.

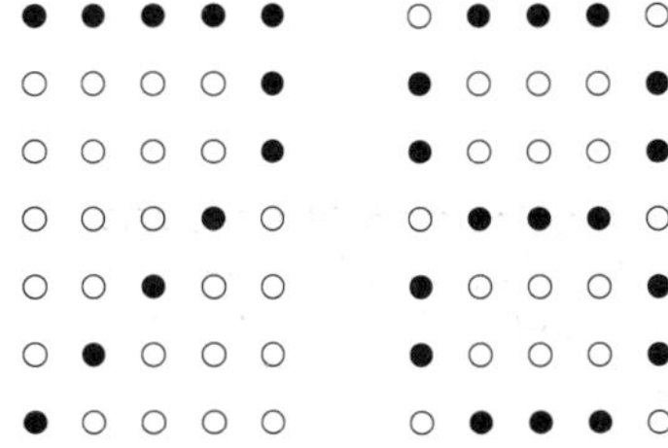

The video screen is normally used with a keyboard, so the visual display unit looks like those used at Villa Park, the London Penta Hotel and by the Mickie system which we saw in Chapter 2.

Printers

Of course, the two examples above do not provide a permanent record. Very many computer users require 'hard copy', and this implies using some form of printing device.

Continuous stationery

The paper used in printers is continuous stationery as you can see in the photograph below. The sprocket holes allow the paper to be moved through the printer in fixed steps. The sprocket drives can be adjusted to allow differing widths of paper to be used.

Continuous stationery in a line printer

Character printers

The slower printers reproduce one character at a time, moving from one end of a line to the other, rather like a typewriter. Many ingenious means of printing have been developed: some spray a pattern of ink on to the paper, others use a fast rotating wheel, called a daisy wheel, containing embossed characters. As this wheel rotates, a hammer operates as the required letter passes by and presses the character against a carbon ribbon.

Daisy wheel

Daisy-wheel printer

A slow printer in common use is that which forms characters by a dot matrix. The head consists of a column of seven hammers which are activated a number of times to produce a pattern of dots. If a 5 × 7 matrix is used there are seven hammers and the print head must operate five times for each character.

Dot-matrix printers can operate at speeds of up to 300 lines a minute.

THE DOT-MATRIX PRINTER

Print head

```
* TESCO WELLINGBOROUGH *
      TESCO COFFEE     .75
      SALAD CREAM      .26½
      LUNCH MEAT       .16
      PUDDING MIX      .11½
      TRIFLE           .29½
      HEINZ SOUP       .16½
      PROCESS PEAS     .18
      MEAT ROLL        .23
      CAN SAUSAGES     .37
      PILCHARDS        .33
      QUICK-JEL        .09½
      PKT CAKE MIX     .26½
      SUGAR STRNDS     .17
      TOTAL           3.39

      CSH TEND        3.50
      CHG DUE          .11

17/06/78 10:37  3368/ 3
*CHECK OUT TESCO PRICES*
```

You can see how the characters are formed from this sales receipt produced by a dot-matrix printer at a Tesco supermarket

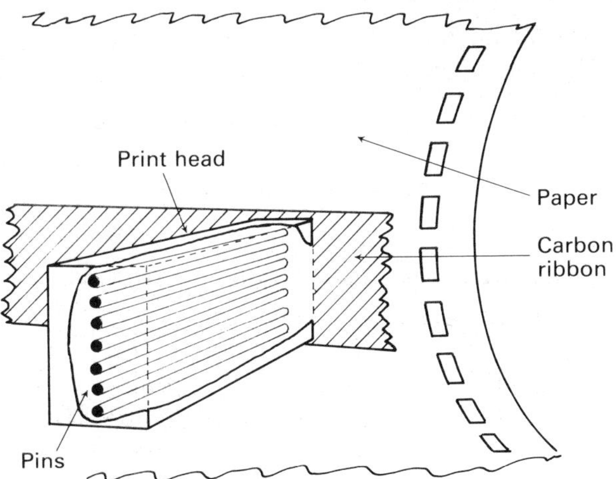

Above Diagram of dot-matrix printer
Below Example of how the number 3 is built up

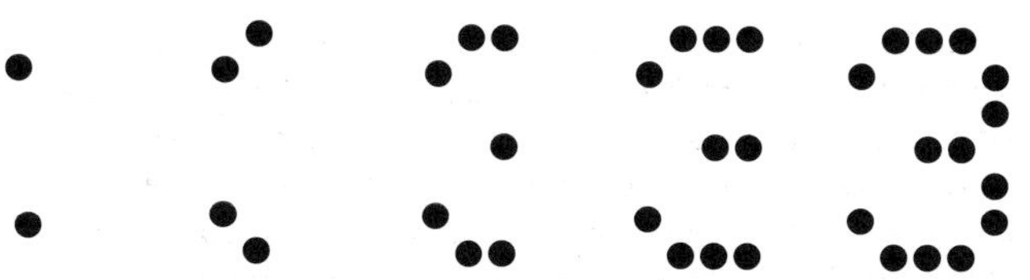

Line printers

The faster printers are line printers **because they print a line at a time instead of a character at a time.**

The chain printer **consists of a fast rotating band of characters passing along the line to be printed. As a character passes the position where it is to be printed, a hammer hits the paper and carbon against the character on the band.**

Chain printer – the band of characters *(above)* and an overhead view *(below)*

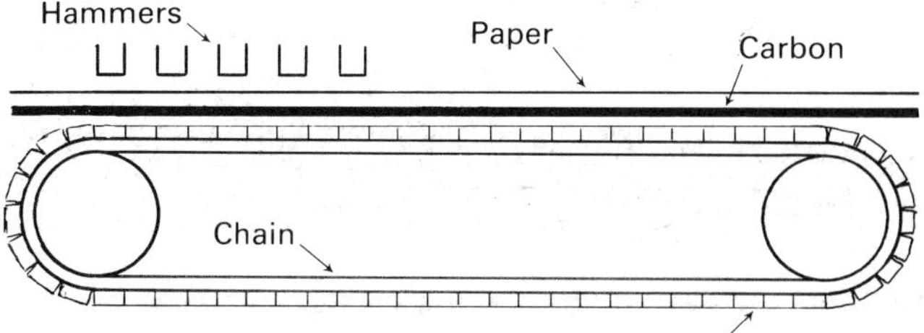

The photograph below shows a train printer, **similar in operation to a chain printer, but with a train of characters embossed on a continuous band of metal.**

Barrel printers **have a complete set of characters for each printing position. The characters are embossed on a cylinder which rotates at a very high speed. As the required character passes by, the hammer hits the paper and the carbon against the barrel. A line of print is built up as successive rows of characters pass the print hammers. First all the A's are printed, then all the B's and so on, until the last character (which is an @ symbol) has been printed. In practice, of course, the printer starts from whichever character is nearest on the barrel.**

THE BARREL PRINTER

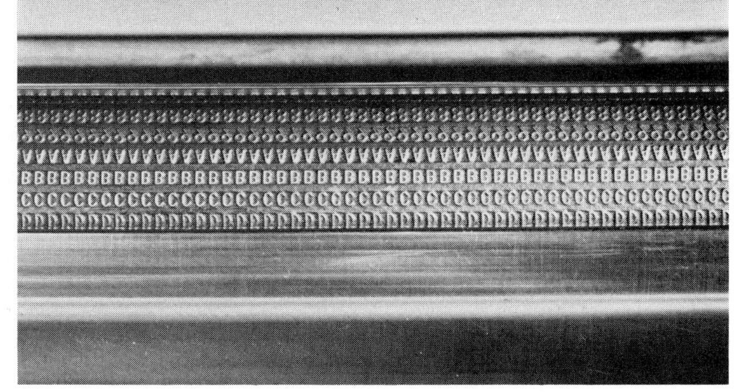

Cylinder with characters

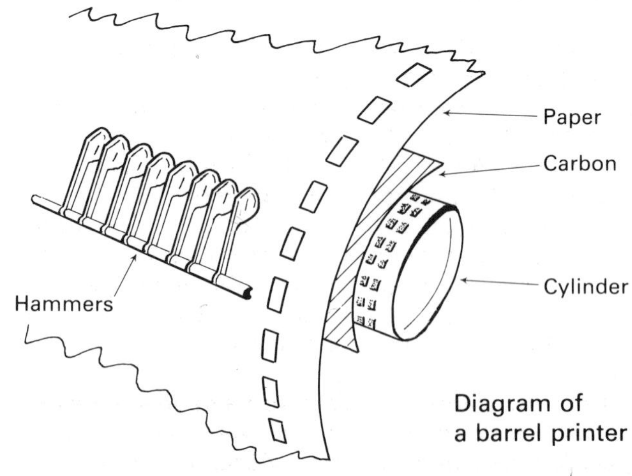

Diagram of a barrel printer

```
 A        A  A
 A       BABBA   B         B
C A      BABBA   B      C  B
C A      BABBA   B    D C  B
C A   E  BABBA E B    DECE BE
C A   E  BABBAGE B    DECE BE
CHA   E  BABBAGE B    DECE BE
CHA LE   BABBAGE B    DECE BE
CHA LE   BABBAGE B    DECEMBE
CHA LE   BABBAGE B  N DECEMBE
CHA LE   BABBAGE BO N DECEMBE
CHARLE   BABBAGE BORN DECEMBER
CHARLES  BABBAGE BORN DECEMBER
CHARLES  BABBAGE BORN DECEMBER    1  1
CHARLES  BABBAGE BORN DECEMBER 2  1  1
CHARLES  BABBAGE BORN DECEMBER 26 1  1
CHARLES  BABBAGE BORN DECEMBER 26 17 1
CHARLES  BABBAGE BORN DECEMBER 26 1791
```

Example of how a line is built up

Off-line printing

If a computer user requires a large amount of printed output it is common practice to output all data to magnetic disc. The discs may then be read and their information printed by a device which is not connected to the computer (i.e. is not 'on line'). This is known as off-line printing.

The computer may output data at up to 800 000 characters per second to a magnetic disc; if the computer is connected directly to a printer it must output at a maximum speed of 40 000 characters per second – the fastest rate at which the printer can operate.

Clearly, if the computer is outputting to a magnetic disc, it is able to spend less time merely outputting, which leaves more time for processing.

Page printers

Line printers may seem fast, but they are still slow when compared with the speed of the CPU which feeds them with data, so large installations need several printers to keep up with the output demands of a single processor. Two new forms of printer have been developed.

A very fast device has been developed that can operate at speeds of up to 27 000 lines per minute. This is called a laser printer **and it forms a page of print by projecting a beam of light on to an electrostatic drum. This collects ink in the shape of the projected characters and prints them.**

Another device is available that can output up to 18 000 lines per minute. It is called a page printing system **and is controlled by its own mini-computer.**

Output data is first put on to magnetic tape, as for normal off-line printing. The page printing system reads the data from magnetic tape and prints it electrostatically on special dielectric paper. Characters are formed by first electrically charging the pattern of each character on the paper; as the paper passes by the printing liquid, the ink is drawn on to the paper in the areas that have been charged.

Character types, character size and positioning of the output on the paper are all controlled by the page printer's mini-computer. Form layouts and standard headings can be printed at the same time

Diagram of a page-printing system

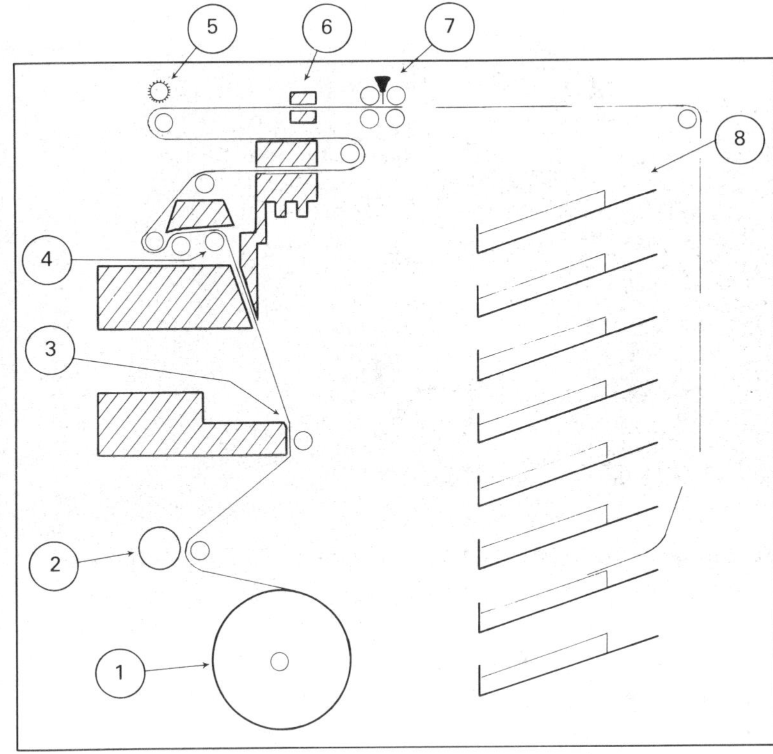

1. PAPER ROLL – rolls of paper simplify the transportation mechanism
2. FORM CYLINDER – exchangeable cylinders eliminate the need to stock pre-printed stationery
3. CHARACTER FORMATION – electrostatic charging of paper
4. LIQUID TONER – colour options are allowed
5. PERFORATOR – for vertical perforations on a page
6. PUNCH – two or three holes punched on the top or side
7. FORM CUTTER – for cutting various page widths
8. STACKER/COLLATOR – 8 to 32 output pockets are available

Page-printing system

by inserting specially prepared cylinders in the printer. Various other tasks may also be performed: holes can be punched for filing, output is cut to size and the system sorts and collates different pages into separate trays, as on the right-hand side of the photograph.

Such systems are of course expensive, and are only suitable for organizations producing more than 400 000 pages of output in a month.

Questions

1. Name some of the things that a computer-operated flight system needs to control.
2. Which of the following kinds of computer output would not require hard copy?
   (a) signals to control blood sampling equipment,
   (b) details of a firm's monthly sales figures,
   (c) information about an individual's wages,
   (d) gas bills.
3. Why is off-line printing necessary if large amounts of output are to be produced?
4. Show how the message COMPUTER CENTRE would be printed by a barrel printer.
5. Draw 5×7 dot matrix diagrams of the symbols +, −, *, and /.
6. List the advantages of using a page printing system.
7. Why might it be necessary to extend the output trays of a page printing system from 8 to 32?
8. Why is it necessary to develop faster printing peripherals?

Vocabulary

barrel printer
chain printer
continuous stationery
daisy wheel printer
dot matrix printer
laser printer
light-emitting diode (LED)
line printer
off-line printing
page printing system
train printer

12 Information Retrieval

Computer storage

When we examined the central processor we saw the need for an immediate access store. However, this is not suitable for storing all the data necessary for, say, processing rate demands or electricity bills. For these two particular applications vast amounts of data are needed, and the cost of immediate access storage would be great. Computer systems therefore need a means of storing large amounts of data in a cheap and convenient way.

If you consider the job of your school secretary you will see that she refers to a great deal of information. As she is unable to remember it all she needs to store it in an organized way, in a filing system.

If the secretary is asked by the headteacher to prepare a list of all fourth-year pupils who travel by bus, then she goes to her filing cabinet and finds the correct records. Having collected the information she wants, she passes it to the headteacher.

In a similar way the computer system makes use of its backing store. **Items of data can be transferred from the backing store to the immediate access store, or returned from the immediate access store to the backing store.**

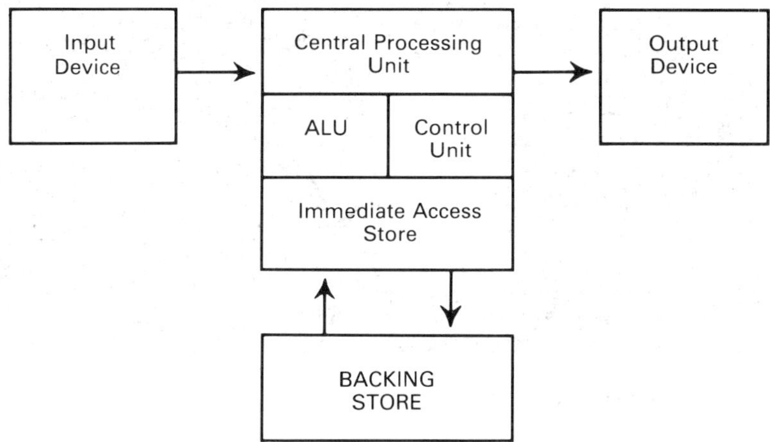

Consider, for example, seat booking at Villa Park. The backing store holds the information necessary to find out how many seats are available. If two seats are sold the information must be updated to reduce the number of seats available. Thus there must be a two-way flow between the backing store and the CPU.

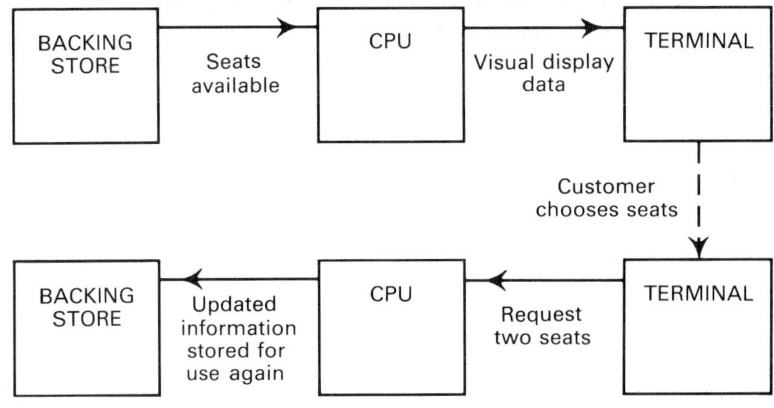

Tape or disc?

If you are a music fan you have the choice of buying albums as LPs or as cassette tapes. What would affect your choice? On a tape the songs are held serially, which means that they follow one another. You cannot get at the song you want straight away unless it is the first one on the tape.

The groove on the LP spirals into the centre and is one continuous track. But there are visible bands between the items, which means that you can lift the stylus to the correct track to save time. This makes the finding of your piece of music more direct.

Computers use both magnetic tapes and a form of magnetic disc as their backing store. Both tape and disc are coated with a ferric oxide which retains the binary codes as either magnetized or non-magnetized areas.

Many applications require that data should be made *immediately* available from a backing store. Obviously, this is not possible if you have to read through a lot of data just to get to the item you want, as you have to if the data is stored on magnetic tape. It can take up to four minutes to find an item of data stored serially. Therefore, magnetic disc units, which provide direct access to data, are more suitable when immediate access is needed.

In a disc system, magnetic discs are used as the computer's backing store. Information is stored on tracks arranged in concentric circles on the disc: each track contains the same number of characters, so tracks near the centre of the disc are more closely packed with characters than the outer ones.

Data is arranged in blocks on the tracks, and these are lined up in sectors, as in the diagram.

Several discs are held in one 'pack', and a central spindle rotates the discs at speed (perhaps 2700 revolutions per minute). There is a read/write head for each surface (except the top and bottom) and these move in and out together between the discs.

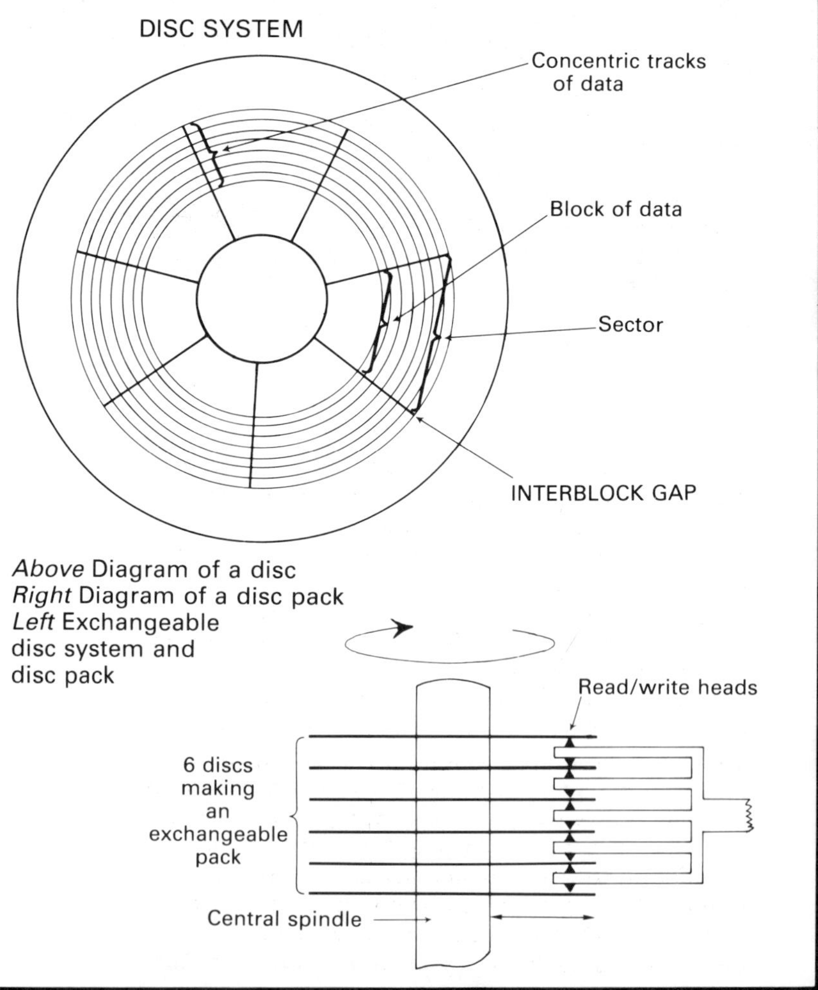

Above Diagram of a disc
Right Diagram of a disc pack
Left Exchangeable disc system and disc pack

Mass storage system

Nevertheless, tape does have the advantage that it generally takes up a great deal less space than discs. So for certain kinds of storage it is clearly more economical. Many organizations need to store vast quantities of data, and this is often done on magnetic tapes. They often have rooms full of these tapes, which have to be fetched as they are needed by the tape librarian.

This is convenient in terms of storage space, but we have seen that it is not very convenient when immediate access is required. So a new system for mass storage has been developed, which stores the data in tape cartridges. The cartridges are fetched and loaded mechanically, and then the data is transferred to magnetic disc, which can provide immediate access. This mass storage system can store up to 472 billion characters, which is equivalent to 4720 disc packs or a library of 47 200 reels of tape.

Information retrieval

Almost all computers store information and the recalling of it is known as information retrieval. British Telecom has developed a system which allows both commercial and private users to store and retrieve information from a computer via a telephone line. Many other firms have developed information retrieval systems that can be used by others, but the British Telecom system is the first available to everyone. The system is called Prestel. Because the system is used by a wide variety of people it is simple to operate and should be cheap to use.

Prestel in action

The user has a modified television set connected to the telephone network by a special jack socket installed by British Telecom, along with a key pad. Adaptors are being developed to allow any TV set to receive Prestel through its aerial socket.

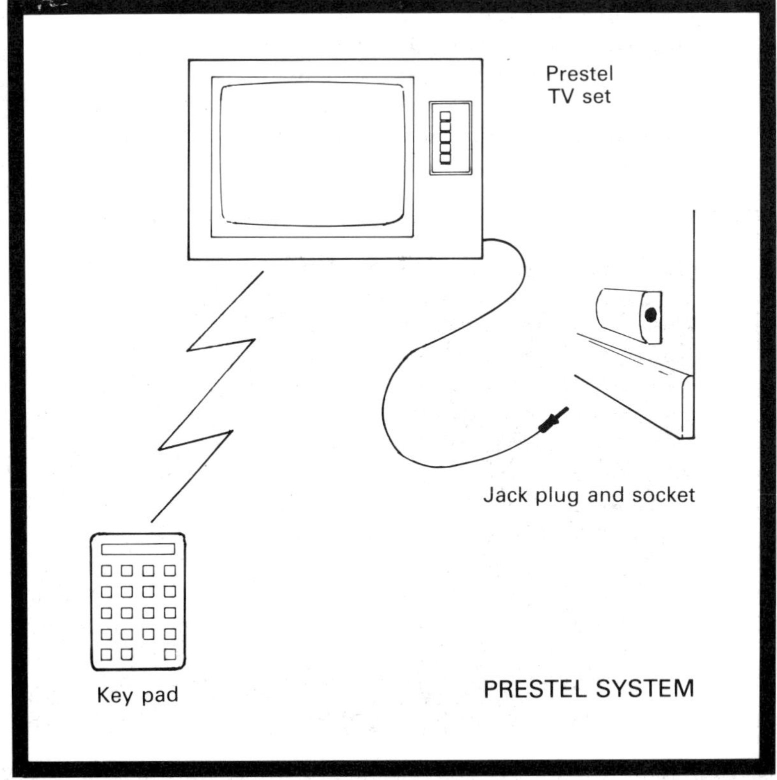

PRESTEL SYSTEM

Television screen showing the Prestel welcome page

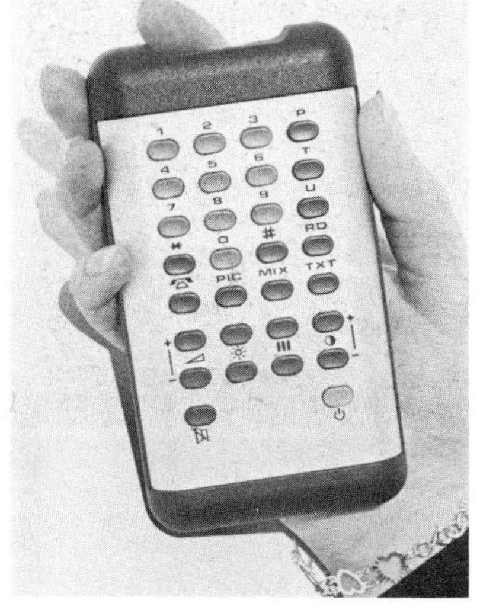

Prestel keypad

To access Prestel, the user presses a special button on the key pad, and then hears a dialling tone from the loudspeaker of the television set. When he presses the button a second time, the set automatically dials the Prestel computer centre.

When the computer answers the call, it sends a signal to switch the TV over to Prestel. Having switched, the television set signals the computer that it is ready to communicate.

The user's number is automatically transmitted to the computer, where it is checked to make sure that it is valid, and to ensure that the correct customer is charged for use of the system.

If the user's number is valid, the computer normally transmits the Prestel welcome page unless the user has programmed a password into the system, for additional security. In this case the user has to key in the correct password before the welcome page is displayed.

Each page is numbered, the index page being 0a. Each section is then subdivided by numbers. The user may refer to the index for the section he wants, and then turn to the section listing, eventually finding the page he wants, or he may use a directory supplied by Prestel.

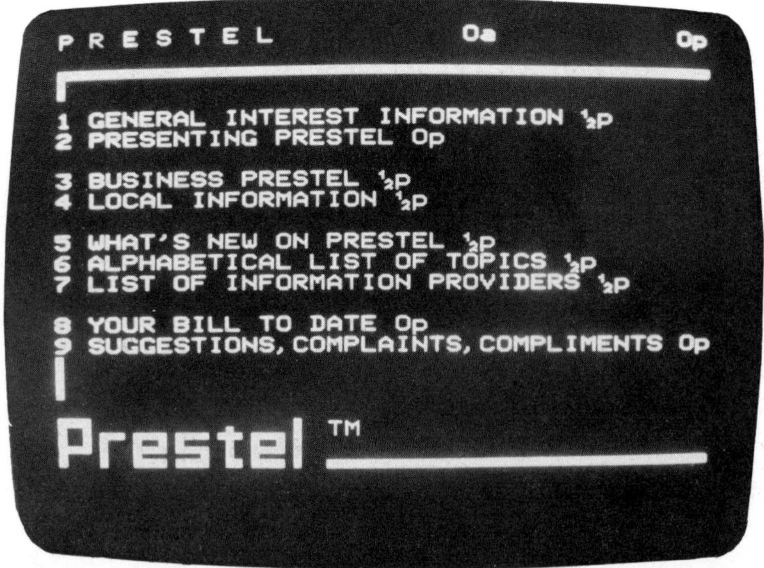

To retrieve information the user keys in *PAGE NUMBER#. For example, to obtain a weather chart, *20990# is keyed in.

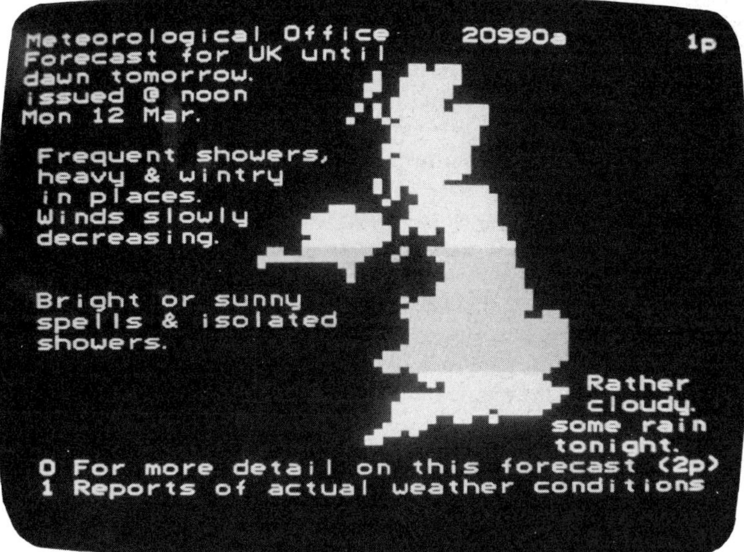

The *Birmingham Post and Mail* Company has put an 'electronic newspaper' on the Prestel system. This contains 2000 pages. To read it the 'Viewtel' title-page must be called, which is 202a.

From now on the user merely keys in the number of the item that he wants. To obtain the 'news index', 0 is keyed and the index is displayed.

To find out what foreign news is available the user enters the number 2, causing 'foreign news' headlines to be displayed.

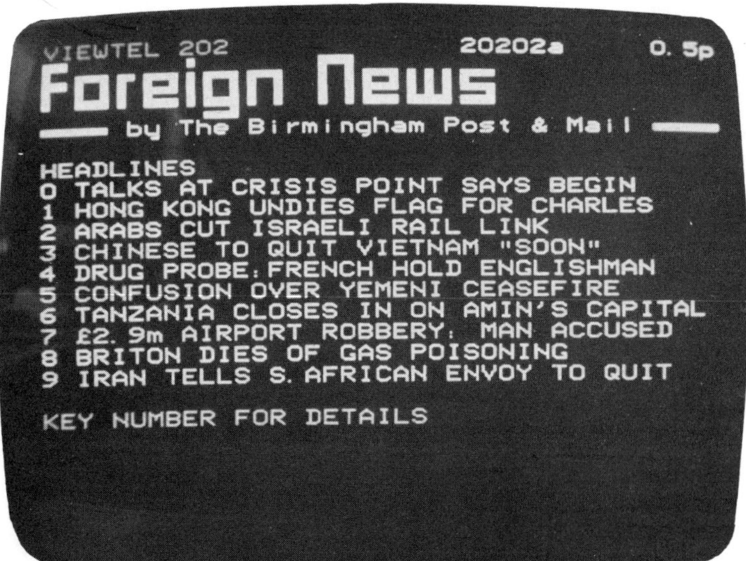

Another service available from Prestel is travel information from British Rail. The first frame is merely an introduction to the BR system and keying in 0 gives the British Rail index: for further information the same procedure is followed as before.

British Rail 2219a 0. 5p

British Rail

welcome you to the Marylebone Reference Library and to PRESTEL

We hope you find our Information useful in planning journeys and holidays

Besides our Inter-City trains such as Inter-City 125 on holiday routes to the West Country, Wales, North East and Scotland we offer many inclusive deals like Golden Rail holidays

If you are taking the car then avoid that tiring drive - go Motorail
Key 0 for British Rail index
If you dont find the information you want this library has our timetable

The system is new, and all its uses have still to be developed. In addition to the information retrieval system, it may soon be used also for computer-assisted learning (CAL), as a message transmitter from user to user, and as a calculator.

The regional centres are linked to the central computer to allow information to pass between them. This means that a user in any region can obtain local and national news and information from the other regional centres.

Disc storage is absolutely essential in such systems, because data in the form of Prestel pages must be made immediately available. Prestel is thus an excellent example of discs used for direct access.

When the Prestel computer receives a request for information, it is decoded and a signal is sent to the disc drive to retrieve a block of data from a particular surface, track and sector.

1. The read/write arms are moved to a position over the required track,
2. the read/write head over the required track is activated,
3. when the correct sector comes round, the data on it is read,
4. then the data is sent to the computer, which in turn sends the information to the user.

The Prestel disc pack contains 5 discs, which are $35\frac{1}{2}$ cm in diameter. Only 8 surfaces are used, because the outside surfaces are kept blank. Each surface has 816 tracks with 34 sectors on each track. Data is recorded at an average of 240 characters per centimetre of track.

The disc rotates at 3600 revolutions per minute, which means that the outside of the disc is moving at 240 kilometres per hour. The disc rotates at this high speed so that any particular block does not take long to come under the read/write head.

The Prestel system makes use of 5 main programs, called INPUT, GATE, TASK, DISC, and OUTPUT. In the flowchart on the next page the programs are illustrated along with their uses.

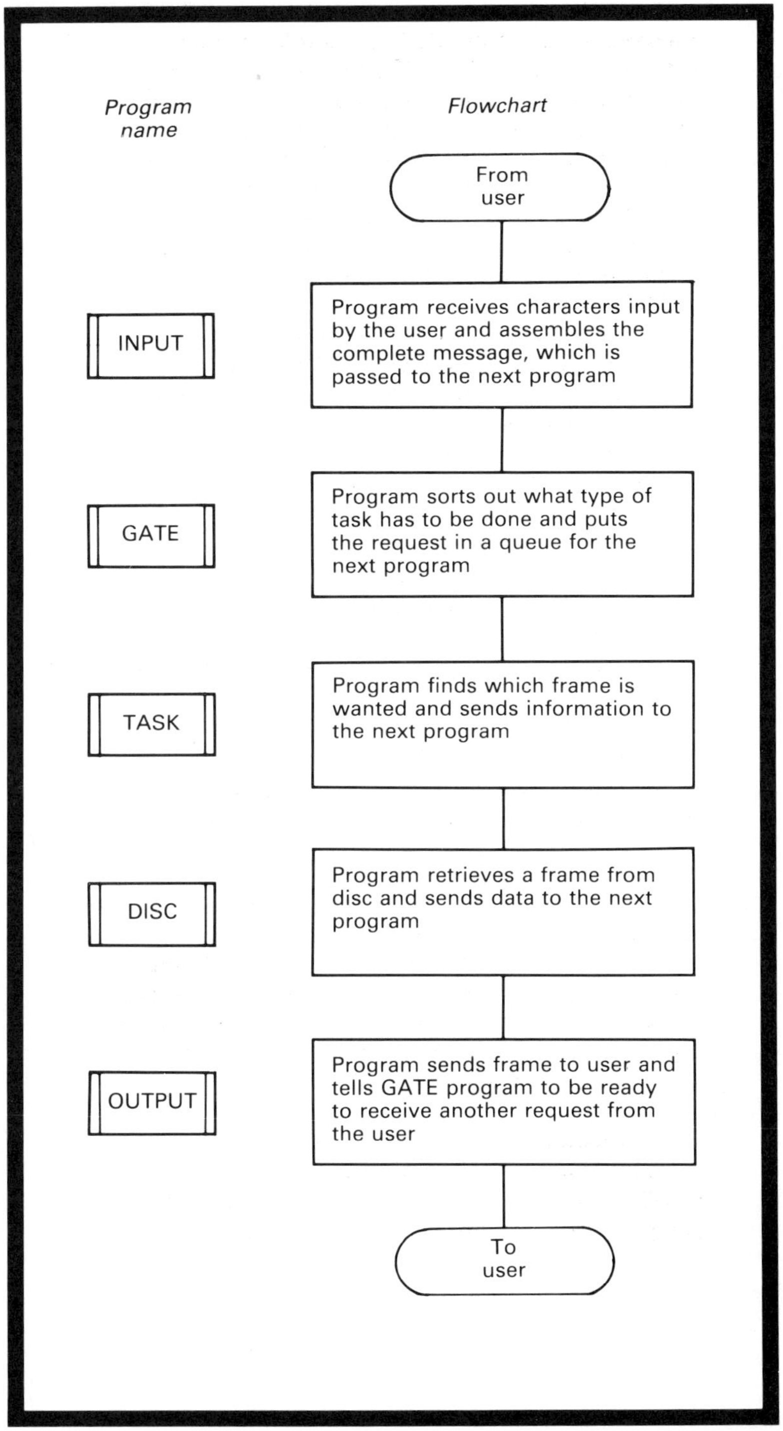

Program name	Flowchart
	From user
INPUT	Program receives characters input by the user and assembles the complete message, which is passed to the next program
GATE	Program sorts out what type of task has to be done and puts the request in a queue for the next program
TASK	Program finds which frame is wanted and sends information to the next program
DISC	Program retrieves a frame from disc and sends data to the next program
OUTPUT	Program sends frame to user and tells GATE program to be ready to receive another request from the user
	To user

Questions

1. What is the main hardware requirement of an information retrieval system?
   (a) large computer,
   (b) good quality terminals,
   (c) magnetic disc unit,
   (d) television set,
   (e) magnetic tape unit.
2. As most frames on the Prestel system have to be paid for (you can see the charge in the corner of each page), how can a regular user save money?
3. Why were the television set and telephone made the basis of the Prestel system?
4. What other peripherals do you think would be used at the computer centre? Give reasons for your answers.
5. Do you think that the 'electronic newspaper' will replace the conventional type of newspaper? Give reasons for your answer.
6. Why would magnetic tape not be a suitable medium for the Prestel system?
7. Only an average figure is given for the number of characters per centimetre of track on a magnetic disc. Why is this so?

Vocabulary

backing store
block
direct access
exchangeable disc system
information retrieval
magnetic disc unit
mass storage system
Prestel
sector
serial access
track

13 The History of Calculating Machines

INDEX	0	1	2	3	4	5	6	7	8	9
0	0/0	0/0	0/0	0/0	0/0	0/0	0/0	0/0	0/0	0/0
1	0/0	0/1	0/2	0/3	0/4	0/5	0/6	0/7	0/8	0/9
2	0/0	0/2	0/4	0/6	0/8	1/0	1/2	1/4	1/6	1/8
3	0/0	0/3	0/6	0/9	1/2	1/5	1/8	2/1	2/4	2/7
4	0/0	0/4	0/8	1/2	1/6	2/0	2/4	2/8	3/2	3/6
5	0/0	0/5	1/0	1/5	2/0	2/5	3/0	3/5	4/0	4/5
6	0/0	0/6	1/2	1/8	2/4	3/0	3/6	4/2	4/8	5/4
7	0/0	0/7	1/4	2/1	2/8	3/5	4/2	4/9	5/6	6/3
8	0/0	0/8	1/6	2/4	3/2	4/0	4/8	5/6	6/4	7/2
9	0/0	0/9	1/8	2/7	3/6	4/5	5/4	6/3	7/2	8/1

Left Napier's system set up
Below Napier's rods

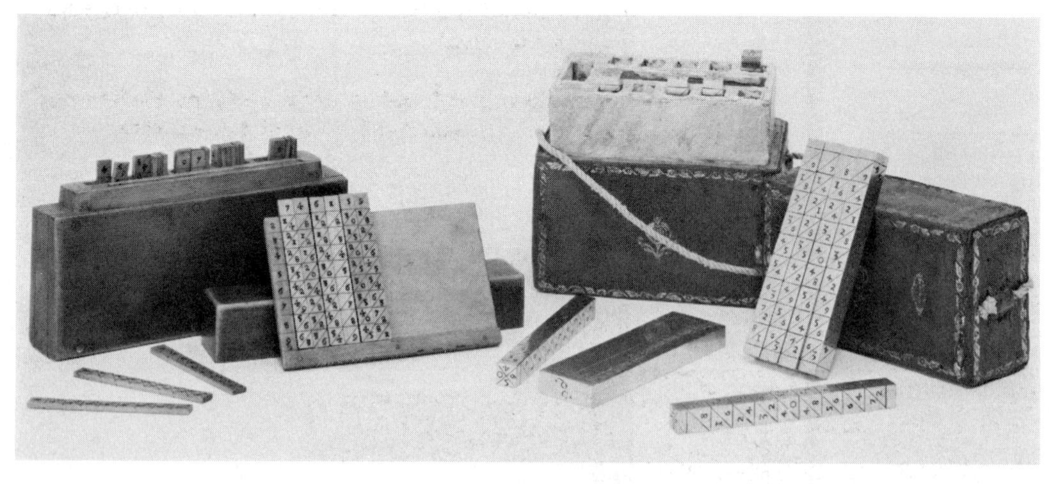

Until quite recently the abacus was the most widely used calculating device. It was not until the seventeenth century that any alternative was available.

In 1617 John Napier, a Scottish mathematician, invented a set of rods which enabled multiplication to be done more quickly. He carved multiplication tables on a set of sheep's bones then laid them side by side and read off the answers to the multiplication. Later these bones were replaced by wooden rods, as shown in the photograph.
The only calculation required to find the answer was addition. The rods were drawn as shown on the left.

You could make a copy of the rods on card, cut out each strip and then use them to perform a multiplication.

Arrangement of rods for multiplying 427 by 4

INDEX	4	2	7
1	0/4	0/2	0/7
2	0/8	0/4	1/4
3	1/2	0/6	2/1
4	1/6	0/8	2/8
5	2/0	1/0	3/5
6	2/4	1/2	4/2
7	2/8	1/4	4/9
8	3/2	1/6	5/6
9	3/6	1/8	6/3

To do the multiplication 4 × 427, the rods 4, 2 and 7 are first arranged together as shown on the previous page. Numbers are added along the diagonals as shown below.

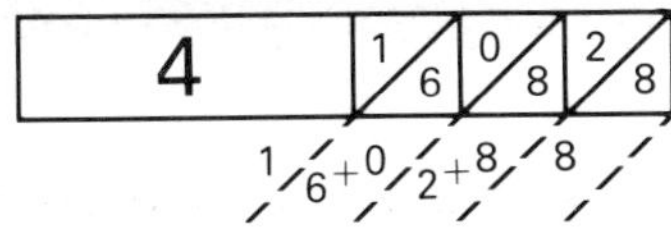

The first diagonal yields 8; the next produces 10, so 1 is carried as in ordinary addition and added on to the 6 in the next diagonal. The fourth diagonal gives 1. Thus the answer is 1708.

More difficult multiplication problems like 827 × 36 must be done in two stages.
First work out 827 × 3.

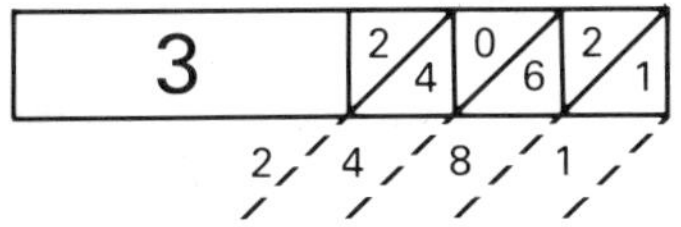

Thus 827 × 3 = 2481.
So 827 × 30 = 24 810 (add a nought).
Then work out 827 × 6.

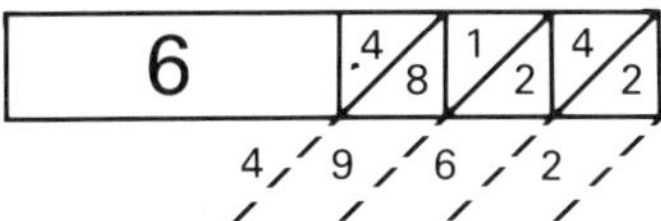

The result is 4962.
To obtain the answer to the whole problem, these two figures must be added:

24 810
+4 962
29 772

Napier was also responsible for the invention of logarithms, which make complex multiplications easier. To multiply two numbers you add their logarithms.

Example Calculate 2.56 × 3.72

Number	Logarithm
2.56	0.408
3.72	0.571
	0.979

This gives an answer of 9.42.

William Oughtred, in 1621, used Napier's logarithms as the basis of his slide rule. Instead of the logarithms being added, the lengths of two logarithmic scales (or rules) are placed alongside each other. The result may be read off directly from the scales.

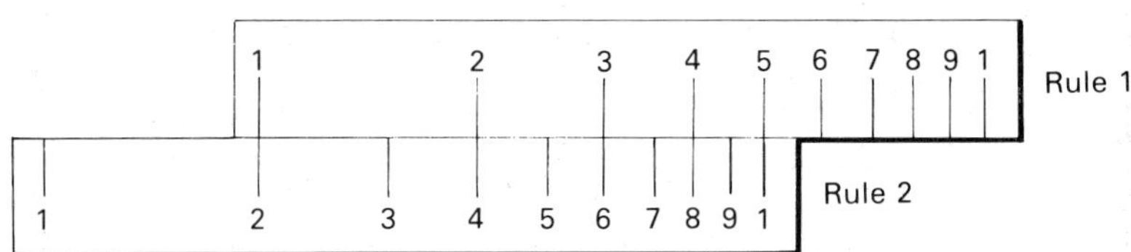

Simple slide rule

Length 2 on rule 1 and length 4 on rule 2 added together give a total length 8 on rule 2, i.e. 2 × 4 = 8.

This is an example of an analog device **where the logarithms of the two numbers are represented by lengths on a scale.**

The photograph below shows 2.56 multiplied by 3.72 on a slide rule that we might use today.

Modern slide rule

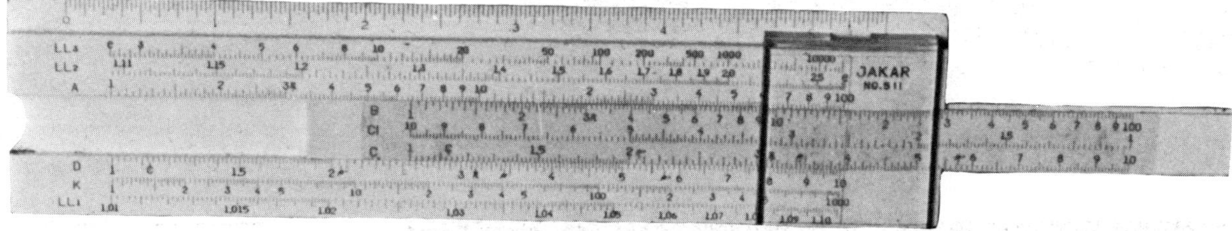

The first calculating machine was invented by Blaise Pascal in 1642, when he was 19 years old. His father was a customs official in France and needed to do many calculations in his work. Pascal designed and built a machine to help him. This consisted of cogged wheels, gears and dials. Each wheel was divided into ten sections, representing numbers, and the mechanism allowed a carry from one wheel to the next. Pascal's machine was only capable of addition.

The engraving shows Pascal's calculating machine in use. The stylus in the left hand of the user is for setting the numbers on the dials.

Pascal's calculating machine

Many other inventors made calculating machines after this, but it was not until 1671 that the first machine was constructed which was capable of multiplying. The machine was invented by another famous mathematician, Gottfried Leibniz. He used a 'stepped wheel' which allowed long multiplication and division to be done. The process of multiplication involved repeated addition.

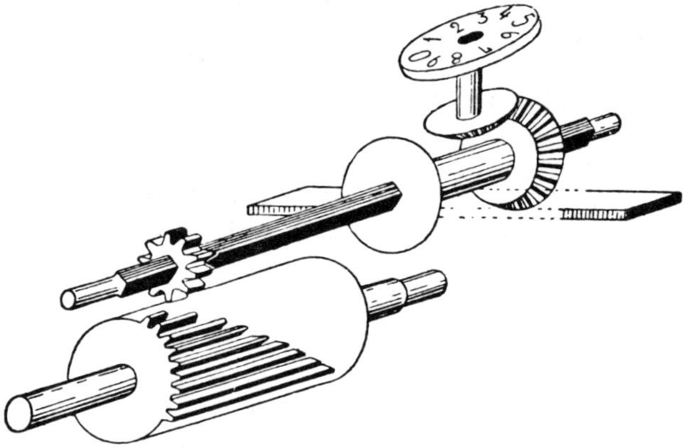

Construction of Leibniz's stepped wheel

Leibniz's calculator

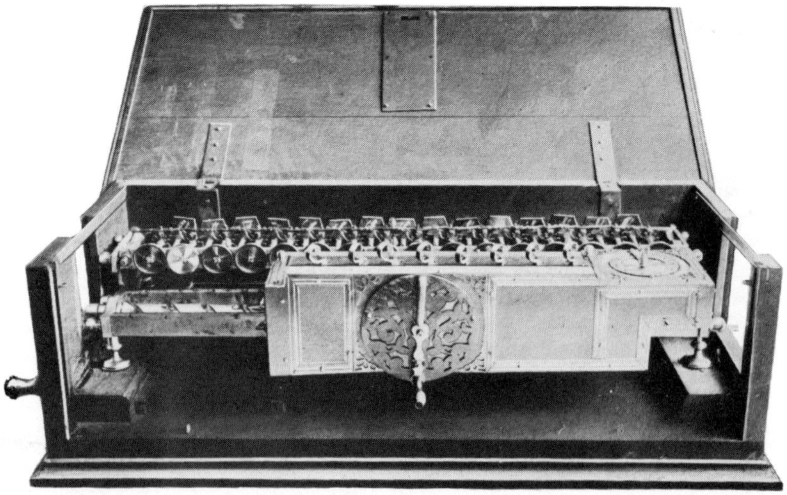

Unfortunately Leibniz's machine was unreliable, as were most of the early calculators. It was very difficult in those days to make the parts to the required precision. Because of this problem mechanical calculators did not become popular for many years, and it was not until the late nineteenth century that they became widely used in business. At that time one of the most popular calculators was the 'Millionaire', shown below, of which over two thousand were sold.

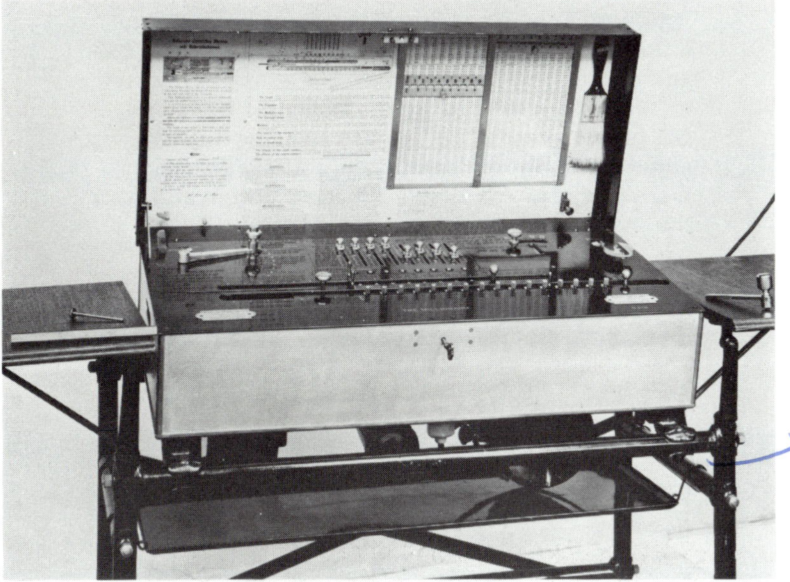

'Millionaire' calculating machine

In 1792 Charles Babbage was born in Devon; he was to become a forward-thinking and controversial mathematician. He was a professor of mathematics at Cambridge for eleven years, during which time he succeeded in giving no lectures at all.

However, his great achievement was the design of a calculating machine called the 'Difference Engine'. He knew that the logarithm tables he used were full of mistakes, and so the Difference Engine was to be made to calculate various mathematical functions. At that time calculations were done by hand by a team of clerks, and the results were subsequently checked by another team.

Charles Babbage

A common method of calculation in those days involved drawing up a table of differences.

Consider, for example, the function $y = x^2 + 3x + 2$.

If we give the value 1 to x, y becomes 6 [that is, $1^2 + (3 \times 1) + 2$].

Various values of x give the table below.

x	y	First difference	Second difference
0	2		
		}4	
1	6		}2
		}6	
2	12		}2
		}8	
3	20		}2
		}10	
4	30		}2
		}12	
5	42		}2
		}14	
6	56		

The second difference between the y values is a constant and thus we can find the next first difference and hence the next value of y:

next first difference = 2 + 14 = 16
next value of y = 16 + 56 = 72

This method of differences is most useful with very complicated functions that may not produce a constant value until the fifth or sixth difference.

Babbage designed his calculator so that once the

initial values were set it would produce the next few thousand values without error.

He managed to build a small machine which had three registers and was accurate to eight decimal places. He was given a grant by the government to construct a full-size machine, but it was never built, although about £17 000 was spent. Babbage became interested in extending his ideas, which delayed his work until eventually his grant was withdrawn. Much of Babbage's work from that point was financed by himself.

George Scheutz, a Swedish engineer, built two difference engines. The first was completed in 1855 and was shipped to America. The second was built in 1859 and was used by the Registrar General's Office to compute the 'English Lifetime Tables', annuities and premiums. Both of these machines were less complex than Babbage's design and were therefore easier to make.

Babbage's Difference Engine

Scheutz's Difference Engine

In 1833 Babbage began work on an 'Analytical Engine'. He believed that it would be possible to program the machine to do any type of calculation and then automatically print out the result. The most impressive thing about the Analytical Engine is that it contained all the main features of a modern computer.

Babbage's Analytical Engine

Babbage's design consisted of five parts.

Store	**This held data for the various calculations and the numbers generated during the calculations.**
Arithmetic unit	**Babbage called this the 'mill' and this term is still used today to cost computer time or 'mill time'. The mill was to perform arithmetic operations on stored numbers. This was to be achieved automatically by the use of gears and wheels.**
Control unit	**This was to organize the work in the correct sequences and control the transfer of data from the store to the mill.**
Input device	**This passed instructions and data into the machine by using punched cards. The idea of punched cards was borrowed from Joseph Jacquard, who was a weaver and who first used them on his loom.**
Output device	**Here the results were to be displayed either in the form of print, moulds from which printing blocks could be made, or on punched cards.**

Punched cards would represent operations (add, subtract, etc.) or numbers. A photograph of such a card is shown below.

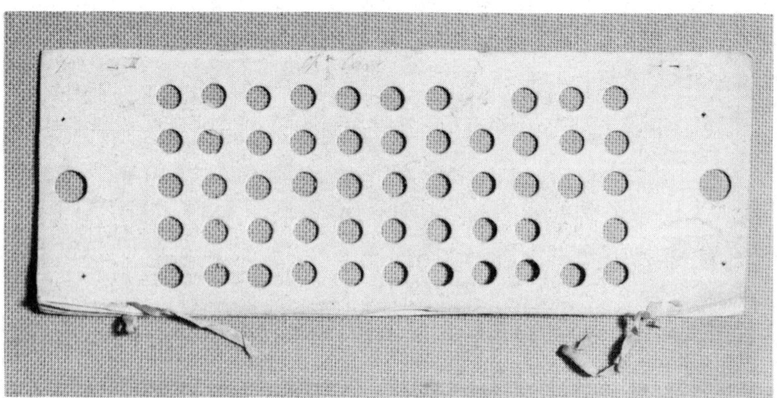

Engraving of the Countess of Lovelace (*c.* 1839)

Babbage gave a paper in Turin on his Analytical Engine in 1842. The Countess of Lovelace (daughter of Lord Byron) translated this into English and added her own detailed notes. She became a great friend and colleague of Charles Babbage and she helped him by planning sequences of operations to be put on punched cards for input to the machine. Because of this she is often referred to as 'the first programmer'. Lady Lovelace once said, 'The Analytical Engine weaves algebraic patterns just as Jacquard's loom weaves flowers and leaves.'

The Analytical Engine was never completed even though Babbage worked on it until his death in 1871.

It was more than seventy years before Babbage's advanced ideas became a reality. In 1944 Howard Aitken of Harvard University in the U.S.A. completed the world's first fully automatic calculator. It was known as the Automatic Sequence Controlled Calculator (ASCC). This machine combined Babbage's mechanical and design ideas with modern electronic technology.

The main memory consisted of 72 registers, driven from a single shaft. It was programmed by punching instructions on 24-hole tape. Addresses and operations were held on 80-column cards, and typewriters or punched cards were used for output. Numbers were stored by using wheels which could be set to any of ten positions, and the position of any of the wheels was sensed by electrical contacts.

ASCC was enormous and consisted of over three-quarters of a million parts, yet it was very reliable, and it was used constantly for fifteen years. Relays were used to send signals around the machine, and it was said to sound like 'a roomful of ladies knitting'.

It also contained tables for such things as logarithms and sines and could add in 0.3 seconds while multiplication and division took 6 and 12 seconds respectively.

The stage was now set for the first completely electric computer.

Questions

1. Why was Lady Lovelace called 'the first programmer'?
2. Give an example of an analog device.
3. Babbage designed two calculators which were never completed.
   (a) What were these two machines called?
   (b) Why were they not completed?
   (c) As his machines were not practical successes, why was he considered a computer pioneer?
4. What was the form of input to the ASCC and what was the form of output?
5. How many registers were there in the ASCC and what did they consist of?
6. Write a brief account of the following:
   (a) calculating aids invented by John Napier,
   (b) Blaise Pascal,
   (c) the Leibniz calculator.

Vocabulary

analog device
analytical engine
Automatic Sequence Controlled Calculator (ASCC)
difference engine
Leibniz's calculator
Napier's bones
Pascal's calculator
Scheutz's engine

14 Computer Logic

In Chapter 6 it was stated that to do arithmetic in the central processor all that was basically required was an electric power supply and circuits for switching and adding. It would not be practical, of course, to have many thousands of ordinary switches inside the CPU of a modern computer: either they would have to be operated by leprechauns or the machinery would be far too large.

To see how the principle works we shall look first at simple switching circuits.

Look at the diagram below of a switching circuit with a battery and a lamp.

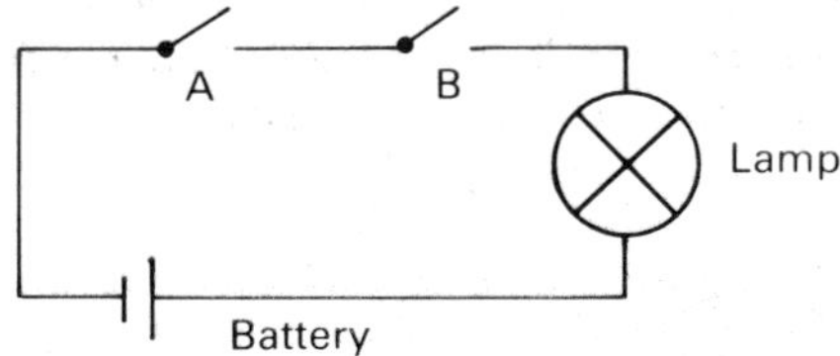

The switches are in series and shown open. There are four different ways of setting the switches.

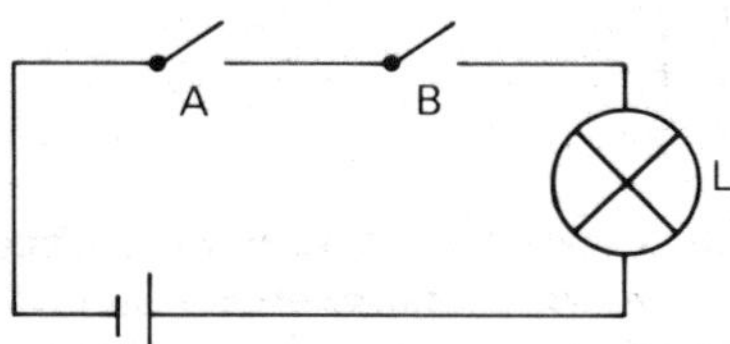

When switches A and B are both open the lamp does not light.

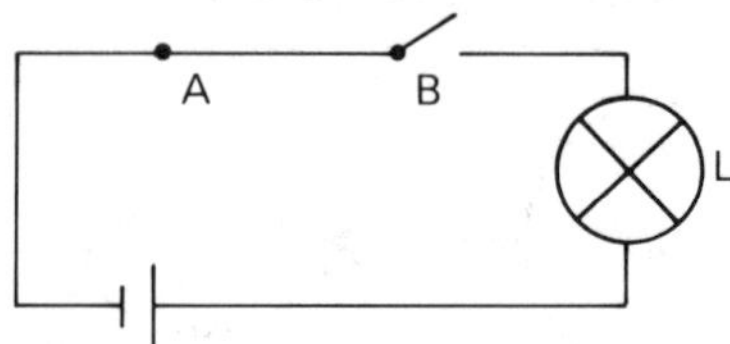

When switch A only is closed the lamp does not light.

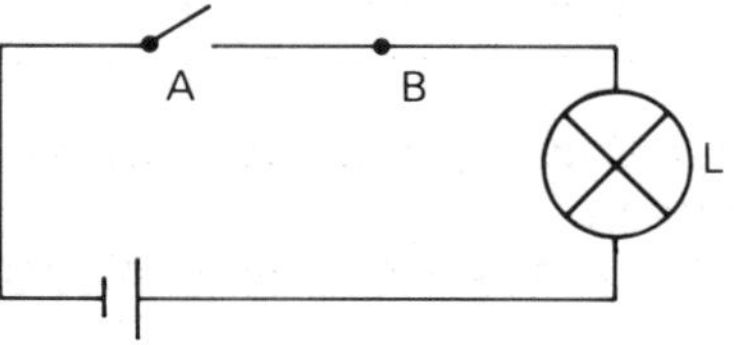

When switch B only is closed the lamp does not light.

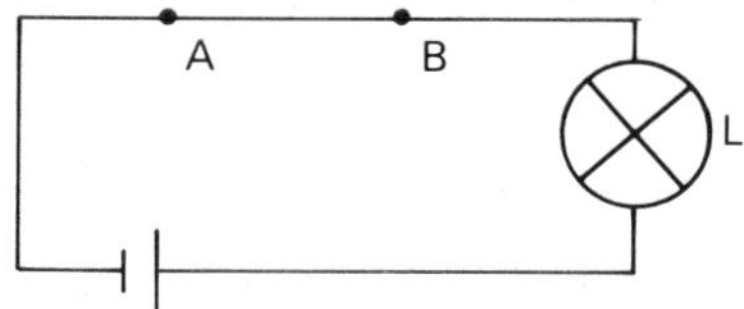

When switches A and B are both closed the lamp does light.

These circuits take quite a long time to draw, so truth tables are used to summarize their results.

Here the lamp is represented by 0 for off and by 1 for on. Similarly the switches are represented by 0 for open and 1 for closed.

Switch A	Switch B	Lamp L
Open	Open	Off
Open	Closed	Off
Closed	Open	Off
Closed	Closed	On

Truth table

A	B	L
0	0	0
0	1	0
1	0	0
1	1	1

This shows clearly that the light is on only when switches A and B are both closed.

When the switches are wired in parallel the circuit and truth tables are as follows:

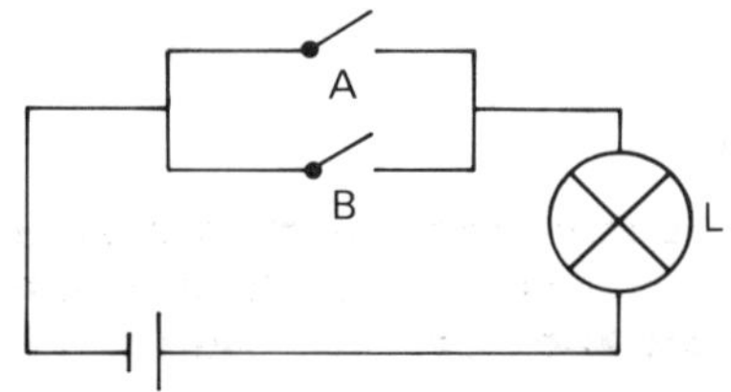

Switch A	Switch B	Lamp L
Open	Open	Off
Open	Closed	On
Closed	Open	On
Closed	Closed	On

A	B	L
0	0	0
0	1	1
1	0	1
1	1	1

We have seen that two switches may be set in four different ways.

Three switches can be set in eight different ways:

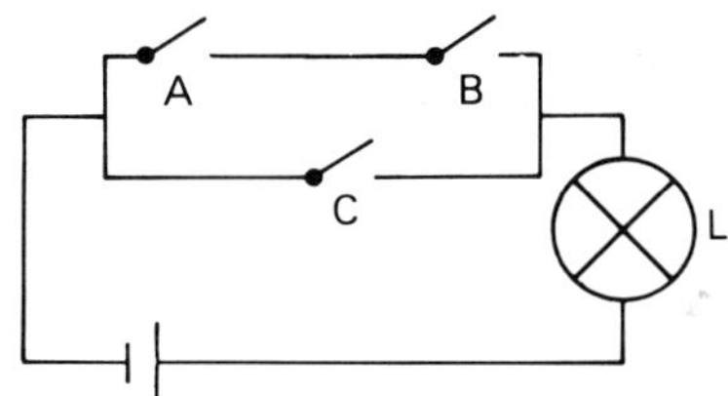

Switch A	Switch B	Switch C	Lamp L
Open	Open	Open	Off
Open	Open	Closed	On
Open	Closed	Open	Off
Open	Closed	Closed	On
Closed	Open	Open	Off
Closed	Open	Closed	On
Closed	Closed	Open	On
Closed	Closed	Closed	On

A	B	C	L
0	0	0	0
0	0	1	1
0	1	0	0
0	1	1	1
1	0	0	0
1	0	1	1
1	1	0	1
1	1	1	1

Logic gates

Some small electronic components can be used to make up series and parallel switching circuits. These circuits are known as logic gates.

Remember that switches in series give an output of 1 only when both inputs A and B are set to 1. This is given diagrammatically as:

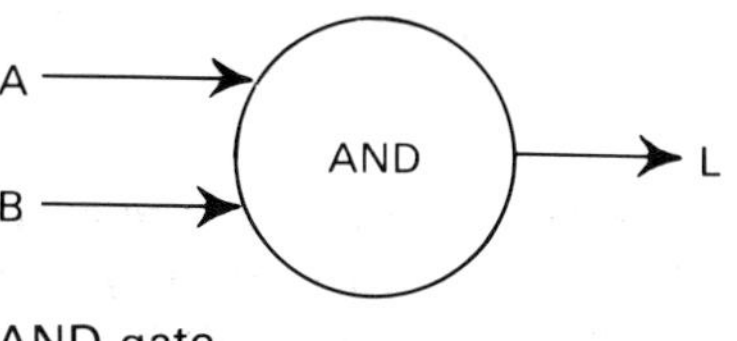

AND gate

Parallel switches give an output of 1 when either input A, input B or both are set to 1.

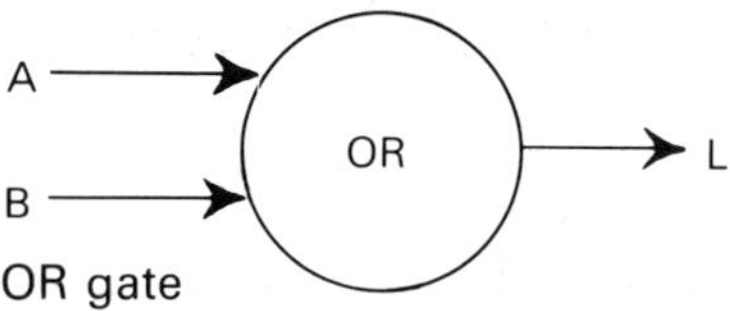

OR gate

One more logic gate is required to enable a computer logic circuit to be built. This is a NOT gate. Its truth table is shown below.

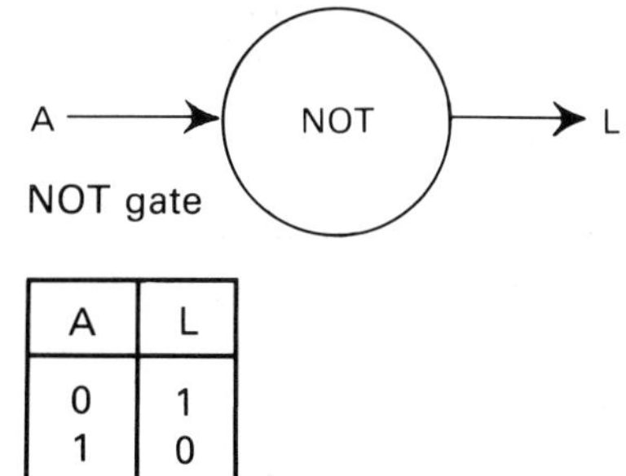

NOT gate

A	L
0	1
1	0

In a switching circuit this would mean that the lamp would be on when the switch was open and vice versa. A NOT gate therefore complements or negates the input.

Examine the logic diagram below.

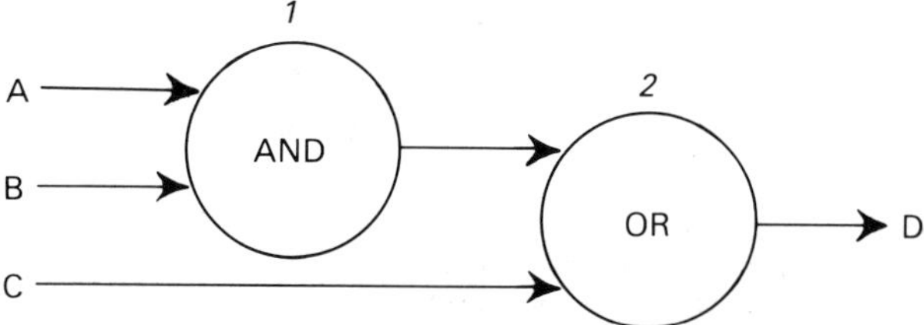

The truth table may be built up as shown below.

A	B	C	1 A AND B	2 1 OR C
0	0	0	0	0
0	0	1	0	1
0	1	0	0	0
0	1	1	0	1
1	0	0	0	0
1	0	1	0	1
1	1	0	1	1
1	1	1	1	1

Or more simply as

A	B	C	D
0	0	0	0
0	0	1	1
0	1	0	0
0	1	1	1
1	0	0	0
1	0	1	1
1	1	0	1
1	1	1	1

Writing numbers over the logic gates will enable you to get the order correct and also help you to build up the truth table. Here is another example:

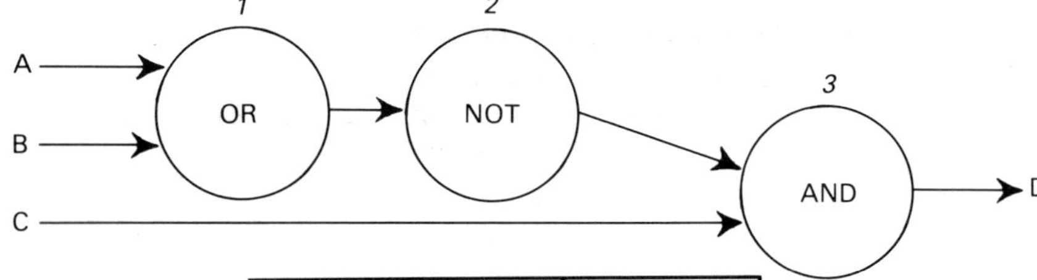

A	B	C	1 A OR B	2 NOT 1	3 2 AND C
0	0	0	0	1	0
0	0	1	0	1	1
0	1	0	1	0	0
0	1	1	1	0	0
1	0	0	1	0	0
1	0	1	1	0	0
1	1	0	1	0	0
1	1	1	1	0	0

A	B	C	D
0	0	0	0
0	0	1	1
0	1	0	0
0	1	1	0
1	0	0	0
1	0	1	0
1	1	0	0
1	1	1	0

Using logic circuits

Having studied these simple logic circuits we can now attempt to design a circuit that will add together two binary numbers.

Look at the logic diagram below.

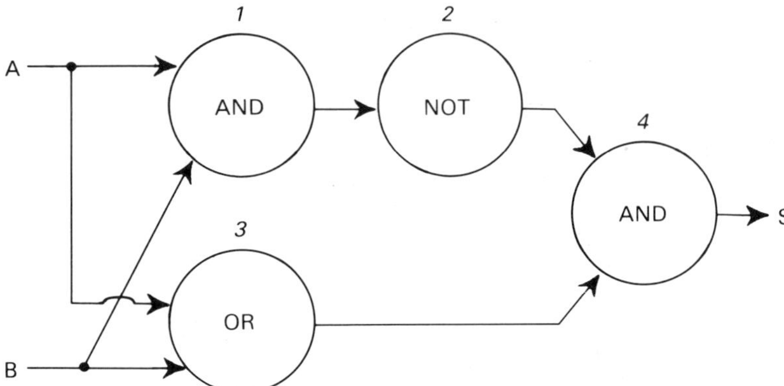

Here is the construction of the truth table:

INPUTS		1	2	3	OUTPUT 4
A	B	A AND B	NOT 1	A OR B	2 AND 3
0	0	0	1	0	0
0	1	0	1	1	1
1	0	0	1	1	1
1	1	1	0	1	0

Examine the completed truth table on the right and see if you can discover why output S is useful.

A	B	S
0	0	0
0	1	1
1	0	1
1	1	0

S represents the *sum* of two bits. When A and B are both 1 the sum is 0 and the carry is ignored at this stage.

$$\begin{array}{r}0\\+0\\\hline 0\end{array}\qquad\begin{array}{r}0\\+1\\\hline 1\end{array}\qquad\begin{array}{r}1\\+0\\\hline 1\end{array}\qquad\begin{array}{r}1\\+1\\\hline 0\end{array}$$

This circuit enables us to add together two bits and produce a sum. However to make this circuit more useful we must be able to produce a carry bit when the arithmetic requires it, e.g. 1 + 1 = 1 (carry) 0 (sum)

The half adder

You will recall that an AND gate gives an output of 1 when both inputs are 1. If you look carefully at the logic diagram again you should discover an AND gate that will serve this purpose.

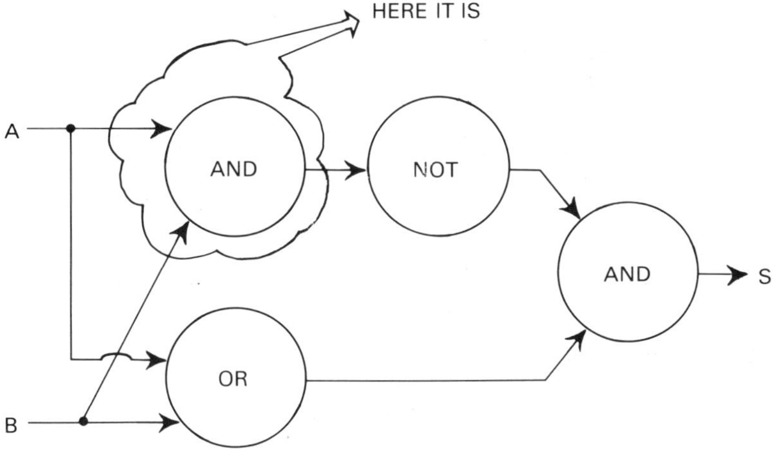

To produce a carry in the circuit we must 'tap off' after this point, giving the logic circuit shown below.

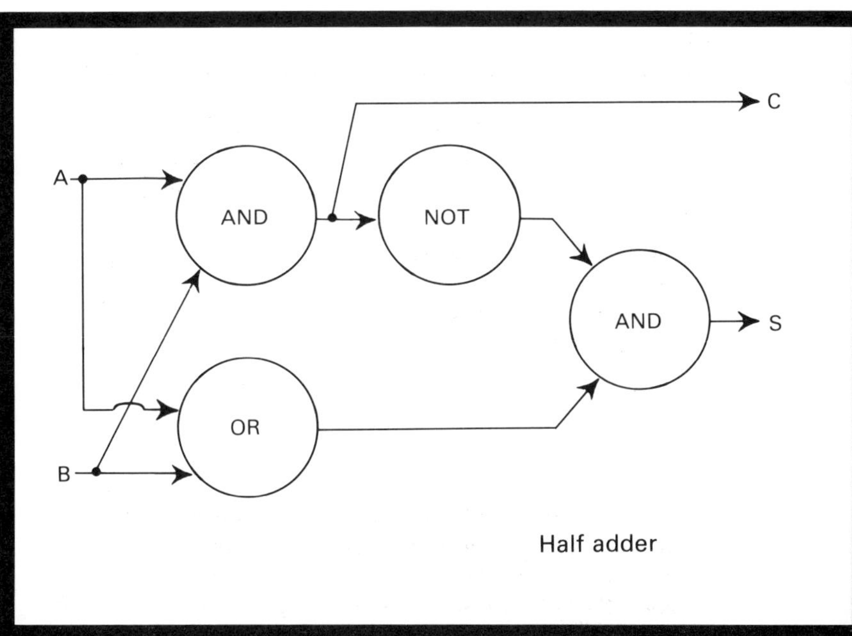

Half adder

The truth table then looks like this.

A	B	C	S
0	0	0	0
0	1	0	1
1	0	0	1
1	1	1	0

Now we can successfully add together two bits to give a sum bit **and a** carry bit.

This circuit is known as a half adder. **Its limitation is that it can add only two bits together and would be useful for adding only the first (right-hand) bits of two binary numbers.**

The full adder

Now look at the addition below.

3rd	2nd	1st	bit positions
1	0	1	two binary numbers (A and B)
+1	1	1	being added
		0	sum
	1		carry

What other operation is required at the second bit position?

Not only must two bits be added but the carry from the previous circuit must also be added.

The next diagram illustrates this more clearly.

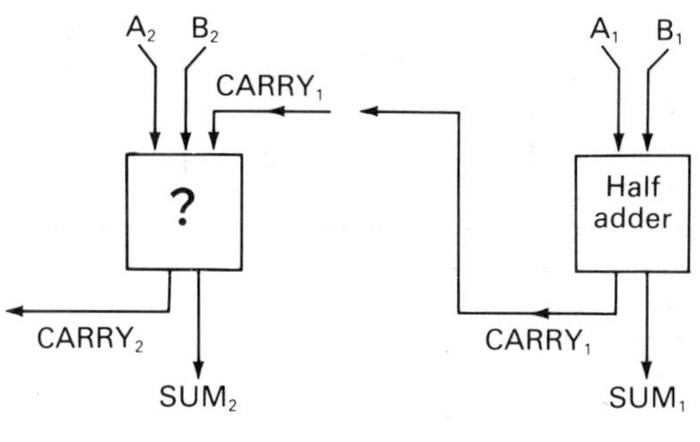

The circuit that adds two bits, together with the carry from the previous sum, and then gives the sum and the carry to the next bit position is called a full adder.

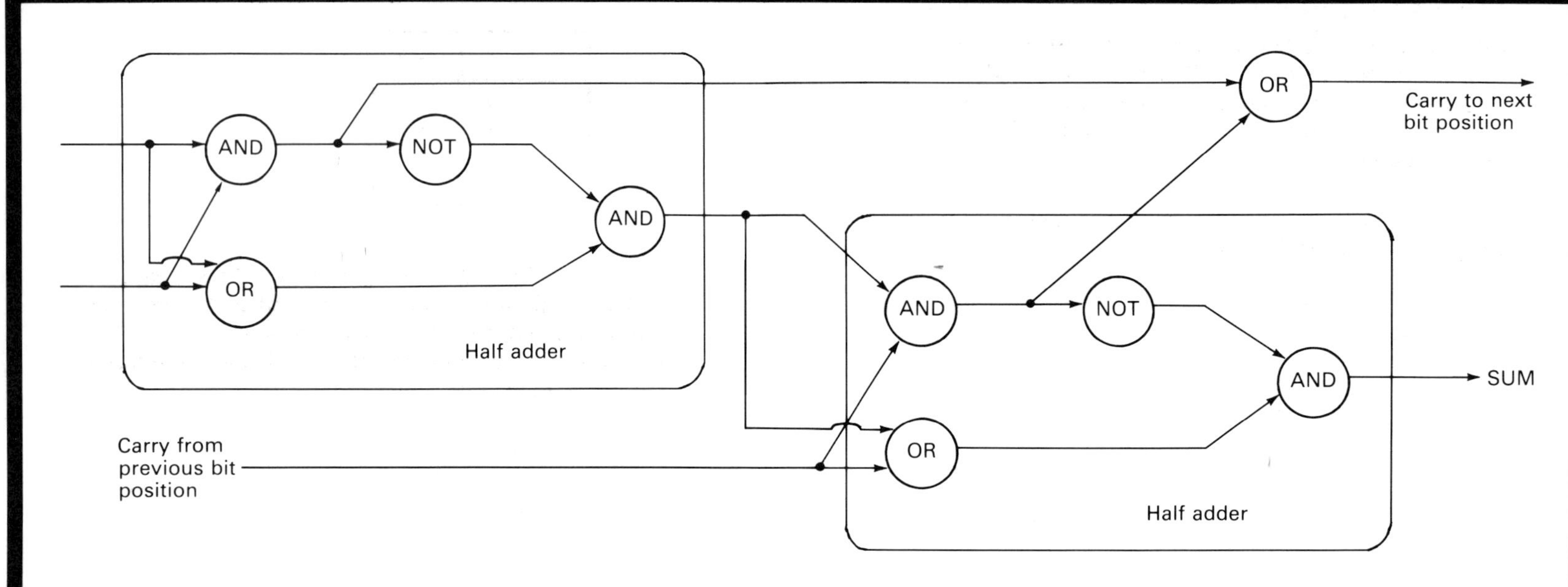

Full adder – two half adders joined together with an OR gate

Above is a logic diagram for a full adder. This looks very much like two half adders joined together with an extra OR gate to produce the next carry.

Now we are in a position to add together two binary numbers, using what is called a binary adder. **We have only to ensure that we have enough full adders to cater for the size of the numbers.**

For adding two three-bit numbers together we need one half adder and two full adders. The process is illustrated below.

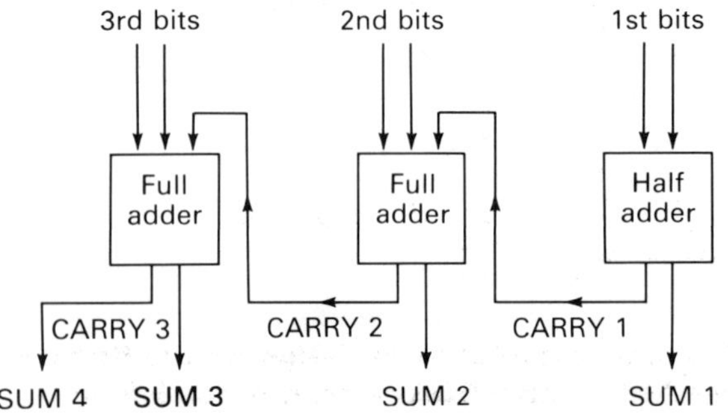

As an example, we will draw a diagram to show how the binary numbers 111 and 101 may be added using half and full adders.

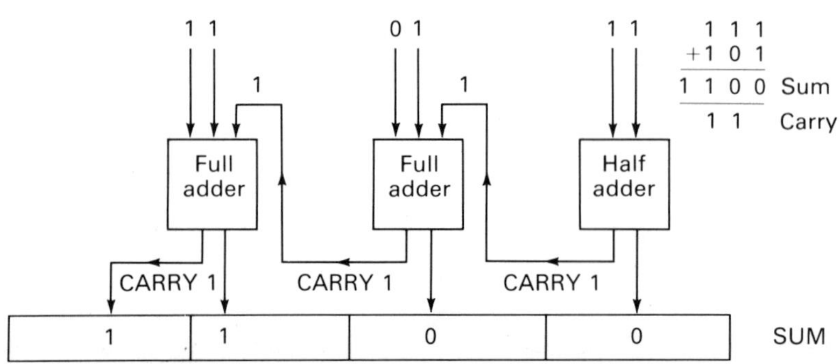

Further logic gates

All computer circuitry could be designed from the three basic logic gates (AND, OR and NOT). There are, however, other gates which are widely used. Three main examples are NAND, NOR and NOT EQUIVALENT.

The NAND gate is produced by negating the output from an AND gate.

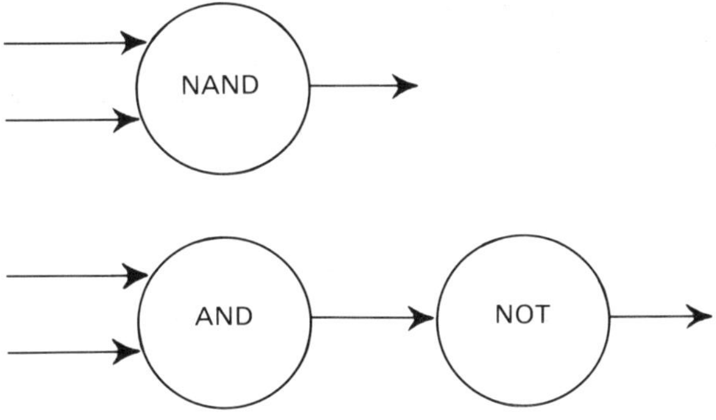

Truth table

A	B	NAND
0	0	1
0	1	1
1	0	1
1	1	0

The NOR gate is produced by negating the output from an OR gate.

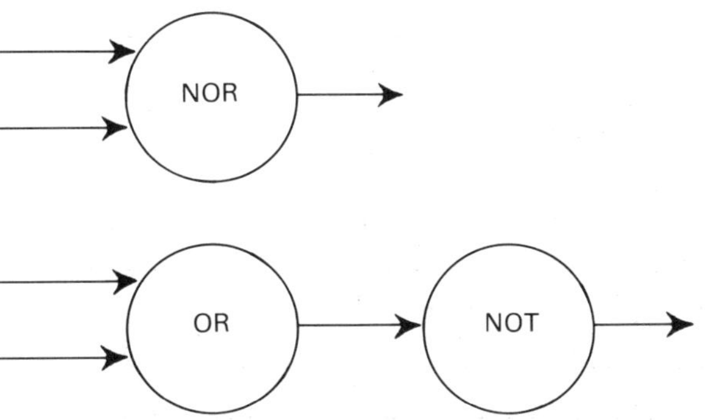

Truth table

A	B	NOR
0	0	1
0	1	0
1	0	0
1	1	0

The NOT EQUIVALENT gate (sometimes called EXCLUSIVE OR) produces an output of 1 when the inputs are not the same. (The symbol used in mathematics for 'equivalent' is ≡. Thus the symbol for 'not equivalent' is ≢.)

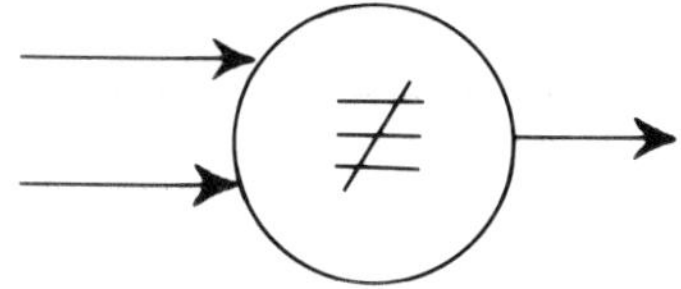

Truth table

A	B	≢
0	0	0
0	1	1
1	0	1
1	1	0

Notice that the output from the last truth table gives the sum of two bits. This means that the logic circuit for the half adder can be simplified. Only two gates are now required.

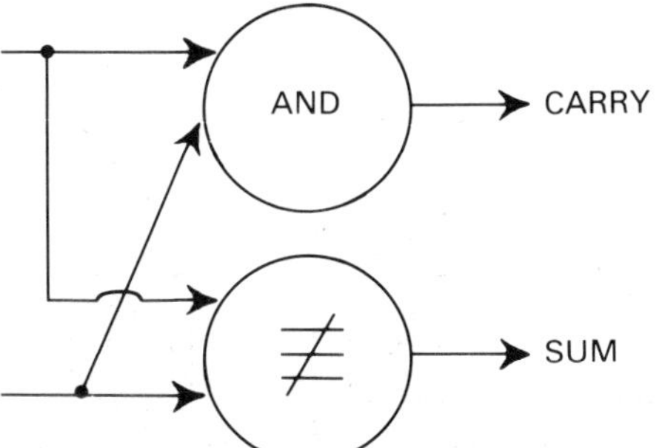

Computer manufacturers design circuits that use only NAND or only NOR gates. It is possible to

construct all other types of gates from NAND gates only, as we see from the diagrams below.

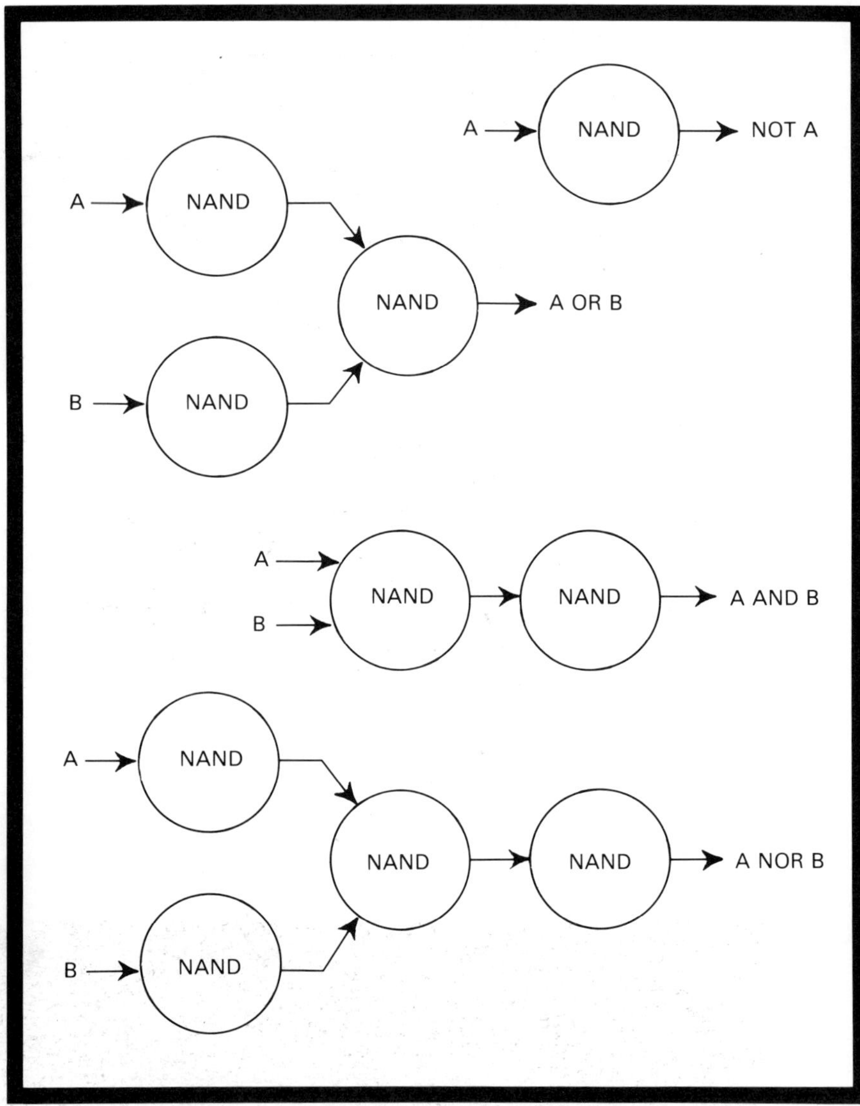

If you are feeling confident and a little brave, try to draw logic diagrams for NOT, AND, OR and NAND gates, but this time using NOR gates only.

It is impossible to identify individual gates in modern computer circuitry, because many thousands of components may be built into a very small silicon chip.

Questions

1. How many possible switch combinations are there for four switches?
2. Draw truth tables for the circuits below.

a

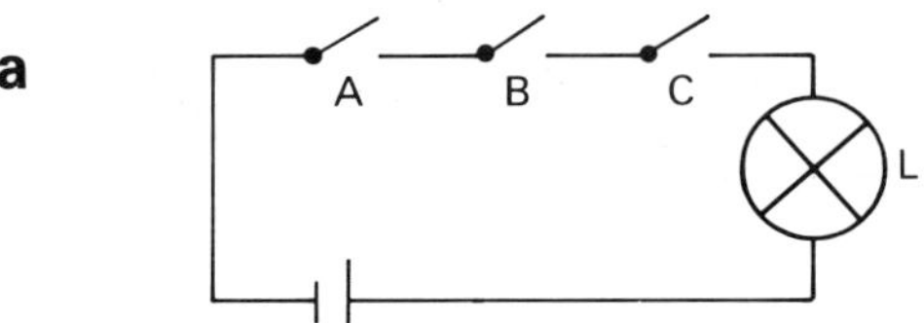

b

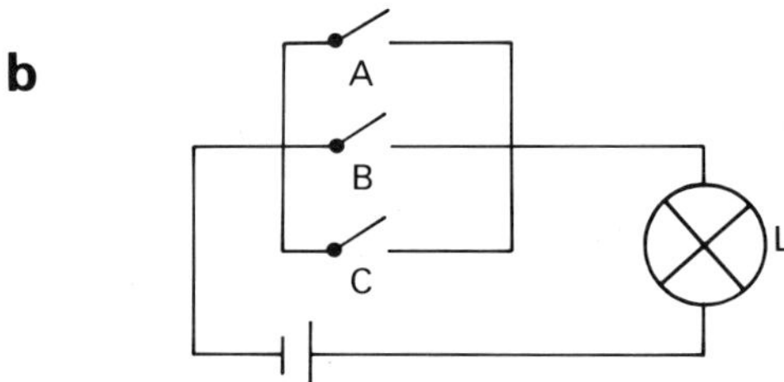

c

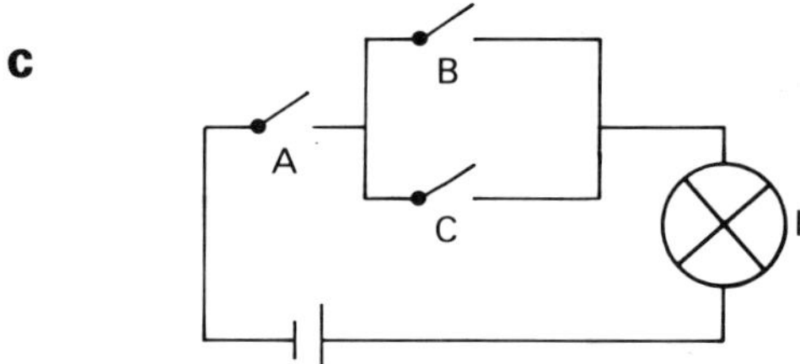

d

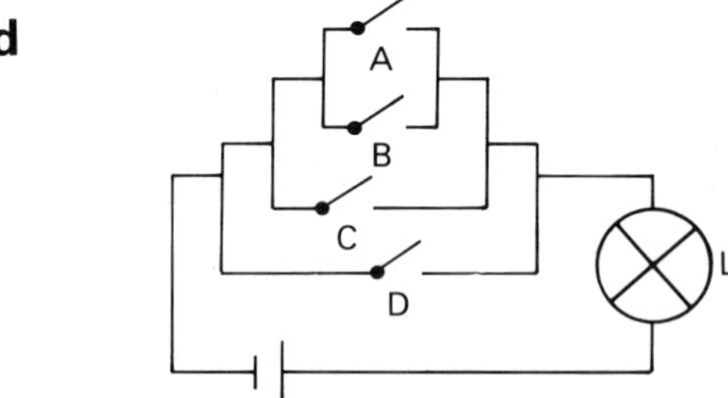

e

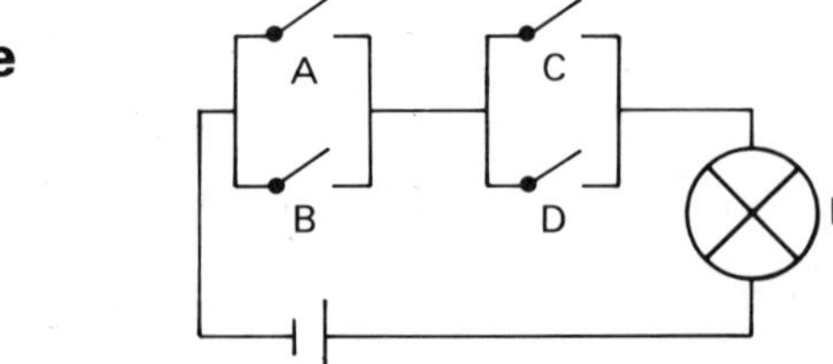

3. Construct truth tables for the logic diagrams below.

a

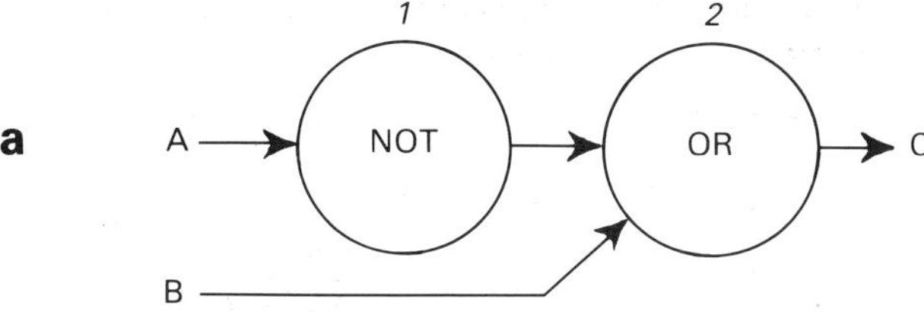

b

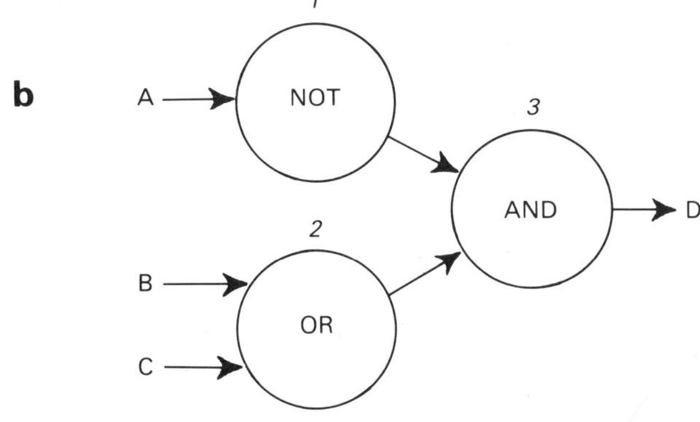

c

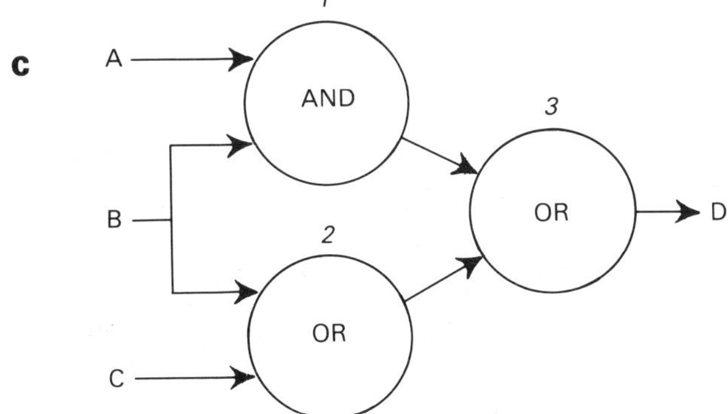

d

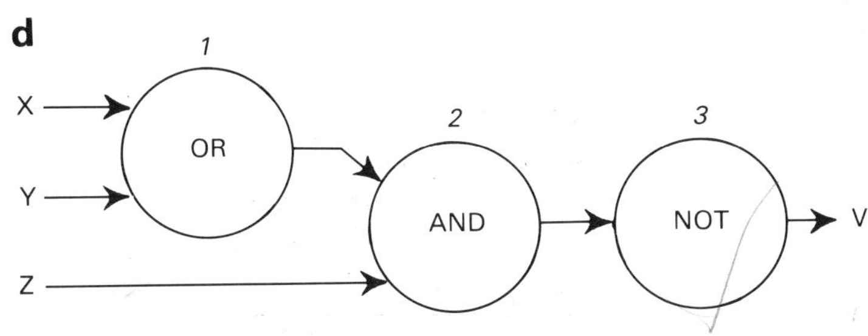

e

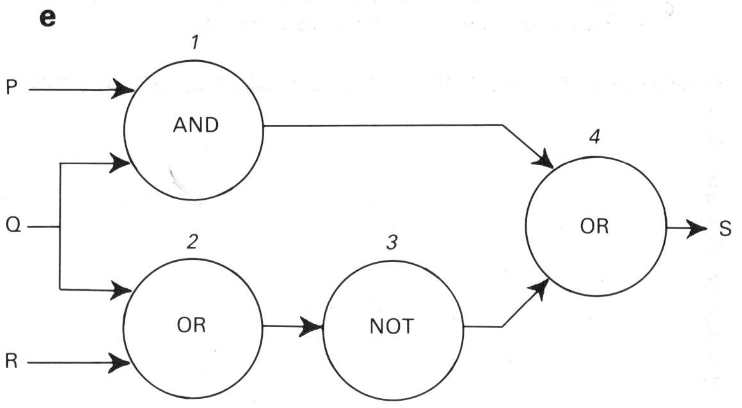

f

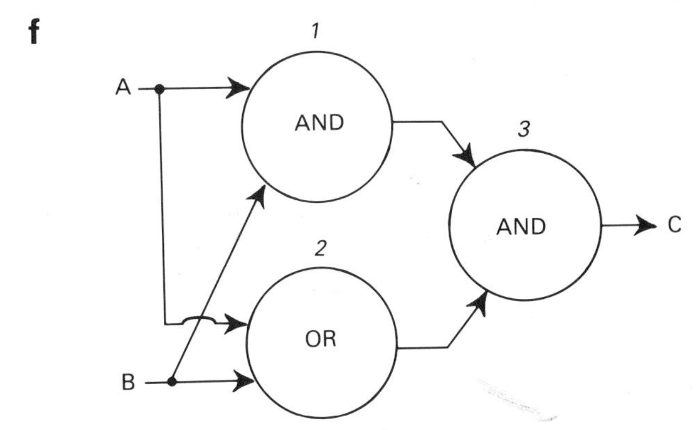

Vocabulary

AND gate	NAND gate
binary adder	NOR gate
carry bit	NOT gate
full adder	OR gate
half adder	sum bit
logic gate	truth table

15 Software

The machines illustrated above work automatically. By this we mean that they do the job for which they were designed without us having to do anything. However, is this completely true?

Consider the tea-maker. Before it can work automatically it must

1. be connected to a power supply,
2. be set to the correct time,
3. have the time set for the alarm to work,
4. have the alarm switched on,
5. have water and tea put in it.

Make a list of things you must do to the automatic washing-machine and record-player in order for them to work properly.

If we bought a computer direct from a manufacturer it also would not work unless it were set up properly first. It consists only of pieces of plastic and metal which cannot function until someone instructs the machine to do something. Someone must first prepare programs which the computer can accept and then act upon.

A computer system may be thought of in two parts, hardware and software. Hardware consists of the machines and devices which allow us to process data. It has been described as 'anything in a computer room that you can trip over'. Software consists of the programs that a computer needs in order to operate properly. It is not the tape or cards that the programs are written on.

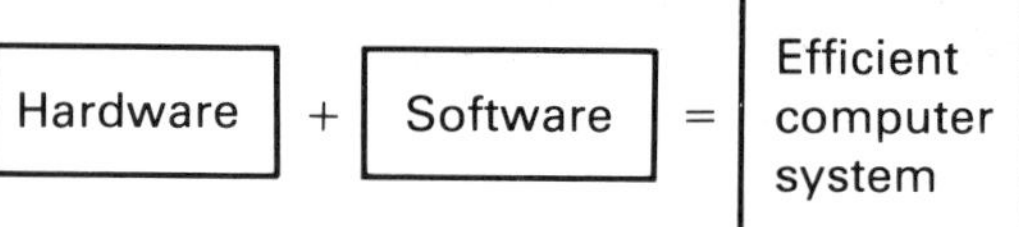

An orchestra may contain many fine musicians, but it will produce good music only if a conductor is there doing his job as well. Similarly, the hardware of a computer system may be fast operating and capable of doing many complicated tasks, but it will not function properly unless good software is provided.

Computer languages

In earlier chapters we said that a computer must first be programmed and that these instructions must ultimately be in the form of binary patterns. Here is an example of a binary-code program:

```
111  010  000  000
001  000  000  101
001  000  000  110
001  000  000  111
011  000  001  000
```

It would be tedious for us to write binary code (also called machine code) programs all the time. It would take a long time and mistakes would be extremely likely.

For these reasons computer manufacturers produce details of a 'low-level language' which can be used with their hardware. Such low-level languages allow us to use mnemonics and different number systems.

Look at the program on the right, which is written in a low-level language called PAL III.

```
CLA
TAD  A
TAD  B
TAD  C
DCA  D
```

This language has been designed for a particular mini-computer. It would not be possible to run this program on other models of computer because they are designed differently. Each individual computer system has its own low-level language.

If we can learn the mnemonic code of the low-level language being used, it will be far easier for us to write programs.

To enable the computer to use such languages we must now have some software called an assembler, **which will translate the low-level language into machine code. The instructions and data may then be stored and obeyed.**

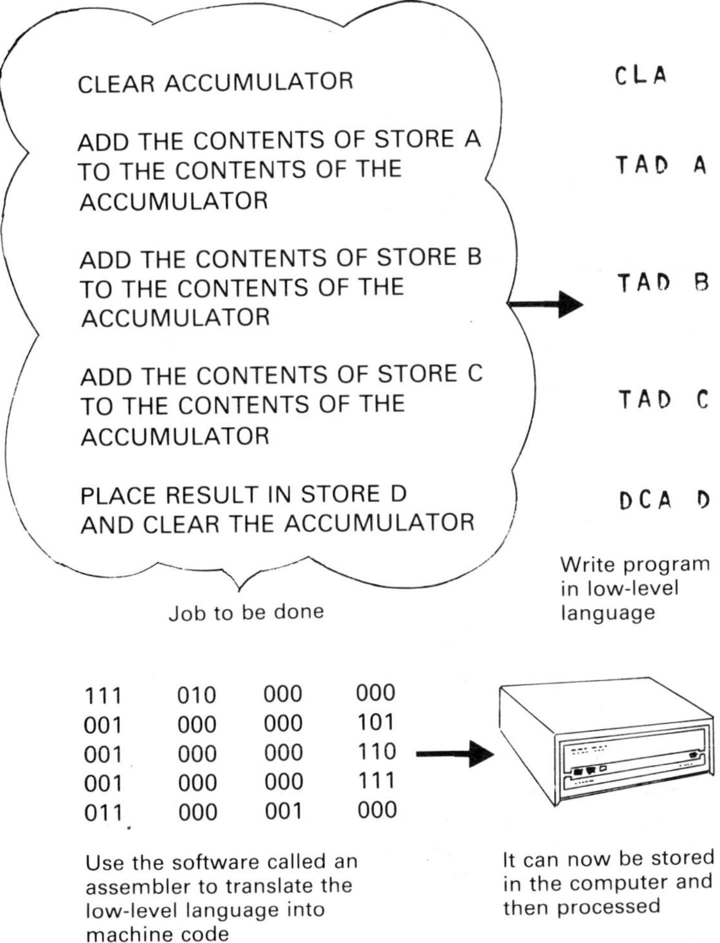

CLEAR ACCUMULATOR
ADD THE CONTENTS OF STORE A TO THE CONTENTS OF THE ACCUMULATOR
ADD THE CONTENTS OF STORE B TO THE CONTENTS OF THE ACCUMULATOR
ADD THE CONTENTS OF STORE C TO THE CONTENTS OF THE ACCUMULATOR
PLACE RESULT IN STORE D AND CLEAR THE ACCUMULATOR
CLA
TAD A
TAD B
TAD C
DCA D
111 010 000 000
001 000 000 101
001 000 000 110
001 000 000 111
011 000 001 000

Job to be done

Write program in low-level language

Use the software called an assembler to translate the low-level language into machine code

It can now be stored in the computer and then processed

Each low-level language instruction is turned into *one* machine-code instruction by the assembler.

Even with the use of assemblers, programs may be long, and the programmer still needs to do most of the work in setting up the instructions. Programmers using a low-level language still need to know a great deal about how a computer works. But many users of computers do not know how they function. They need more complex languages, such as FORTRAN, COBOL or ALGOL, which are closer to normal English or to mathematics, but further from the computer's machine code.

FORTRAN listing

```
      PROGRAM(CODE)
      USE 1=ED1/DIRECT
      INPUT 2=CR0
      INPUT 3=CR1
      OUTPUT 4=LP0
      OUTPUT 5=LP1
      ABNORMAL FUNCTIONS
      COMPACT DATA MIXED SEGMENTS
      END
      MASTER SUBLISTS
      COMMON/BLOCKA/ICODE(16)/BLOCKB/ISCODE(32)/BLOCKC/ISN,ILN,ION
      DIMENSION ISUBNAME(63,3),NAME(6),NAME1(6),IPT(63),ISO(250,4),
     1IOPT(15),ISUB(16),LINE(12),ILEVEL(4)
      DEFINE FILE 1(2500,14,0,IPN)
      DATA EOC/'££'/,ISPAC/'        '/
C
C       READ IN LEVEL,SET & OPTION NAMES - ECHO ON LPO
C
      WRITE(4,4000)
 4000 FORMAT(28H1 LEVEL AND SET/OPTION NAMES,///)
      READ(2,2000) (ILEVEL(I),I=1,4)
 2000 FORMAT(A8)
      WRITE(4,4001)  (ILEVEL(I),I=1,4)
 4001 FORMAT(2X,A8)
      READ(2,2000)  (IOPT(I),I=1,15)
      WRITE(4,4001)  (IOPT(I),I=1,15)
C
C       READ, COMPACT & ECHO SUBJECT CODES & NAMES ON LPO
C
      WRITE(4,4002)
 4002 FORMAT(26H1  SUBJECT CODES AND NAMES,//)
      IN=1
   10 READ(2,2001) SCODE,(ISURNAME(IN,I),I=1,3)
 2001 FORMAT(A2,3A8)
      CALL COMPAC(SCODE,IN)
      IF(SCODE.EQ.EOC) GOTO 20
      WRITE(4,4003) SCODE,(ISURNAME(IN,I),I=1,3)
 4003 FORMAT(1X,A2,4X,3A8)
      IN=IN+1
      GOTO 10
C
C       CONSTRUCT LOOK UP TABLE OF SUBJECT CODES
C
   20 CALL ENCODE
C
C       READ PUPIL DATA & CONSTRUCT OUTPUT FILE
C
      WRITE(4,4004)
 4004 FORMAT(15H1  ERROR REPORT,//)
      IR=1
```

```
           03 PAGENO           PIC 9(3).
           03 FILLER           PIC X(9) VALUE SPACES.
       01  BLANKS              PIC X(132).
       PROCEDURE DIVISION.
       INITIALIZE.
           OPEN INPUT CARDR, OUTPUT PRNFIL.
           MOVE SPACES TO OUTAREA.
           WRITE PRNTLINE FROM BLANKS BEFORE PAGE.
           PERFORM NEWPAGE.
       LOOP.
           READ CARDR INTO INAREA AT END GO TO ENDOFF.
           MOVE CORRESPONDING INAREA TO OUTAREA.
           PERFORM PRINTIT.
           GO TO LOOP.
       ENDOFF.
           CLOSE CARDR, PRNFIL.
           STOP RUN.
      *
       PRINTIT.
           WRITE PRNTLINE FROM OUTAREA BEFORE 1 AT EOP PERFORM NEWPAGE.
```

COBOL listing

```
#LISTING OF :JC2BSD9MSHBY.ALGOL15(1/OUTP)   PRODUCED ON 17DEC75 AT 22.23.18

#OUTPUT BY BHAM 6A   JB':JC2BSD9MSHBY.ALGOL15' ON 17DEC75 AT 22.23.19

DOCUMENT    :JC2BSD9MSHBY.ALGOL15(/OUTP)

HEATEQ2 'WITH' CUGHOST 'FROM' :LIB.GRAHP68
'BEGIN'    'REAL'H,A,C,U1,U2;[0:10]'REAL'U; READ((H,C));
PAPER(1);PSPACE(0.1,0.9,0.1,0.9); MAP(0.0,1.05,-1.0,22.0);
AXES;CTRSET(1);CTRSIZ(1);
    'WHILE' (READ(A);A>0) 'DO'
    'BEGIN' 'FOR' I 'FROM' 0 'TO' 10 'DO'
         'IF' I<6 'THEN' U[I]:=C*H*I 'ELSE' U[I]:=C*H*(10-I) 'FI';
     POSITN(0,U[0]+15); 'FOR' I 'FROM' 1 'TO' 10 'DO' JOIN(I*H,U[I]+15);
    'FOR' J 'FROM' 14 'BY' -1 'TO' 1 'DO'
        'BEGIN'   U1:=0;
         'FOR' I 'FROM' 1 'TO' 9 'DO' (U2:=A*U[I-1]+(1-2*A)*U[I]+A*U[I+1];
         'IF' U1>0 'THEN' U[I-1]:=U1 'FI'; U1:=U2); U[9]:=U2;
         POSITN(0,U[0]+J);
         'FOR' I 'FROM' 1 'TO' 10 'DO' JOIN(I*H,U[I]+J)
         'END';
    PLOTAS(0.7,20,"A= "); TYPENF(A,3);FRAME;AXES
    'END';
GREND
'END'
'FINISH'
```

ALGOL listing

To be able to understand such languages the computer requires a translation stage, just as an Englishman might need an interpreter to understand somebody talking in a foreign language.

High-level languages like BASIC, FORTRAN, ALGOL and COBOL are foreign to the computer. With software called a compiler* **the computer takes each high-level language instruction and turns it into several machine-code instructions, which it can then understand. We say that high-level languages are 'user oriented' because they are designed for the user of the computer and not the computer itself.**

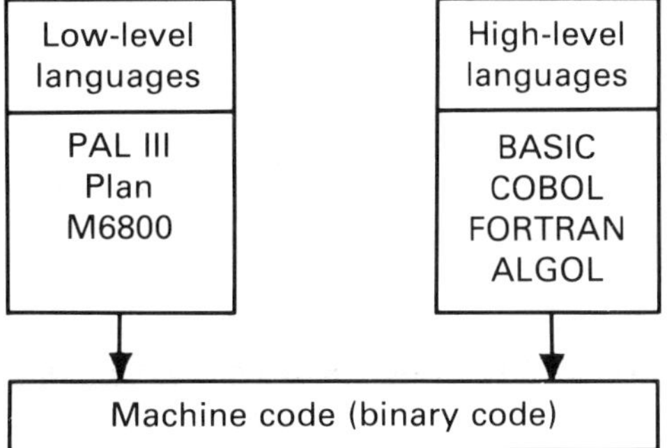

The source program, that is, the program written in a low- or high-level language, thus requires one of two software programs: an assembler or a compiler.

The assembler takes each low-level instruction and translates it into machine code for the computer to deal with. It must be written in machine code and can be used only on the computer for which it was designed. Because the programmer does most of the work in producing low-level programs, the assembler takes up little room in the computer's store. Hence the object program **will be quickly processed.**

The compiler takes each high-level instruction and translates it into *several* machine-code instructions. The compiler takes up much more computer storage because it has far more work to do. Compilers are written for each different type of computer and for each high-level language.

The object program produced by the compiler is stored inside the computer in binary code. Compilation (the process of compiling) takes much longer than the assembly process.

**BASIC can also be translated using an interpreter. See Addenda, p. 159.*

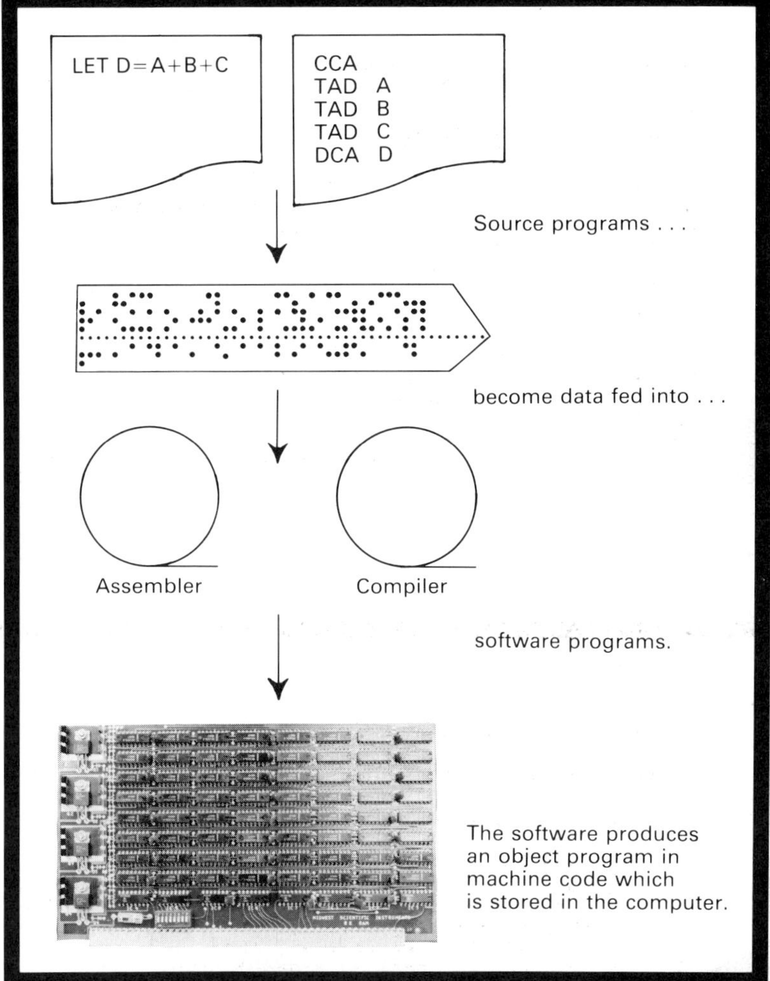

Multi-programming

Using assemblers and compilers to translate source programs takes very little time compared with the time it takes to read in programs via an input device or to print out results from an output device.

It doesn't take long for us to eat our Sunday lunch, but a great deal of time has been spent in preparing it. It also takes a long time to wash up and then dry the pots, pans and plates afterwards. If we did nothing but eat all day long we should need an array of cooks and servants to keep us supplied.

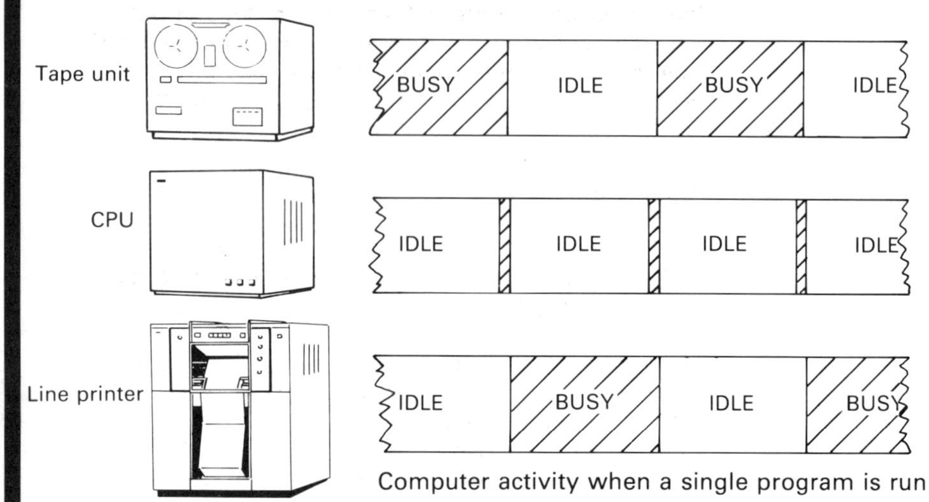

Tape unit
CPU
Line printer

Computer activity when a single program is run

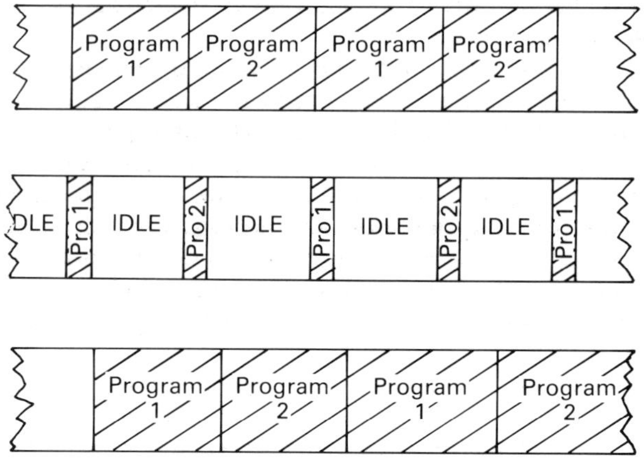

Two programs being run together

Fortunately, three meals a day are all we require. If we fed a central processor only three times a day, the computer company concerned would soon be bankrupt.

Running an efficient computer system involves keeping the CPU busy, because it is a very fast and expensive item of hardware. In order to do this we have to solve the problem of the slow speeds of peripherals. If the central processor has to wait for data to be input before it can begin processing, and then wait again while results are output, it is of little use having a CPU that can execute instructions in microseconds (1/1 000 000 sec).

We can see from the left-hand diagram above how little time is used by the central processor in processing the program compared with the time taken by the peripherals for input and output.

One solution to the problem is to let the computer work on several programs at the same time. This is called multi-programming. While one program is being processed in the CPU, another program may be receiving data from a tape reader, and a third program may be having its results printed on a line printer.

The other diagram shows the computer working on two programs (although it is possible to work on many more programs than this) at the same time.

The software which is responsible for organizing the use of the computer by several user programs is called an operating system. The operating system may be thought of as a master program which directs other programs to do the jobs required.

In any organization there must be someone at the top who is responsible for the way things are done. The headteacher at a school directs the teachers, caretaker, secretary and school cook. He is able to leave his staff to see to their particular jobs and call on their help as and when he wants it.

The operating system acts in a similar manner, calling in other items of software to help when needed. We will now look at some of the programs which are part of or related to the operating system.

System software

The supervisor (or executive) keeps track of the programs that are being run and the peripherals and files that these programs need. The computer operator needs to know the state of jobs being run, so the supervisor will communicate with him on a special terminal, called the operator's console. Messages that are typed on this terminal make up what is known as the computer's log.

The monitor allows the operator to give

commands to other programs in the operating system. For instance, the operator may use a monitor command to instruct the computer to abandon a run.

The scheduler is a program which organizes the timetable of the CPU. It decides which programs may use the CPU at any time. The time given to any program can depend upon the amount of calculating to be done, or it may be that a particular program is more important and requires more time. We say that programs may have a greater priority and the scheduler is responsible for seeing that programs with the highest priority are given more time.

Additional software is usually available and may be used when relevant. Here are some examples.

The editor is used to make alterations to files of data or programs.

Utility programs are needed very often for routine tasks such as sorting and merging files, calculating 'Pay As You Earn' deductions, making copies of programs or listing contents of magnetic tapes.

Applications packages are used in various applications like calculating salaries and wages, bus scheduling, school timetabling and highway design.

Programmers may write subroutines within their own programs. However, many subroutines are available in the computer library and can be called up by the programmer to be used even though he has not written them. Examples would be to find square roots or to produce random numbers.

The final piece of software we need to know about is very important because without it no other programs could be used by the computer. Remember that the computer is only a machine and is not capable of doing anything unless instructed. To begin with it will not 'know' how to load programs because it has not as yet been instructed to get data from cards or tape. So the very first, basic instructions cannot be input like this.

A loading program must be set up manually; the operator must enter the program by means of switches. These programs are called bootstraps and at the beginning of each working day a bootstrap loader must be 'toggled in', or input by switches. This then allows the operating system to be entered into the computer's store. The operating system may be the only software which is permanently resident when the computer is working.

It is possible, with more modern technology, for loaders or bootstraps to be built into the computer circuitry. The loader is then said to be 'hard wired'. The loader may also be available as part of the computer's memory which cannot be erased. This is called read only memory (ROM).

Modes of processing

There are two principal ways in which the operating system allows users' programs to be run. These are called batch processing and real-time processing.

Batch processing involves collecting all the data together before running the program. Once a program has been started the user has no further control: the operating system takes over. This mode of operation is ideal when large numbers of similar jobs are to be processed. Batch processing is therefore used for such things as electricity and gas billing and wages calculation.

With real-time processing, an immediate response is given to any input to the computer. This allows continuous control over the program being run. Input and output may be via a peripheral called an analog/digital converter. This takes readings from instruments like thermometers, altimeters, speedometers and voltmeters and converts them into binary codes. By such means a computer can be used to control such things as chemical processes, electronic devices and machinery.

To make real-time processing very useful, many operating systems will allow several terminals to be connected at the same time. Each separate user will have freedom to use the computer independently. This system is called time-sharing. Each user believes that he alone is using the system because an immediate response is given to his commands. However, time slices are given to users' programs so that their programs and the software required by them will be swapped in and out of the CPU.

This is not the same as multi-programming, which involves giving each user a section of the store. Time-sharing allows each user to have the whole of the CPU at his disposal, but only during his allocated time slice.

Hotel reservation, seat booking and airline reservation systems are all examples of time-shared real-time processing.

Questions

1. Look up the word 'mnemonic' in a dictionary and see what it means and what its origin is.
2. What language would an assembler be written in?
3. Which is easier for the programmer, a high-level language or a low-level language?
4. What type of program must have been previously stored in a computer before a BASIC program can be run?
   (a) utility program,
   (b) compiler,
   (c) supervisor,
   (d) assembler.
5. Which of the following items of software does *not* assist with the running of a user program?
   (a) monitor,
   (b) scheduler,
   (c) supervisor,
   (d) editor.
6. Which of the following applications would be best run on a real-time system?
   (a) updating bank accounts,
   (b) season ticket booking at Villa Park,
   (c) processing wages and salaries,
   (d) producing gas bills.
7. Why is a compiler slower at translating programs than an assembler?
8. How does multi-programming lead to efficient use of a computer system?
9. What mode of processing would be used for telephone billing? Why would this system be used?
10. Explain carefully the differences between multi-programming and time-sharing.
11. 'User software' is the name given to the software which the user requires to run his program. 'System software' refers to the programs required by the computer itself. Write down a list of the software programs given in this chapter, and beside each indicate whether it is user or system software.

Vocabulary

applications package
assembler
batch processing
bootstrap
compiler
editor
hardware
machine code
mnemonic
monitor
multi-programming
object program
operating system
operator's console
read only memory (ROM)
real-time processing
scheduler
software
source program
subroutine
supervisor
time-sharing
time slice
utilities

16 Further Flowcharting

The majority of jobs for which computers are used involve files of data. This data may be lists of football matches, details of guests at a hotel, the products stocked by a supermarket or details of a gas company's accounts. Such files may be held on magnetic tape, magnetic discs or (less likely) on paper tape or punched cards.

However the files are stored, various operations must be performed on them at times.

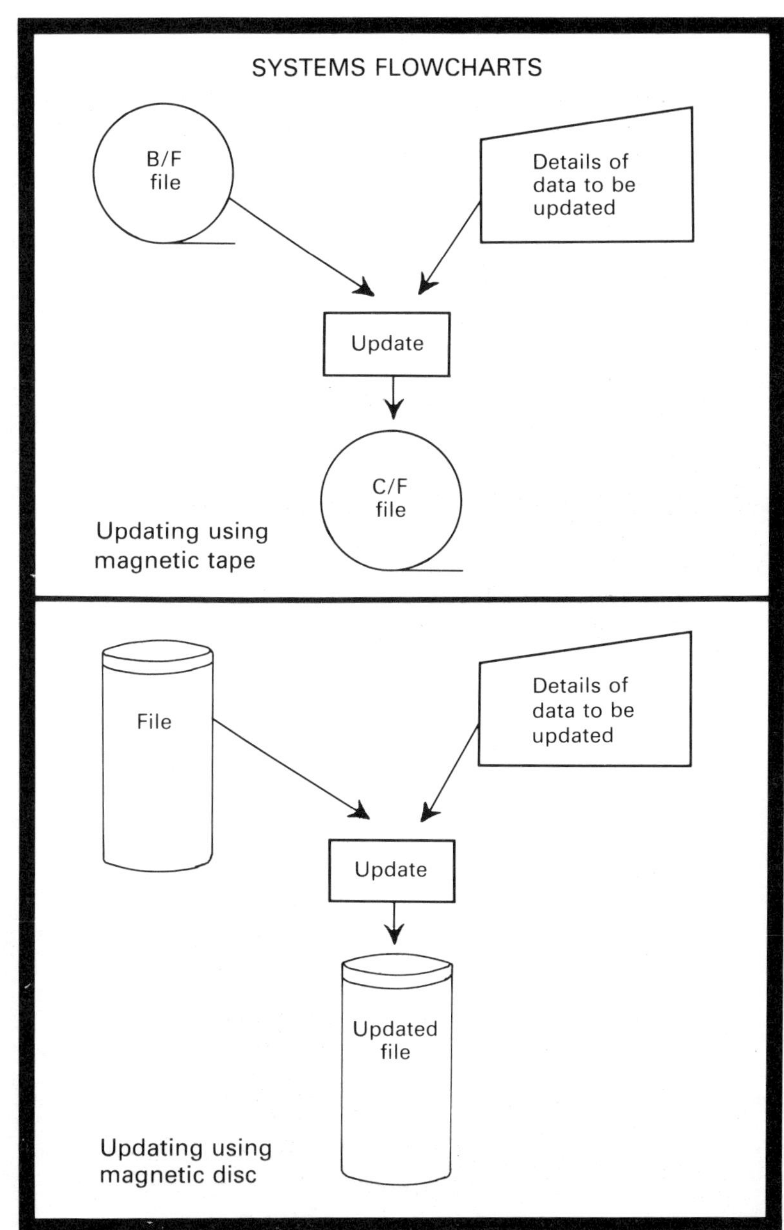

Updating files

Data on files is likely to change at some time. What do you think might change on files containing the following information?

1. A list of football matches to be played in a season.
2. Details of customers in a gas company area.
3. Details of the products stocked by a supermarket.
4. Details about each of the rooms in an hotel.

When information held on a file is changed it is said to be updated. A class register is a file containing pupils' names, their attendance records and addresses. If your address changed your class register would need to be updated. Updating may involve changing information, adding new information or deleting information.

If a magnetic tape file is updated, a whole new file has to be made. The old file is called the brought-forward file **(B/F)** and the new file the carried-forward file **(C/F)**. The next time the file is updated the previous C/F file will become the B/F file.

Old brought-forward files are often kept for security reasons. If a tape should be damaged or corrupted, a user would then be able to go back to the old file, and thus have relatively few records to amend, instead of having to recreate a completely new file.

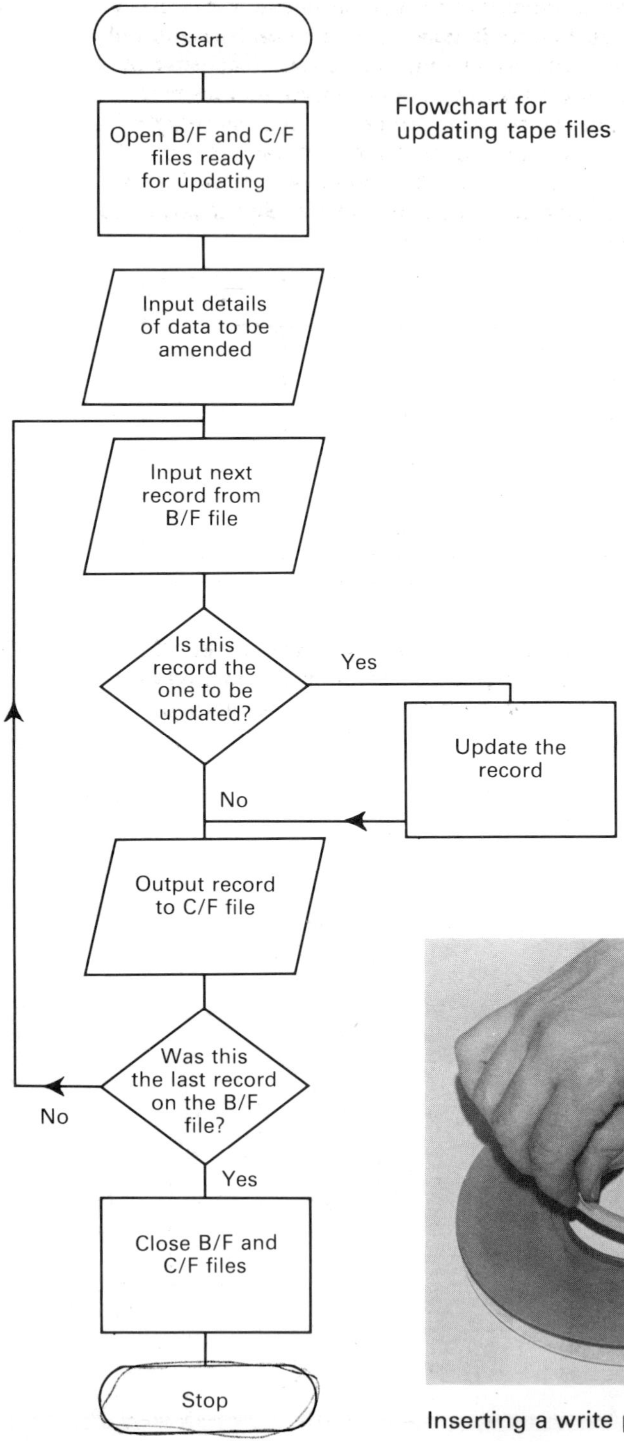

Start

Open B/F and C/F files ready for updating

Input details of data to be amended

Input next record from B/F file

Is this record the one to be updated?

Yes

Update the record

No

Output record to C/F file

Was this the last record on the B/F file?

No

Yes

Close B/F and C/F files

Stop

Flowchart for updating tape files

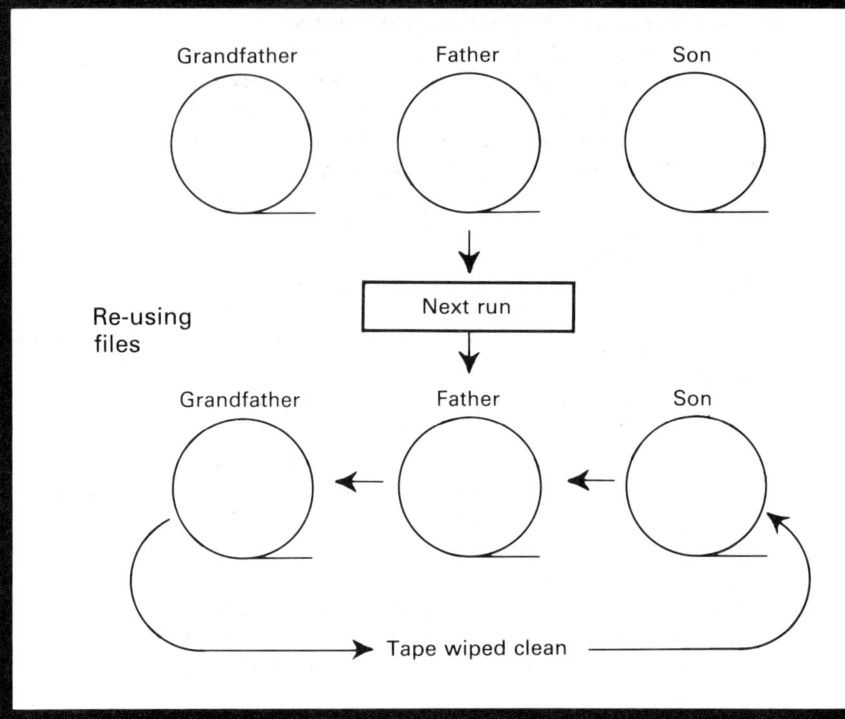

Re-using files

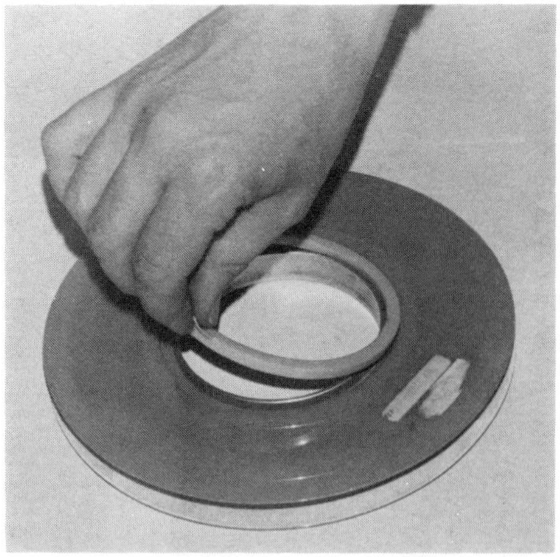

Inserting a write permit ring

'Generations' of tapes are kept, which are referred to as 'grandfather', 'father' and 'son'. The latest file is the 'son', the previous one 'father' and the one before that 'grandfather'. At the next run of the brought-forward file, the 'grandfather' is wiped clean and the tape used again for the new master file, now called the 'son'. By such techniques three generations of important files are kept.

There are two more important security techniques. Important tapes may have a copy kept in a fire-proof safe, for obvious reasons. Secondly, all magnetic tape reels have a 'write permit ring' which can be fitted into a groove on the reel. If this ring is not attached no new data can be written on to that tape.

Searching files

Files frequently have to be searched to find a particular record. When a magnetic tape file is updated a form of search called a serial **or** sequential search **is used. This involves looking at each record**

in turn until the required one is found. This method is used when data held on magnetic tapes or magnetic discs is not in any special order.

If the books in a library were not kept in any special order you would have to search through all of them to find what you wanted. This would take a long time and be inefficient. Similarly, to find a record on magnetic tape using this method could take up to four minutes – a very long time in computer terms.

Files that are searched frequently are held on magnetic disc, so taking advantage of the ability of a disc system to read data from any part of the disc very rapidly.

One way of speeding up a search is to use an index. Library books are often classified using the Dewey system. If you want to find a book in the library the quickest way is to look first in the library index, and then go straight to the shelf indicated by the Dewey index number.

By using an index to a file of employees the computer needs only to search through the index of employee numbers to locate a particular employee file. However, a search still has to be made through the index.

As an alternative to a sequential search a binary search **technique is used, but this can be done only if the records are arranged in order. The order may be numerical (in the case of employee numbers) or alphanumerical (as in the case of a class register).**

Here is a simple example of a binary search. Suppose we have a list of pupils and their forms, and we wish to search the list for 'Sue Oldham' to discover which form she is in.

Name		Form
Abrahams	Bill	3.1
Chalk	Jane	4.2
Daniels	Philip	6.1
Howe	Paul	2.3
Matthews	Jill	3.1
Oldham	Sue	4.1
Rawson	Tanya	5.3
Weston	Jack	2.1

The flowchart below will enable you to find the required name by asking three questions, whereas a sequential search would need five questions.

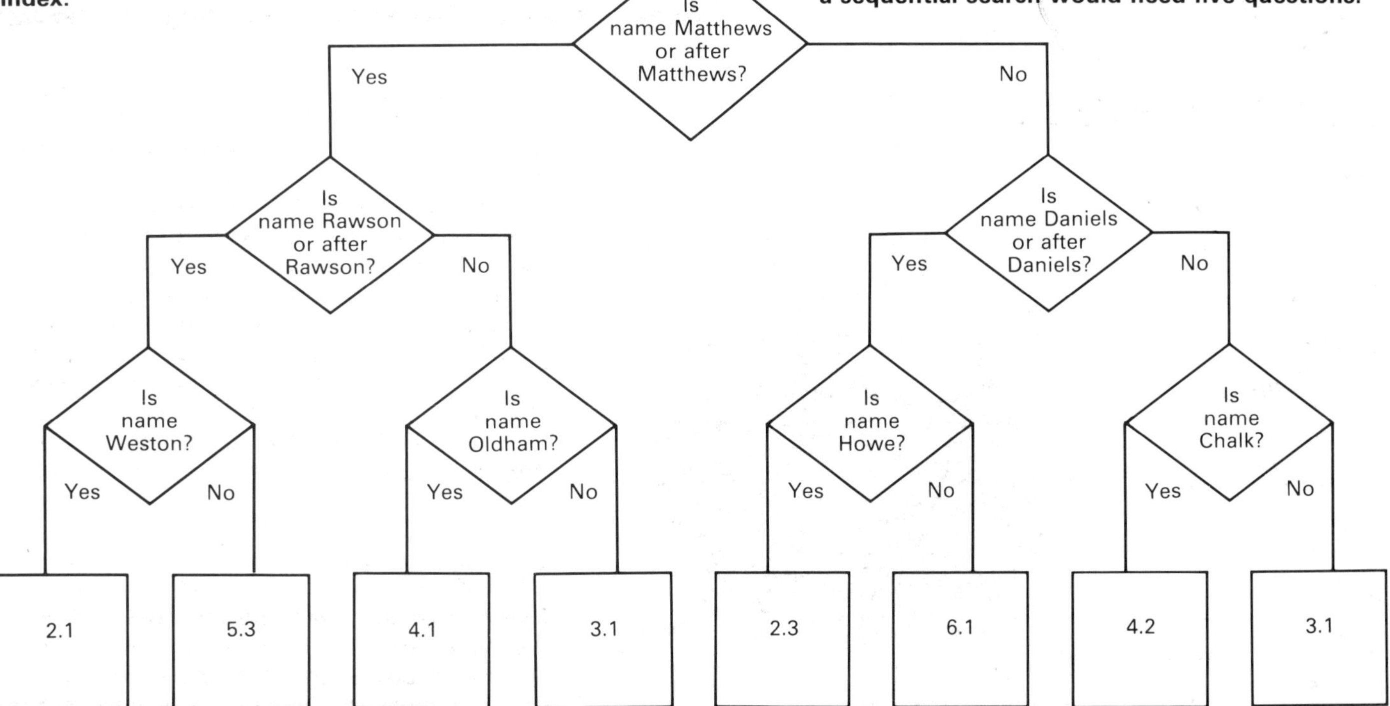

Binary searching can be used on any amount of data and is increasingly efficient compared with sequential searching, as the table below illustrates.

Number of records	Number of questions to be asked in binary search	Number of questions to be asked in sequential search (average)
8	3	4
16	4	8
32	5	16
1000	10	500

Sorting files

If data is to be held in numerical or alphanumerical order it must of course be sorted first. The simplest means of sorting data is by employing a search sort.

Perhaps you might want to sort a list of marks. To do this, you first look down the list of marks and find the highest one, then look down the list again and find the next highest, and so on.

A more efficient method is called a bubble sort. **Follow the flowchart on the right and see how the table is developed. The first two marks are 32 and 4 and no swap is made. The next pair is 4 and 16 and because 16 is bigger than 4 they change places. The next pair is now 4 and 21 and these also change places, so the next pair becomes 4 and 28. This process continues until the end of the list is reached, and the procedure is then repeated from the top of the new list. When no swaps are made in a** pass **then the list has been sorted.**

	Start	1st pass	2nd pass	3rd pass	4th pass
	32	32	32	32	32
	4	16	21	28	28
	16	21	28	21	21
	21	28	19	19	19
	28	19	16	16	16
	19	9	9	9	9
	9	4	4	4	4
Number of swaps	–	5	3	1	0

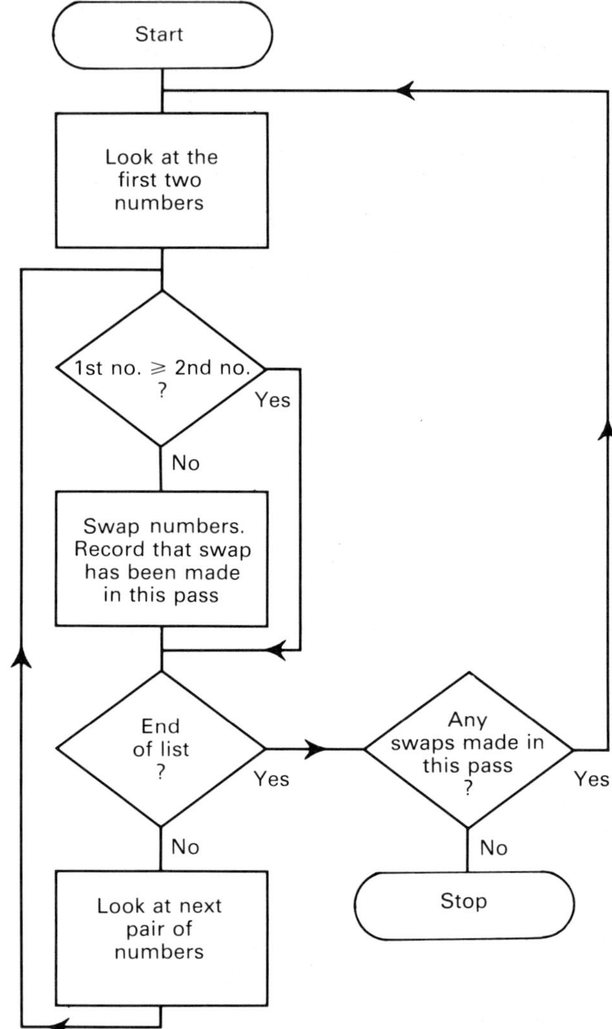

Flowchart for a bubble sort

The table shows the list after each pass. Search and bubble sorts can be used on any data held in the computer's immediate access store or on magnetic disc files, but it is not practical for magnetic tape. Magnetic tapes have to be sorted by far more complex techniques which involve use of three, four or more tapes.

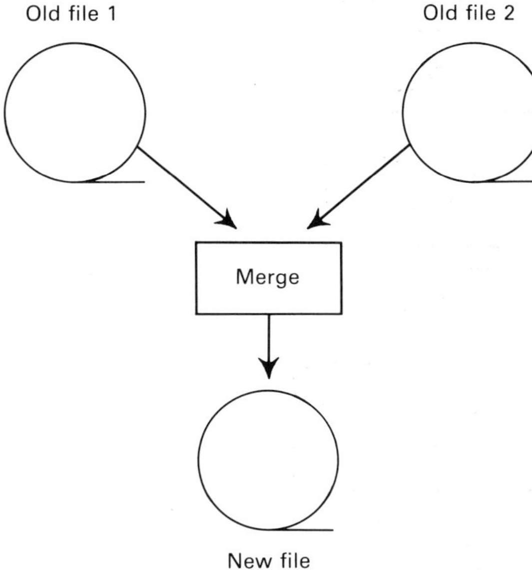

Systems flowchart showing merging

Merging files

The last process we shall consider is that of merging two files of a similar type, that is, bringing together the two files to produce one. Both the two original files and the resulting merged file need to be in order. Any data that appears on both original files will appear only once on the merged file.

Consider the example of a firm wishing to merge files containing product numbers. The original two files are called 'old file 1' and 'old file 2'. The diagram on the left shows what happens.

Systems flowcharts

As you have seen from the systems flowcharts shown in this chapter, symbols are used to represent various items. Systems flowcharts illustrate the way data is used in a computer, whereas a program or a procedure flowchart of the type used in Chapter 5 illustrates the way a result can be obtained from this data.

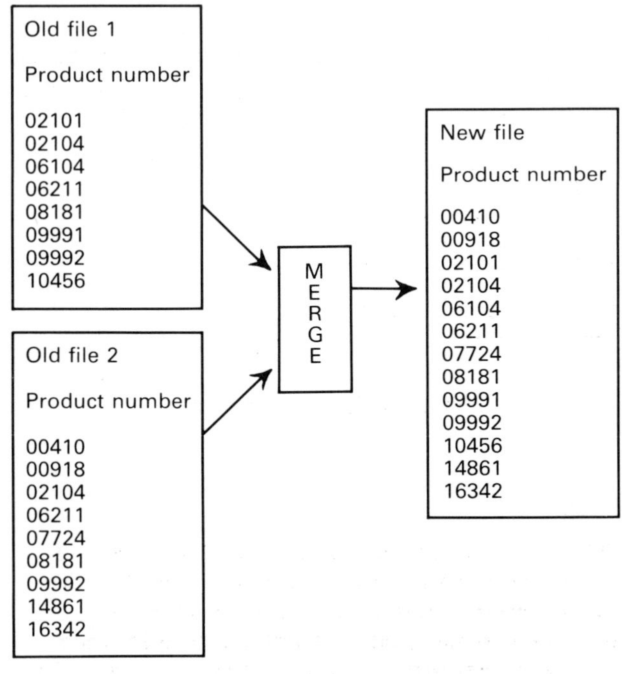

Table showing merged files

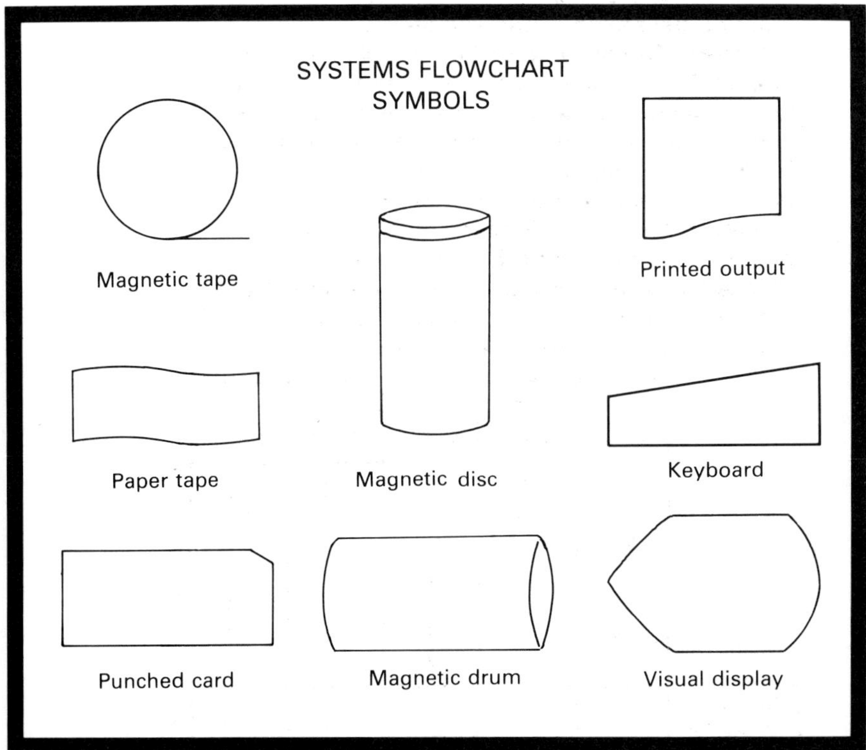

Questions

1. Which of the following items of data would not need to be updated?
   (a) date of birth,
   (b) address,
   (c) name,
   (d) age.
2. What precautions can be taken to ensure security of data on magnetic tapes?
3. Why would you not conduct a binary search on data held on magnetic tape?
4. What do you think is meant by 'opening' and 'closing' files?
5. How many questions would you need to ask in order to do a binary search on 200 items of data?
6. Illustrate how a binary search would be used to find the record 'Andrews' from the following list of names: Andrews, Allen, Braddock, Cartwright, Chester, Fisher, Gough, Heath.
7. Draw up a table showing the number of passes and the number of swaps that would be needed to conduct a bubble sort on the following numbers: 78, 45, 89, 12, 43, 96, 34.
8. Show the result of merging two files which contain the following data:
   File 1 = 23, 45, 67, 89, 90, 98;
   File 2 = 19, 23, 36, 45, 78, 89, 90, 99.

Vocabulary

binary search
brought forward file
bubble sort
carried forward file
file generations
merging files
pass
search files
search sort
sequential search
serial search
sorting files
systems flowchart
updating files

17 Serial Files and Batch Processing

When considering whether to use magnetic disc or tape in Chapter 12 we chose disc because the data was needed randomly (not in any order). However, if a large amount of data is to be processed serially (one after another in order), then tape is better.

Magnetic tape

Magnetic tape unit

Magnetic tape units used for backing stores operate rather like tape-recorders, but instead of recording music the tape holds binary data. The kind of tape used is similar to that on an ordinary recorder or cassette except that it is wider, longer and of better quality. The tape is made from plastic coated with a ferric oxide. Small zones on the tape can then be magnetized clockwise or anticlockwise, by a read/write head, to represent 1 and 0. Binary codes for characters are stored across the tape, in a manner similar to that in which codes are arranged on paper tape. There are, however, either seven or nine tracks on magnetic tape.

Data held on magnetic tape has to be accessed serially and so tape is used when all the data on a file has to be processed. Each record is processed as it is read from the tape, and the data is held in blocks on the tape. If you watch a tape drive working you will see it jerking. This is because the tape is started up to read a block and then stopped while the CPU processes the data read. Data can only be read from and written on to a tape while the tape is travelling at full speed. Because of this, the data is arranged with inter-block gaps.

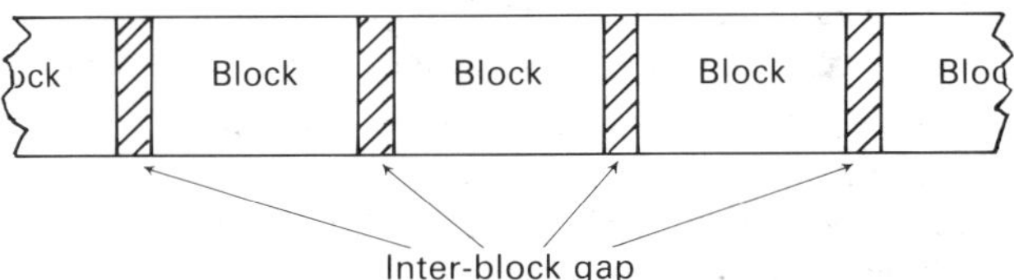

The tape is also fed through vacuum columns so that the continual stopping and starting at high speeds will not rip or damage the tape.

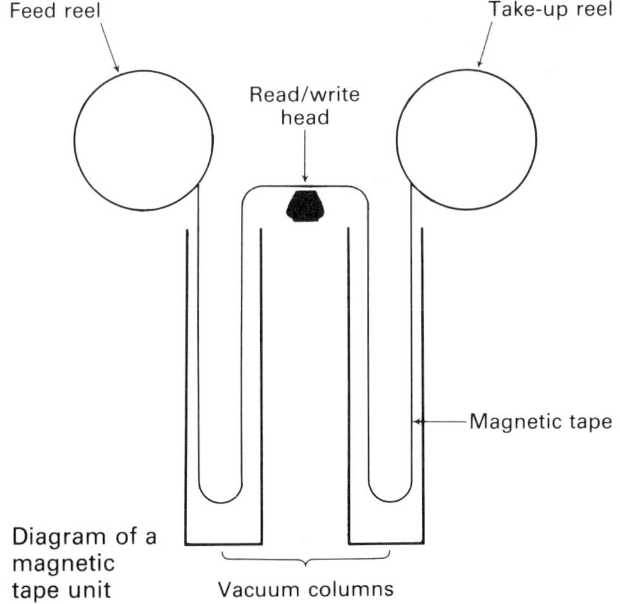

Diagram of a magnetic tape unit

As an application of the use of serial files and large-scale batch processing we shall examine the work of a typical gas board, which we shall call Midshires Gas.

Bear in mind throughout this section that because records are kept in the order of customer reference numbers, there must be several checks built into the system to make sure that these numbers are always correct. Similarly the meter readings must undergo regular checks to make sure they are valid.

Preparing source documents

The photograph shows the familiar scene of the gas meter being read. We have seen in Chapter 8 that this gas board uses mark sensing for meter reading sheets.

Notice that before any mark is put on the form there is already some information on it. Some of this information is for the benefit of the meter reader; other data on this form will be used by the optical mark reader when the meter reading sheets are processed.

The diagram opposite shows the various areas, or fields, on the form and their purpose.

The marks in fields D and G are pre-marked on these computer-produced forms. This means that they may be read by the same machine that deals with the readings marked by the gasman.

Fields A, B, C, F and H are for the benefit of the meter reader. Field B is a note that the meter is outside, for example. This tells the meter reader that he need not gain entrance to the premises.

Field F shows the date by which the batch of forms should be completed.

Field H provides, as a guide, two values between which the reading should fall. The two values have been calculated by reference to previous bills paid by the customer. If the reading falls outside these parameters the meter reader should mark the special code 1 and check the reading again.

Reading a gas meter

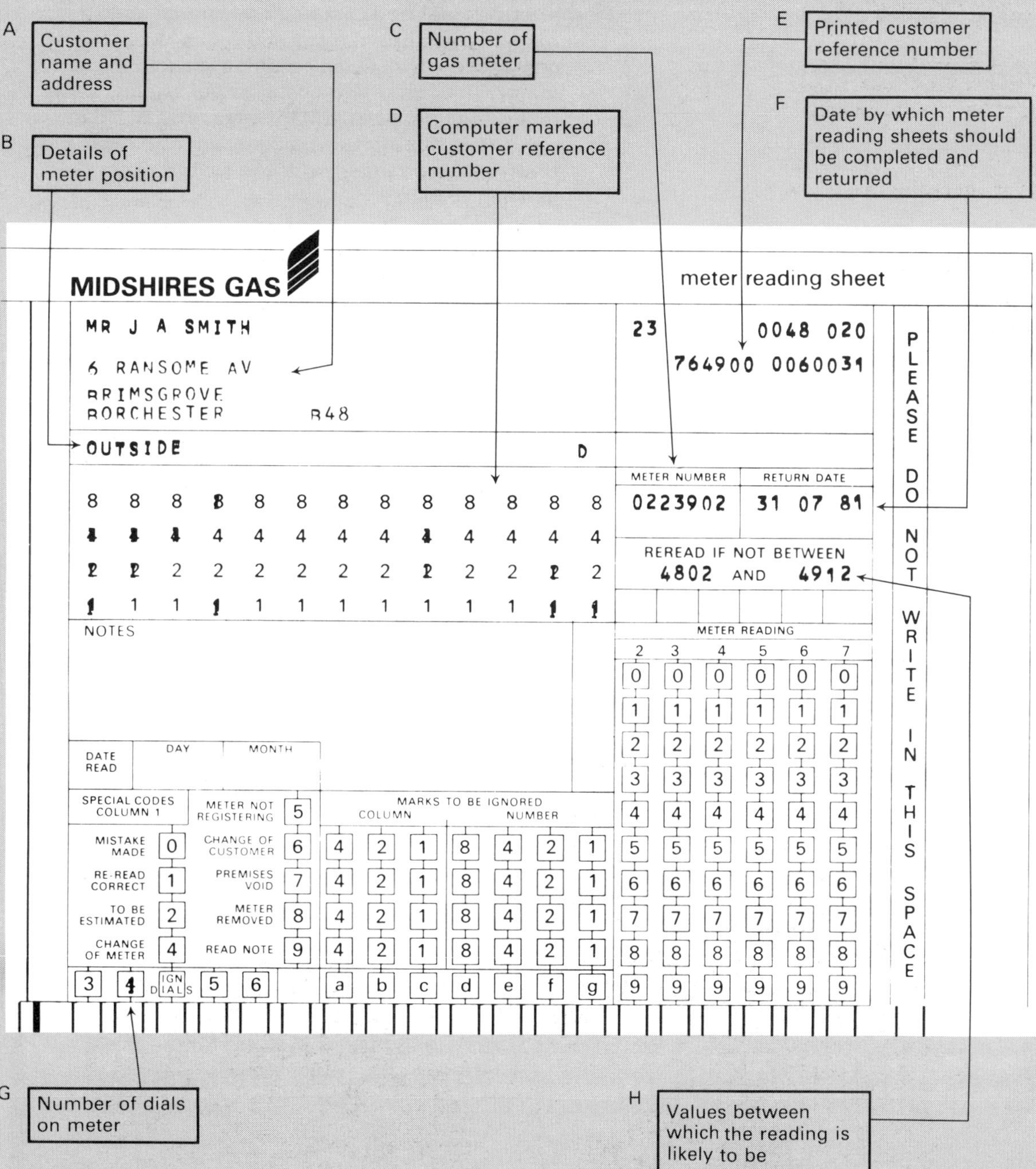

Fields on a meter reading sheet

The reading sheet is marked as shown below. For verification purposes the reading is written in the space above the reading marks, and the date is entered.

Can you think of anything that might go wrong at this stage?

The gas board has over a million customers, and on average 121 625 calls are made each week. Over 13 000 of these customers will be out and the meter will not be read. The readings for such premises will be estimated and special code 2 marked. (The board must make sure that at least one of three scheduled readings is taken for each meter. Thus after two unsuccessful attempts the meter reading sheet will be marked with 'must read'. If at this stage a reading cannot be taken, a time will be arranged with the customer for the gasman to call).

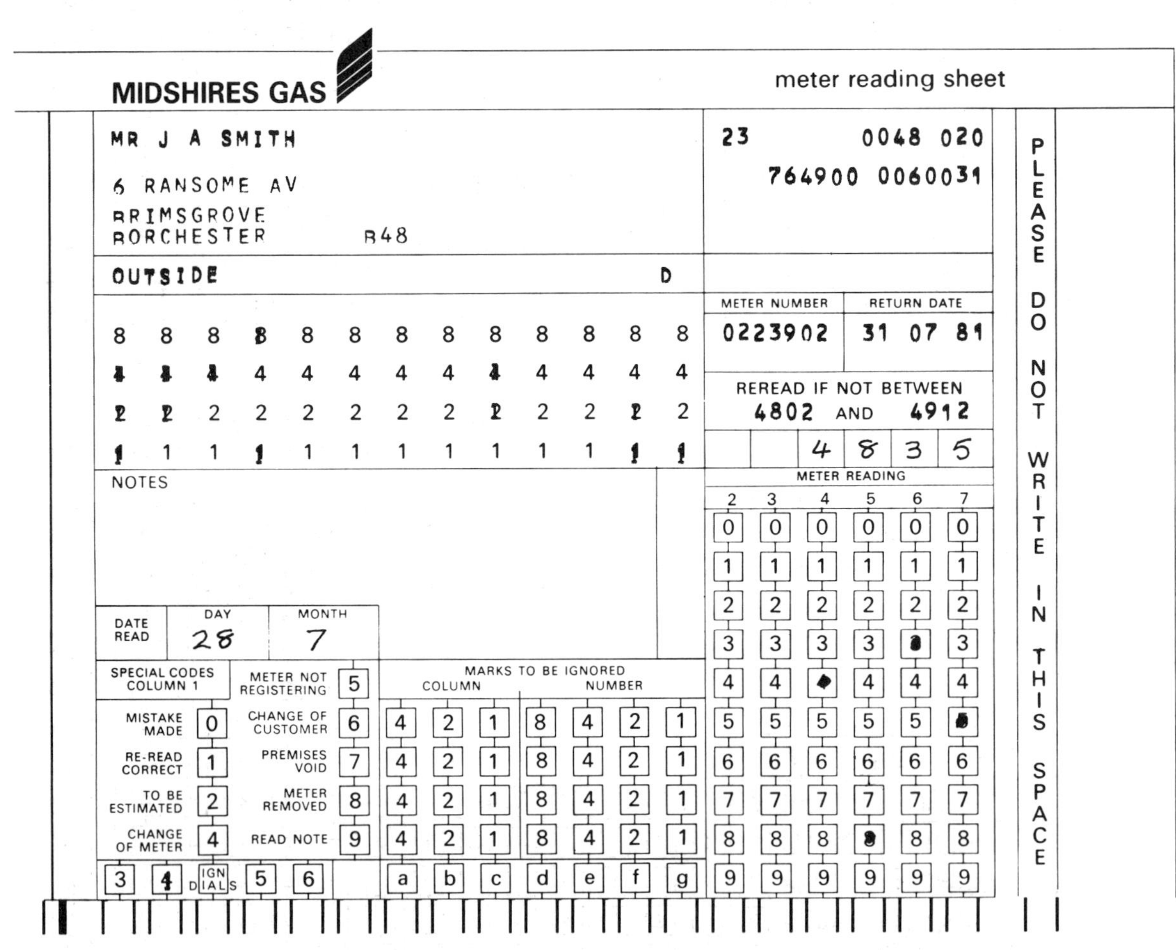

MIDSHIRES GAS — meter reading sheet

MR J A SMITH
6 RANSOME AV
BRIMSGROVE
BORCHESTER B48

OUTSIDE D

23 0048 020
764900 0060031

METER NUMBER	RETURN DATE
0223902	31 07 81

REREAD IF NOT BETWEEN 4802 AND 4912

METER READING: 4 8 3 5

	2	3	4	5	6	7
	0	0	0	0	0	0
	1	1	1	1	1	1
	2	2	2	2	2	2
	3	3	3	3	3	3
	4	4	4	4	4	4
	5	5	5	5	5	5
	6	6	6	6	6	6
	7	7	7	7	7	7
	8	8	8	8	8	8
	9	9	9	9	9	9

NOTES

DATE READ	DAY	MONTH
	28	7

SPECIAL CODES COLUMN 1

MISTAKE MADE	0	METER NOT REGISTERING	5
RE-READ CORRECT	1	CHANGE OF CUSTOMER	6
TO BE ESTIMATED	2	PREMISES VOID	7
CHANGE OF METER	4	METER REMOVED	8
		READ NOTE	9

MARKS TO BE IGNORED — COLUMN: 4 2 1 — NUMBER: 8 4 2 1

3 4 IGN DIALS 5 6 a b c d e f g

PLEASE DO NOT WRITE IN THIS SPACE

Marked meter reading sheet

Special codes are used when some problem arises. If, for example, the meter reader makes a mistake in the reading he marks code 0.

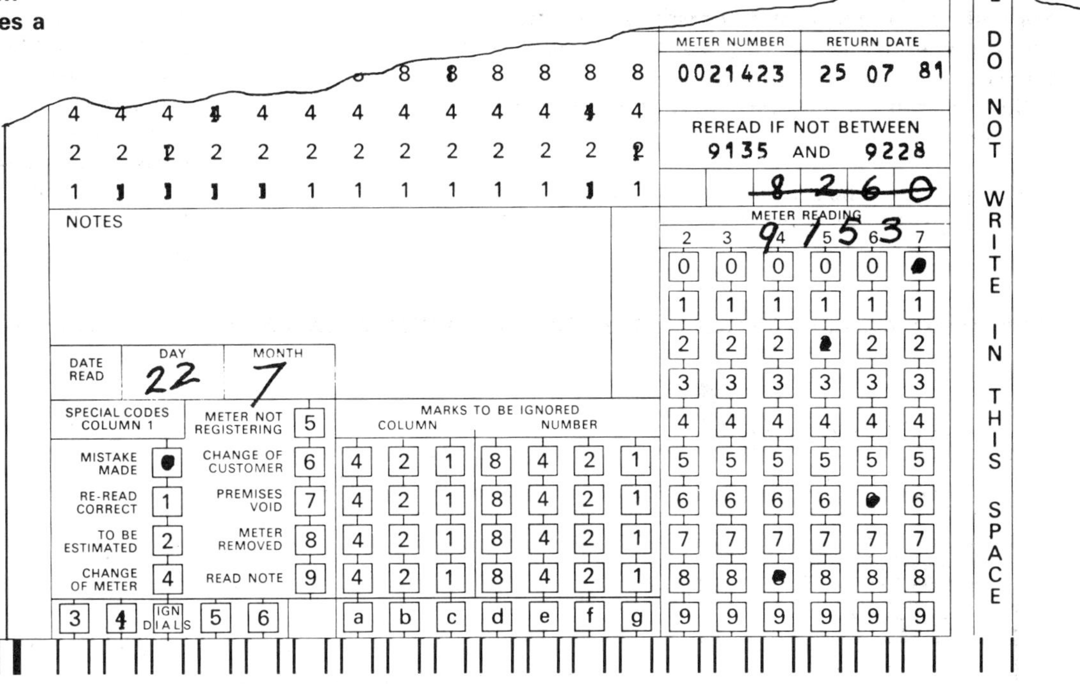

As another example, if the meter reading does not fall between the two parameters given then code 1 is marked.

METER NUMBER
0196701
RETURN DATE
31 07 78
REREAD IF NOT BETWEEN
1360 AND 1468
1489
METER READING
NOTES
DATE READ
DAY
28
MONTH
7
SPECIAL CODES COLUMN 1
MISTAKE MADE
RE-READ CORRECT
TO BE ESTIMATED
CHANGE OF METER
METER NOT REGISTERING
CHANGE OF CUSTOMER
PREMISES VOID
METER REMOVED
READ NOTE
MARKS TO BE IGNORED
COLUMN
NUMBER
IGN DIALS
DO NOT WRITE IN THIS SPACE

The special codes attempt to cover the most likely events. If a particular situation occurs that cannot be recorded by this method, the meter reader marks code 9 and writes a note in the space provided above.

You can see that every effort is made to ensure that the data recorded by the meter reader is correct. We must now consider how this data is processed and how checks are made.

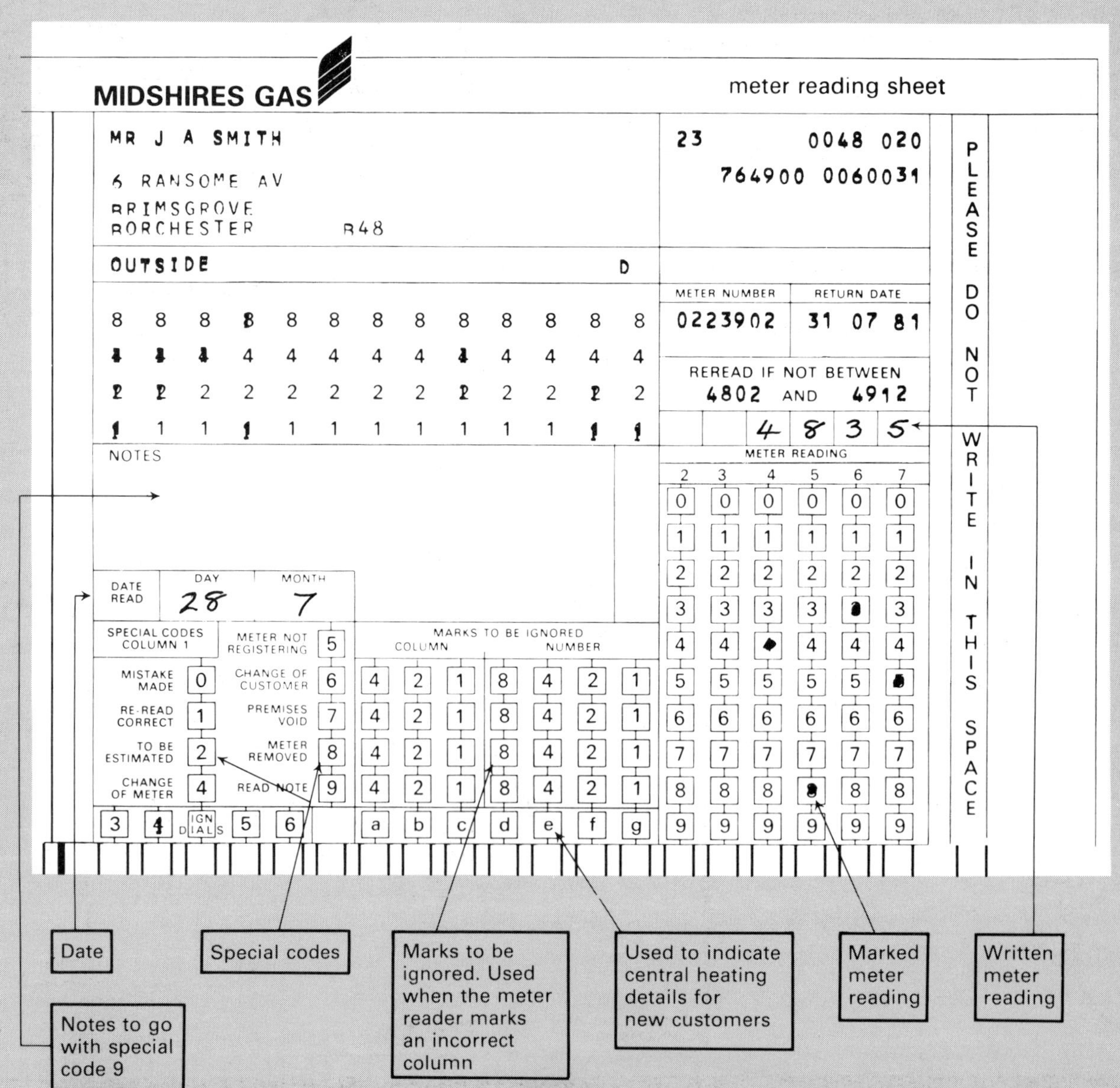

Fields for the use of the meter reader

Checking reading sheets

The meter reading sheets are fed into a universal document reader **(UDR).**

As its name suggests, this peripheral can read many different kinds of input documents. It can be used either as an optical mark reader or as an optical character reader.

The drawing illustrates the layout of a UDR, showing the OM and OC readers.

The meter reading sheets are entered as they come in from meter readers and are not in any specific order at this point. As the meter reading sheets (MRS) are read further checks are made, and any sheets in error will be rejected. Some of these checks are explained below.

THE UNIVERSAL DOCUMENT READER

Optical mark reader

Mechanical rejects

Tracking unit

Feed drum

Feed hopper

Optical character reader

Read drum

Transport to stackers

Stackers

Ungated reject stacker

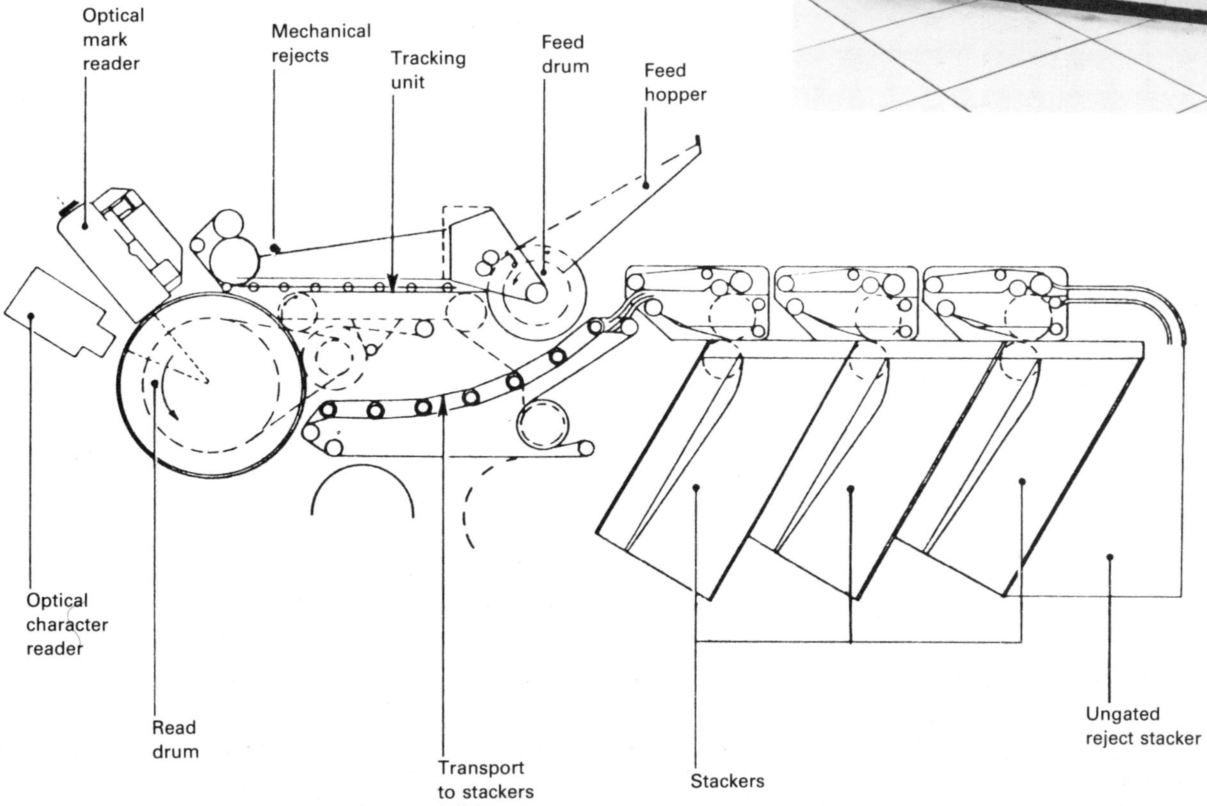

Customer reference number

All customers are given a reference number of thirteen digits. These digits are coded according to the address of the customer and the type of meter. Here is an example for a single meter:

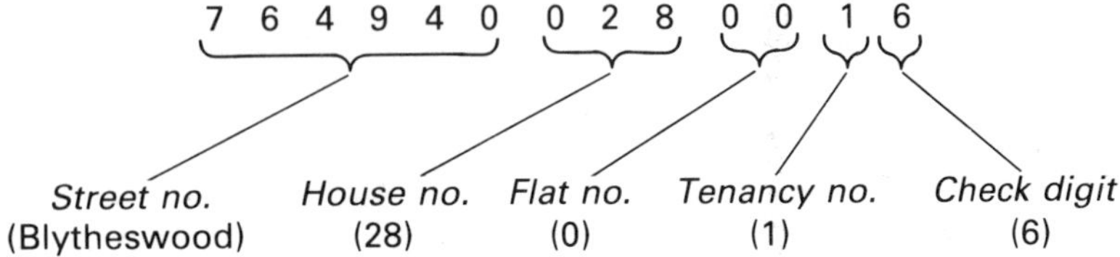

The reference number marked on the MRS is checked to see if the check digit is valid. This is done by dividing the first twelve digits by eleven. The remainder is then the check digit. (Except that for a remainder of 0 the check digit is given as 6, and for a remainder of 10 the check digit is given as 7.)

Thus

11) 764940028001
    69540002545 remainder 6

The 6 is the check digit.

The customer reference number will also be in error if, for example,

1. It contains a non-numeric character.
2. The street number is 999999 or if it is less than 001030.
3. The tenancy digit is 0.
4. The house and the flat number are both zero.

Must read

The UDR is set to pick up the T of 'MUST READ' on the meter reading sheet. If a reading is not present the sheet is rejected.

Mark readings

Sheets will also be rejected if any column has more than one mark in it.

Special codes

Meter reading sheets will be in error if, for example,

1. There is an impossible combination of two codes, e.g. code 1 (reread correct) and code 8 (meter removed).
2. The meter reading is present but codes 2 or 8 are included.
3. The meter reading is absent but the codes include 1 or 4.

Number of dials

In field G no more than one box should be dot-marked. The meter reading could be valid, but if the number of marked columns does not match the number dot-marked in field G then an error is registered.

These are some of the tests to which each MRS must be subjected. Failure to pass these tests means that the offending sheet will be rejected, including, of course, any document that has neither marked readings nor special codes.

Preparing bills

As valid MRS are read by the UDR, the information on them is dumped on to magnetic tape.

Sheets are sometimes rejected because they cannot be processed by the OMR – they can be corrected and their information input by another method (punched cards or a VDU).

Valid and corrected MRS are then sorted into customer reference number order and validated.

We can at this point start to build up a systems diagram of the process. The upper flowchart opposite shows the operations carried out so far.

The sorted movements are now used in the update process. The update process uses the brought-forward version of the master file. After updating the data is transferred to the carried-forward file, which now contains all the latest records. The appropriate calculations are carried out to enable gas bills to be prepared. Details for the production of bills and also various reports are then dumped on to magnetic tape. Bills and reports are then prepared on on-line printers.

Finally the bills, produced on pre-printed stationery, need to be separated and put in envelopes.

In the Midshires area there are 175 meter readers who collect their work from 15 regional offices.

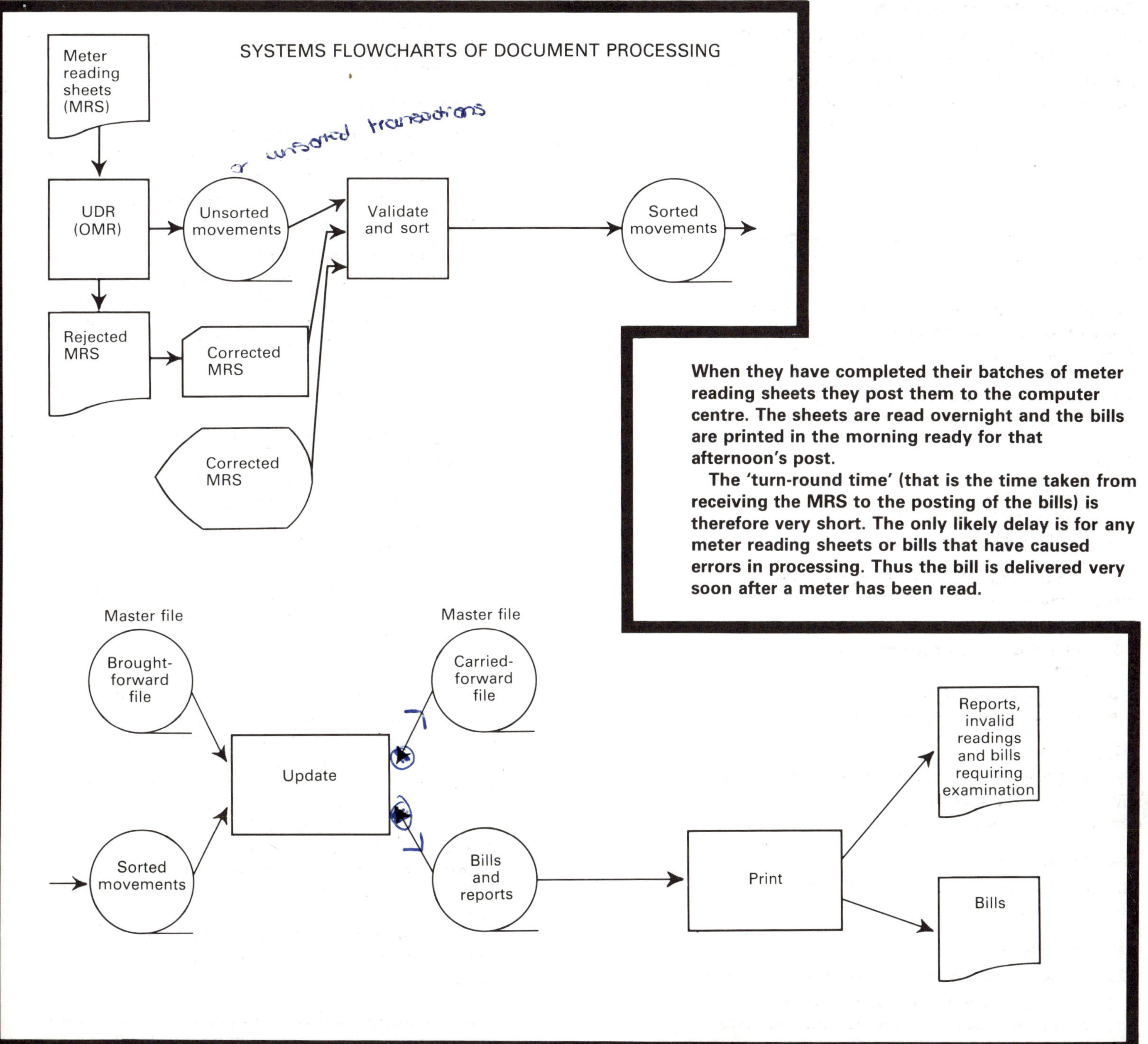

When they have completed their batches of meter reading sheets they post them to the computer centre. The sheets are read overnight and the bills are printed in the morning ready for that afternoon's post.

The 'turn-round time' (that is the time taken from receiving the MRS to the posting of the bills) is therefore very short. The only likely delay is for any meter reading sheets or bills that have caused errors in processing. Thus the bill is delivered very soon after a meter has been read.

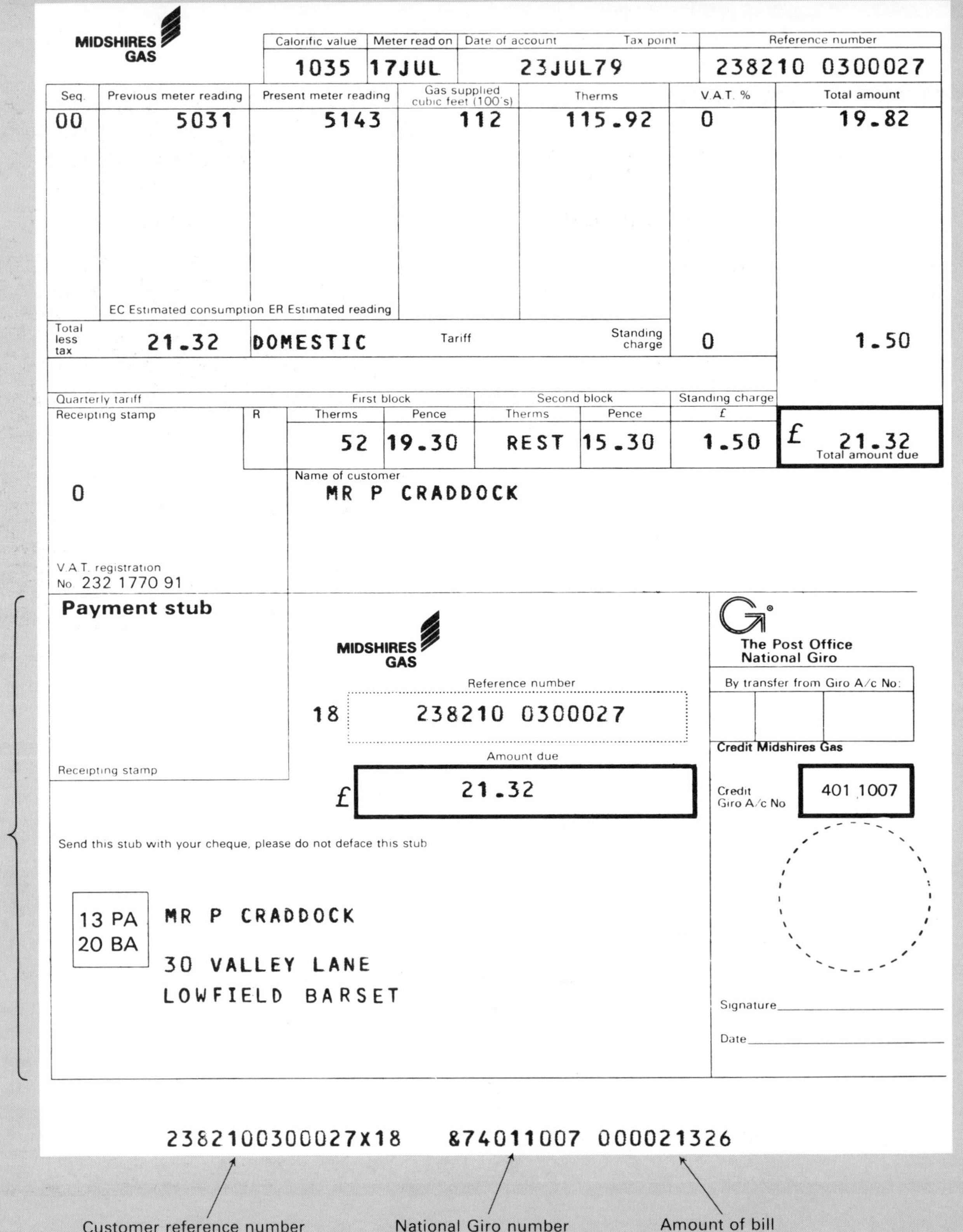
MIDSHIRES GAS

Calorific value	Meter read on	Date of account Tax point	Reference number
1035	17JUL	23JUL79	238210 0300027

Seq.	Previous meter reading	Present meter reading	Gas supplied cubic feet (100's)	Therms	V.A.T. %	Total amount
00	5031	5143	112	115.92	0	19.82

EC Estimated consumption ER Estimated reading

Total less tax 21.32 DOMESTIC Tariff Standing charge 0 1.50

Quarterly tariff	R	First block Therms	First block Pence	Second block Therms	Second block Pence	Standing charge £
Receipting stamp		52	19.30	REST	15.30	1.50

£ 21.32 Total amount due

Name of customer
MR P CRADDOCK

0

V.A.T. registration No. 232 1770 91

Payment stub

MIDSHIRES GAS

Reference number
18 238210 0300027

Amount due
£ 21.32

Receipting stamp

The Post Office National Giro

By transfer from Giro A/c No:

Credit Midshires Gas

Credit Giro A/c No 401 1007

Send this stub with your cheque, please do not deface this stub

13 PA
20 BA

MR P CRADDOCK
30 VALLEY LANE
LOWFIELD BARSET

Signature

Date

2382100300027X18 &74011007 000021326

Typical bill

Processing payments

The customer can now pay the bill either by sending the bill stub and the payment due to the main office of Midshires Gas, or by going to a local gas salesroom.

The bill stub eventually arrives back at the computer centre for processing.

This time the bill stubs are read by the optical character reader within the UDR. The important information is at the bottom of the stub.

The bills are then validated, sorted and updated. Unpaid bills are listed on a line printer and then reminders are printed for those customers who have not paid at this time. The systems flowchart is given below.

The photograph shows staff at the main office of Midshires Gas. They are sitting at special terminals which deal with customer enquiries over telephone lines.

Main office of the gas board

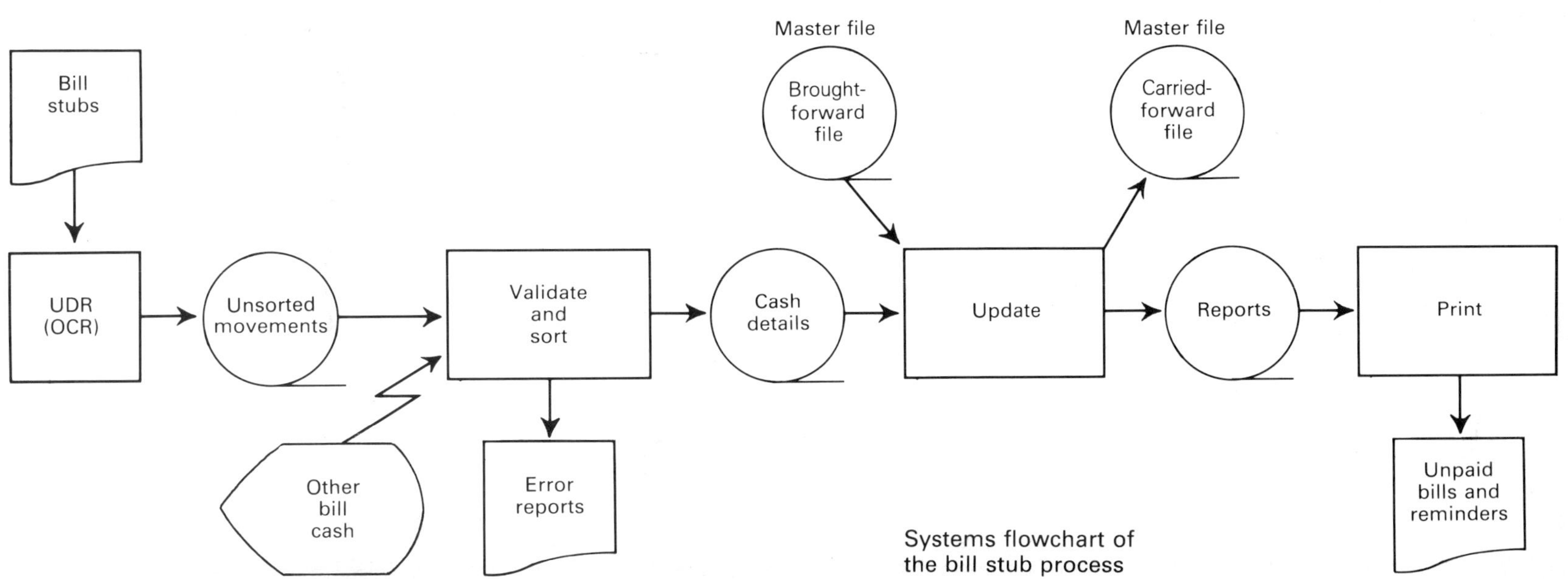

Systems flowchart of the bill stub process

The computer system is also used for various other data processing and development tasks. To deal with all these jobs the hardware includes two large computers. The computer configuration is given in the diagram below.

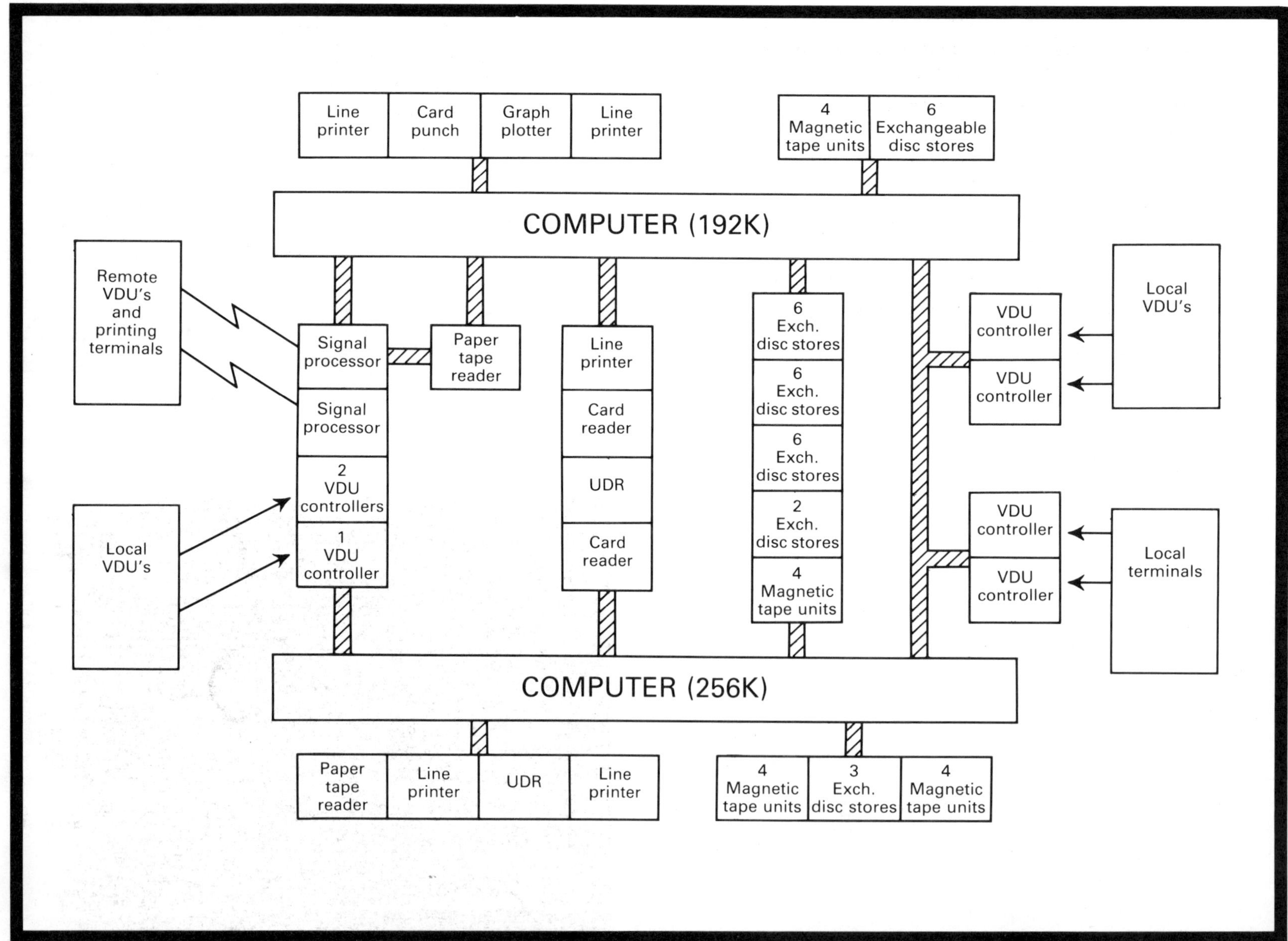

Questions

1. Why are inter-block gaps used on magnetic tape?
2. What is the difference between serial and direct (random) access? Illustrate your answer with labelled diagrams of an exchangeable disc system and a magnetic tape unit.
3. What would be the advantage of increasing the block size on a magnetic tape?
4. Why are mark sensing documents used for meter readings?
5. Give some examples of the fields that are pre-printed on meter reading sheets.
6. What is the purpose of the special codes on the meter reading sheets?
7. Why is the universal document reader so called?
8. (a) Why are meter readings processed in customer reference number order?
   (b) How is this reference number obtained?
9. Why is it necessary to put a check digit at the end of the customer reference number?
10. How are rejected meter reading sheets corrected and re-input?

Vocabulary

dumping
inter-block gap
magnetic tape unit
master file
universal document reader

18 The History of Computers

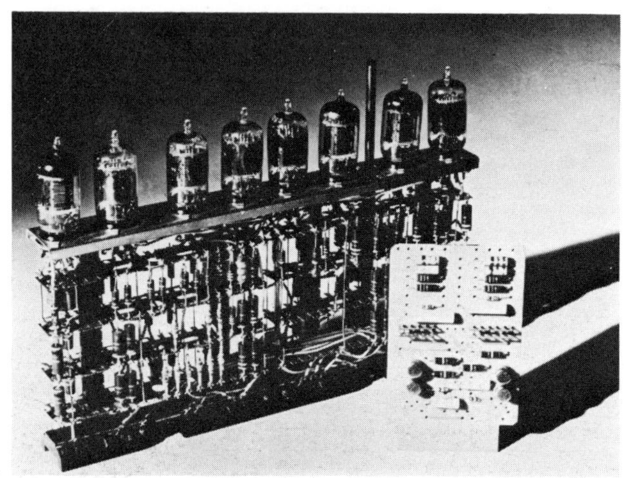

Thermionic valves and a transistor card

Above The Colossus computer
Below General view of ENIAC

The development of the thermionic valve at the start of the century has given rise to a wide variety of electronic devices. It was not until the 1930s, however, that designers began to see that the switch-like property of valves could be used to develop electronic computers.

The computer, like the jet engine, owes much of its development to the Second World War. In 1943 the British started work on a computer which was used to decode enemy signals. A photograph of Colossus, **as it was called, is shown above.**

In 1946 a machine named ENIAC (Electronic Numerical Integrator and Calculator) **was built in America. It was used to calculate the trajectories of bombs and shells. ENIAC could be reset to carry out other types of calculation by altering switch settings and plug and socket connections. This was the first general-purpose digital computer. It consisted of 18 000 valves and consumed 150–200 kilowatts of power, yet it could store only twenty numbers.**

John von Neumann joined the ENIAC team and made a number of proposals for future developments, including the use of a large internal memory to store instructions as well as data.

Mercury delay tube from EDSAC

The first stored-program computer was built at Cambridge University in 1949 and was called EDSAC (Electronic Delay Storage Automatic Computer). **Others followed, including** ACE (Automatic Computing Engine), **designed and built by the National Physical Laboratory, and** EDVAC (Electronic Discrete Variable Automatic Computer), **which was built in Pennsylvania, U.S.A., as a follow-up to ENIAC.**

The ACE computer

All the early computers were built by scientists and mathematicians, but it was not long before computers began to be used commercially for data processing. In 1953 the tea company of J. Lyons and Co. began using a computer called LEO (Lyons Electronic Office) for payroll and accounting. It was the first British commercial computer and it was marketed more widely in 1958: the Inland Revenue and British Railways used LEO for producing tax tables and for working out freight charges.

At about this time the American Census Bureau bought a UNIVAC computer. This was intended for both scientific and commercial applications. It also had the first software available to translate program language to machine code – a compiler.

Many ingenious methods were used in these early computers for internal storage, including vacuum tubes, delay lines and cathode-ray tubes. Input to such machines was via punched paper tape and output was on paper tape, punched cards or typewriter-like printers.

The design of computers was continually frustrated by the limitations of the components that were available. Valves were very unreliable and very few machines could run for more than two hours without needing attention. These computers were extremely large and expensive to operate, so it was not surprising that only a few were installed.

Section of core store, with a chip of the same capacity

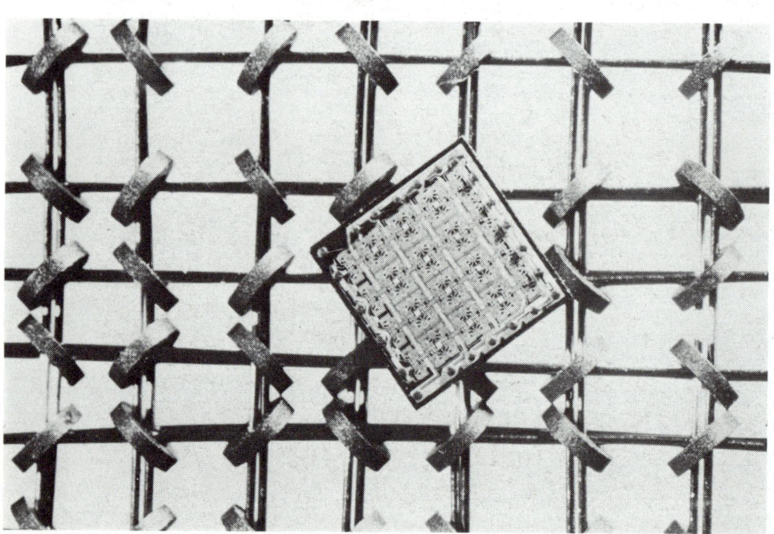

Two developments brought about a rapid increase in the popularity of computers: first, in 1955, came a fast, reliable and acceptably priced form of internal storage, called core store. Then, two years later, transistors became available to replace valves. Transistors, which had been invented in 1947, reduced construction costs and power consumption, and generally increased the reliability of machines.

One further development was the use of magnetic backing stores, in the form of magnetic tape, discs and drums. Magnetic tape was also used for input/output and was many times faster than punched cards and paper tape.

The use of transistors marked the birth of 'second generation' computers, and the number of installations rose from a few hundred to several thousand. Multi-programming and time-sharing were introduced and high-level languages became widely used. New and more powerful peripherals, including line printers, graph plotters and video terminals, became available. Central processors became more powerful and internal stores were much larger. This brought about a move towards big centralized computer bureaux.

Silicon chip compared with a pen nib

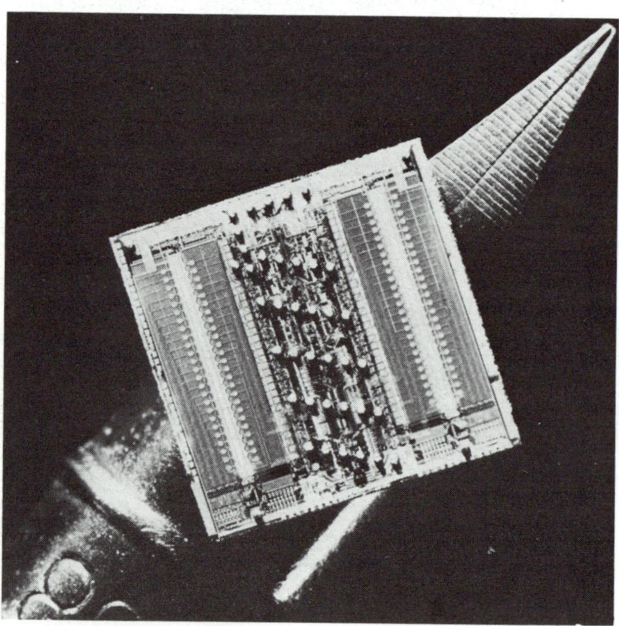

In 1964 another major step forward was taken with the introduction of integrated circuits. These consist of a number of individual electronic components (transistors, resistors, capacitors) fused together to form a single small component. The circuits are formed using thin slices of silicon, and became known as silicon chips. Computer costs were still further reduced, and the speed of operation increased. These 'third generation' computers were even more popular.

Since the early days of integrated circuits, scientists have discovered ways of putting more and more components on a single silicon chip. The photograph opposite shows a modern silicon chip compared with a pen nib. This chip can hold 64 000 individual pieces of information.

In 1971 the first 'computer on a chip' was produced, and there followed a micro-processor revolution. Micro-processor chips contain a central processor, an arithmetic/logic unit and a limited amount of immediate access memory. The photograph below shows the CPU board of a modern micro-processor containing a Z80 micro-processor chip, 32K bytes of RAM (random access memory) and an operating system in ROM (read only memory).

Many everyday devices are now controlled by micro-processors. Some of the items using such a device are: domestic appliances, watches, cars, word processors, TV games, robots, automatic warehouses, traffic-lights, programmed tractors, calculators, pocket thermometers, cameras, vending-machines, deep-freezers and cash registers.

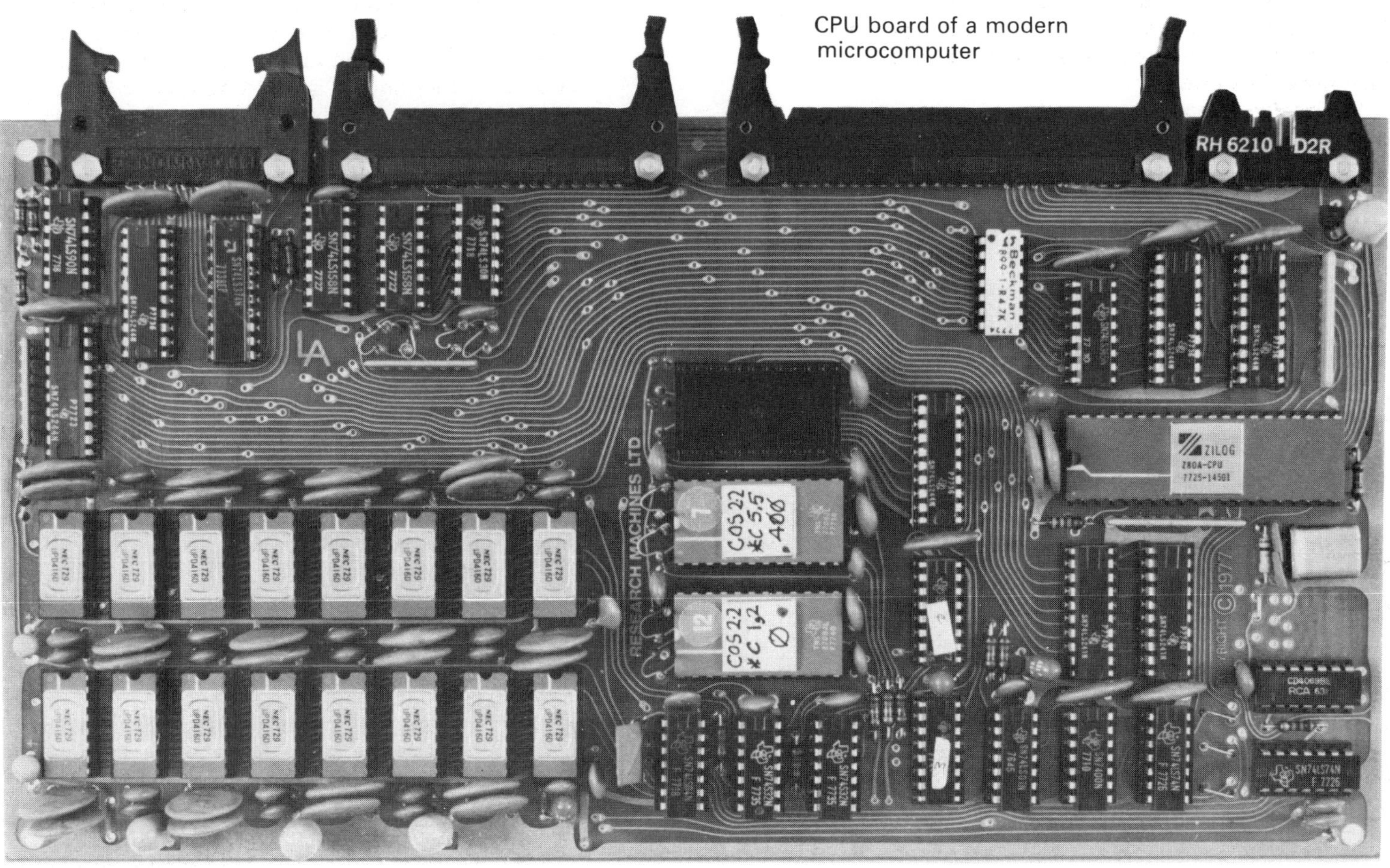

CPU board of a modern microcomputer

Core store has been replaced by memory chips capable of storing 1, 2, 4, 8, 16, or 64K bytes. These memory chips come in various forms. Random access memory (RAM) can be added to and read from. Read only memory is used for programs which must not be erased or overwritten, as data can only be read from this kind of store. Programmable read only memory (PROM) **is a kind of ROM which may have its contents changed by the use of special equipment.** Eraseable programmable read only memory (EPROM) **is similar, but in addition it may have its data erased by the application of ultraviolet light.**

Inexpensive mass-produced computer components have now completely changed the computer world. In the 1960s the trend was towards large main-frame computers that were centralized in big departments; now there are many more small and medium-sized installations. Companies who would previously have hired computer time from bureaux can now afford their own mini- and micro-computers housed in their own offices. Chapter 20 gives some examples of the use of such computers in the supermarket, office and in engineering design. Of course, there is still a place for the large main-frame computer, and Chapter 19 describes a typical situation and the many jobs involved.

Questions

1. Which memory device first made large internal stores possible?
   (a) cathode ray tubes,
   (b) silicon chips,
   (c) core store,
   (d) delay lines.
2. Why did transistors make computers more acceptable?
3. Which of the computers below was the first to use a stored program?
   (a) ENIAC, (b) ACE, (c) EDSAC, (d) Colossus.
4. Computers have passed through three generations. What technological advances marked these stages?
5. Name two computers that were first used commercially.
6. Explain why in the 1960s there was a trend towards large computer centres and why now there is a trend towards mini- and micro-computers.
7. What is meant by the following?
   (a) RAM, (b) ROM, (c) PROM, (d) EPROM.
8. Even though there is a trend towards the use of small computer systems, is there still a need for large main-frame machines?

Vocabulary

Automatic Computing Engine (ACE)
Colossus
core store
Electronic Delay Storage Automatic Computer (EDSAC)
Electronic Discrete Variable Automatic Computer (EDVAC)
Electronic Numerical Integrator and Calculator (ENIAC)
eraseable programmable read only memory (EPROM)
integrated circuits
Lyons Electronic Office (LEO)
micro-processor unit (MPU)
programmable read only memory (PROM)
random access memory (RAM)
read only memory (ROM)
silicon chip

19 A Study of an Organization

Many schools in this country use computing facilities offered by their local authority. The computers used by these authorities will probably be large 'main frames', and so they can usually find some room on their system for a schools computer service. This may involve using either remote access terminals in the schools, or a bureau service.

A bureau service means that programs which have been written on coding sheets by pupils will be punched and processed at the computer centre.

Local authorities, of course, deal with lots of other matters besides education. Because of the wide variety of jobs done there, many schools take their pupils to see the computer centre.

JOBS DONE AT LOCAL-AUTHORITY COMPUTER CENTRES

Wages and salaries	**Processing salaries and wages of local-government employees.**
Rates	**Production of rate demands and the collection of rates.**
Bus passes	**Production of passes for pupils who must travel some distance to school by public transport.**
Libraries	**Production of notices to library members. Library stock management.**
Further education	**Maintenance of student records, fees and statistics.**
Youth employment	**Facilities for record keeping, aptitude tests and job vacancies.**
Poll cards	**Production of poll cards for elections (very often at extremely short notice).**
Bonds	**Issuing and recording local-authority bonds.**
Magistrates, court	**Keeping records of fines and fees.**
Schools service	**Providing computer facilities for schools and colleges.**
Housing allocation	**Keeping records of council houses and the allocation of properties.**
Housing rents	**Keeping records of rented properties and the collection of rents.**
Data base of land and property	**Keeping records of all facts relating to all properties within the local-authority area.**
Communications	**Provision and maintenance of communication systems for computer users of the local authority's machine.**

It is for these reasons that we shall now study the organization of a typical local-authority computer centre.

All matters dealing with local government are of course in the end controlled by councillors, who are your representatives. So, for example, the Education and Housing Departments are answerable to committees of councillors. This makes the organization of local authorities different from that of most business concerns.

The Treasurer's Department is involved in a large number of committees, and it is usually this department that is responsible for the computer centre. Thus the Treasurer and the Assistant Treasurer are in overall charge.

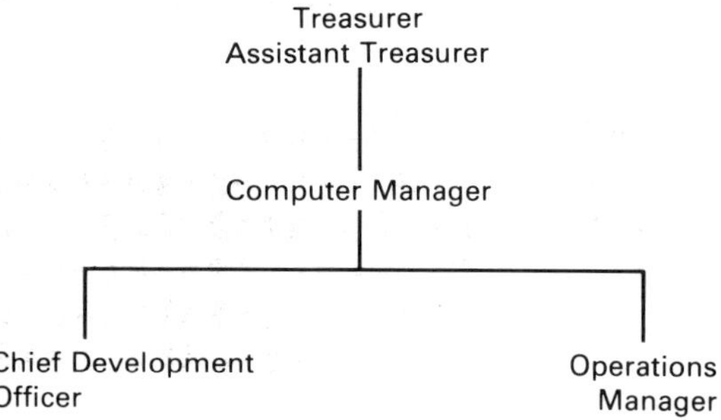

The Computer Manager **is in charge of the computer centre. He is an expert in both management and computer organization. He is responsible to the Treasurer, and makes sure that anything he requires is done. The Treasurer, although highly qualified in financial matters, may not have the knowledge of computing that the manager has.**

There are two main departments in the computer centre: Development and Operations. The Operations Manager **is concerned with the day-to-day running of the computer, while the** Chief Development Officer **is responsible for such things as maintaining current systems and designing and implementing new ones.**

Operations staff

The operations staff consist of computer operators, KDT operators, control clerks and the librarian.

Computer operators

These members of staff are to be found in the computer room. They are responsible for changing magnetic tapes and discs and for putting the correct stationery on the line printers. They have a 'run sheet' which gives them details of the tapes, discs and stationery which will be required for each job.

The operating system 'scans' the tape and disc drives to see if any new files are wanted, and if so whether they are available. Any files that are required are asked for by the operating system. Operators can keep track of requirements by looking at special VDUs that are strategically placed around the computer room.

When a file has been finished with, the operating system notifies the operators through the VDU. To save them looking at each drive in turn, the operating system outputs the number of the actual peripheral concerned.

If a line printer is required but one is not available at that moment, then the output is 'spooled' automatically on to magnetic disc. When the printer is available the operator checks the kind of stationery needed and loads it on the printer. He then uses a loop of punched paper tape in order to ensure that the stationery is 'thrown' the correct distance between pages of output. The size of pre-printed output varies according to the job being output. Samples of the pre-printed stationery used for rate demands, reminders for overdue library books and teachers' wage receipts and salary advice slips are shown overleaf.

The operator then runs tests on the line printer to see that the output is properly aligned on the paper. The section of 'poll card' stationery opposite shows the alignment tests, done using the two characters M and E.

Besides VDUs in the computer room there is an operator's console **which is used to control the operation of programs and peripherals. It gives a print-out of all the operating system messages. In this way a hard copy of all the day's activities can be kept and this is known as the** operator's log.

When a particular job has been printed, the output may be fed through a guillotine to separate out the individual sheets and if required these sheets can be put into envelopes automatically.

MEMEMEMEMEMEMEMEMEMEMEMEMEM
MEMEMEMEMEMEMEMEMEMEMEMEMEM
MEMEMEMEMEMEMEMEMEMEMEMEMEM
MEMEMEMEMEMEMEMEMEMEMEMEMEM

MEME MEMEMEMEMEMEMEMEMEMEMEME
MEMEMEMEMEMEMEMEMEMEMEME
MEMEMEMEMEMEMEMEMEMEMEME

...o 9 p.m.

...Returning Officer

View of the computer room showing the exchangeable disc system on the right and magnetic tape units in the background

MEMEMEMEMEMEMEMEMEMEMEMEMEM
MEMEMEMEMEMEMEMEMEMEMEMEMEM
MEMEMEMEMEMEMEMEMEMEMEMEMEM
MEMEMEMEMEMEMEMEMEMEMEMEMEM
MEMEMEMEMEMEMEMEMEMEMEMEMEM

OFFICIAL POLL CARD

2 POSTAGE PAID SERIAL NO 31

MEMEMEMEMEMEME
MEMEMEMEMEMEMEME

Number on Register MEMEME MEME

Name:—

MEMEMEMEMEMEMEMEMEMEMEMEMEM
MEMEMEMEMEMEMEMEMEMEMEMEMEM
MEMEMEMEMEMEMEMEMEMEMEMEMEM
MEMEMEMEMEMEMEMEMEMEMEMEMEM
MEMEMEMEMEMEMEMEMEMEMEMEMEM
MEMEMEMEMEMEMEMEMEMEMEMEMEM

MEMEMEMEMEMEMEMEME

MEMEMEMEMEMEMEMEME

...will be:-

MEMEMEMEMEMEMEMEME
MEMEMEMEMEMEMEMEME
MEMEMEMEMEMEMEMEME
MEMEMEMEMEMEMEMEME

Polling hours 8 a.m. to 9 p.m.

POLL CARD

2 POSTAGE PAID SERIAL NO 31

MEMEMEMEMEMEMEM
MEMEMEMEMEMEMEMEME

Number on Register MEMEME MEME

Name:—

MEMEMEMEMEMEMEMEMEMEMEMEMEM
MEMEMEMEMEMEMEMEMEMEMEMEMEM
MEMEMEMEMEMEMEMEMEMEMEMEMEM
MEMEMEMEMEMEMEMEMEMEMEMEMEM
MEMEMEMEMEMEMEMEMEMEMEMEMEM
MEMEMEMEMEMEMEMEMEMEMEMEMEM

OFFICIAL POLL CARD

Ward/Electoral Division:—

MEMEMEMEME
MEMEMEMEMEMEMEMEMEMEMEMEME

Polling Day MEMEMEMEMEMEMEMEMEMEMEME

Your Polling Station will be:-

Number MEME

MEMEMEMEMEMEMEMEMEMEME
MEMEMEMEMEMEMEMEMEMEME
MEMEMEMEMEMEMEMEMEMEME
MEMEMEMEMEMEMEMEMEMEME

Polling hours 8 a.m. to 9 p.m.

2 POSTAGE PAID SERIAL NO 31

MEMEMEMEMEMEMEM
MEMEMEMEMEMEMEME

Number on Register MEMEME MEME

Name:—

MEMEMEMEMEMEMEMEMEMEMEMEMEM
MEMEMEMEMEMEMEMEMEMEMEMEMEM
MEMEMEMEMEMEMEMEMEMEMEMEMEM
MEMEMEMEMEMEMEMEMEMEMEMEMEM
MEMEMEMEMEMEMEMEMEMEMEMEMEM
MEMEMEMEMEMEMEMEMEMEMEMEMEM

...rn-Trent Region
Your attention is
and which forms part of
THE AMOUNT

SAMPLES OF PRE-PRINTED STATIONERY

Form Ref. 459

NOTICE—IF THE EMPLOYEE ENTRUSTS THIS PRINTED WAGE RECEIPT TO ANOTHER PERSON HE OR SHE WILL DO SO AT HIS OR HER OWN RISK IN RESPECT OF ANY LOSS THAT MAY OCCUR IN THE COURSE OF COLLECTION

Received of THE TREASURER OF THE CITY *the sum stated below being the amount of wages and extras due to me*

EDUCATION COMMITTEE

BANK No.	WARRANT No.	NAME	BANK A/C No.	PAY POINT	DATE	AMOUNT

This Receipt form must be presented at the branch of the bank indicated in the first column not later than seven days following the date of issue

..........................Signature....................................19..........

SEE OVER FOR KEY TO BANK NUMBERS

P.48295

Deanson Limited 14774

Form Ref. 459

NOTICE—IF THE EMPLOYEE ENTRUSTS THIS PRINTED WAGE RECEIPT TO ...ER PERSON HE OR SHE WILL DO SO AT HIS OR HER OWN RISK IN ... THAT MAY OCCUR IN THE COURSE OF COLLECTION

Received of THE TREASURER OF THE CITY *the sum stated below being the amount of wages and extras due to me*

EDUCATION COMMITTEE

DATE AMOUNT

...ing the date of issue

Deanson Limited 14774

See paragraph overleaf

Date Due

If undelivered please return to
BIRMINGHAM PUBLIC LIBRARIES
CENTRAL LENDING LIBRARY
BIRMINGHAM B3 3HQ.

See paragraph overleaf

Date Due

Deanson Limited 14774

Deanson Limited 855

IN ALL COMMUNICATIONS PLEASE QUOTE YOUR FULL NAME AND THE ROLL NUMBER PRINTED BELOW

ROLL NUMBER	PAY PERIOD WK. Nos.	CLAIM 1 £ p	CLAIM 2 £ p	CLAIM 3 £ p

	MONDAY CODE £ p	TUESDAY CODE £
A.M.		
P.M.		
EVE		

CO...

IN ALL COMMUNICATIONS PLEASE QUOTE YOUR FULL NAME AND THE ROLL NUMBER PRINTED BELOW

ROLL NUMBER	PAY PERIOD WK. Nos.	CLAIM 1 £ p	CLAIM 2 £ p	CLAIM 3 £ p

TUESD...

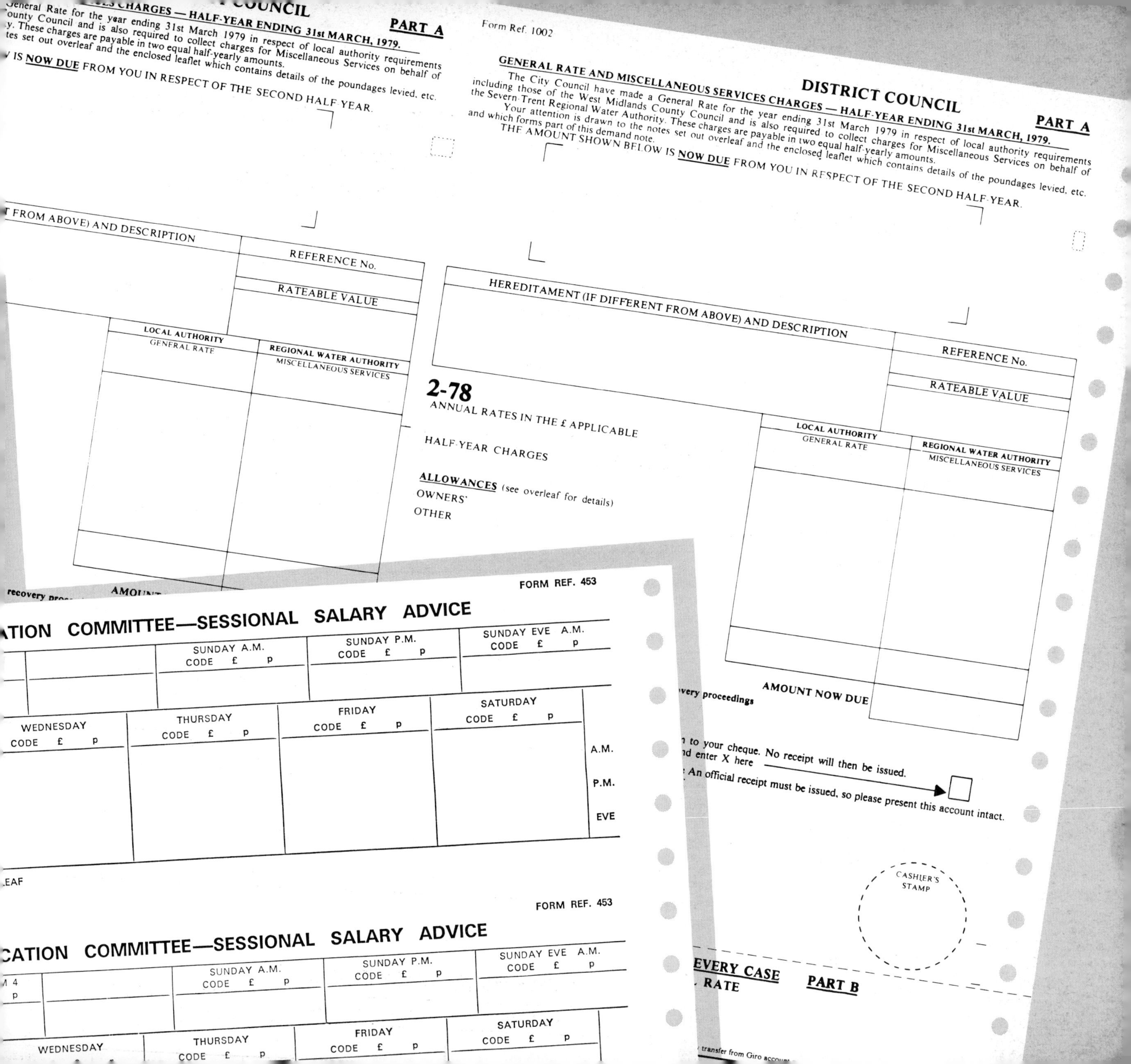

Form Ref. 1002

PART A

GENERAL RATE AND MISCELLANEOUS SERVICES CHARGES — HALF-YEAR ENDING 31st MARCH, 1979.

DISTRICT COUNCIL

PART A

The City Council have made a General Rate for the year ending 31st March 1979 in respect of local authority requirements including those of the West Midlands County Council and is also required to collect charges for Miscellaneous Services on behalf of the Severn-Trent Regional Water Authority. These charges are payable in two equal half-yearly amounts. Your attention is drawn to the notes set out overleaf and the enclosed leaflet which contains details of the poundages levied, etc. and which forms part of this demand note.

THE AMOUNT SHOWN BELOW IS **NOW DUE** FROM YOU IN RESPECT OF THE SECOND HALF-YEAR.

HEREDITAMENT (IF DIFFERENT FROM ABOVE) AND DESCRIPTION

REFERENCE No.

RATEABLE VALUE

2-78

	LOCAL AUTHORITY GENERAL RATE	REGIONAL WATER AUTHORITY MISCELLANEOUS SERVICES
ANNUAL RATES IN THE £ APPLICABLE		
HALF-YEAR CHARGES		
ALLOWANCES (see overleaf for details)		
OWNERS'		
OTHER		
AMOUNT NOW DUE		

...very proceedings

...n to your cheque. No receipt will then be issued.
...nd enter X here

...: An official receipt must be issued, so please present this account intact.

CASHIER'S STAMP

...EVERY CASE

PART B

... RATE

... transfer from Giro account

FORM REF. 453

...ATION COMMITTEE—SESSIONAL SALARY ADVICE

	SUNDAY A.M. CODE £ p	SUNDAY P.M. CODE £ p	SUNDAY EVE A.M. CODE £ p

WEDNESDAY CODE £ p	THURSDAY CODE £ p	FRIDAY CODE £ p	SATURDAY CODE £ p	
				A.M.
				P.M.
				EVE

...EAF

FORM REF. 453

...CATION COMMITTEE—SESSIONAL SALARY ADVICE

...M 4 p		SUNDAY A.M. CODE £ p	SUNDAY P.M. CODE £ p	SUNDAY EVE A.M. CODE £ p

WEDNESDAY	THURSDAY CODE £ p	FRIDAY CODE £ p	SATURDAY CODE £ p

KDT operators

The data preparation is done in the Key to Disc to Tape room. There are over sixty people employed in this department (which illustrates yet again how expensive data preparation is in terms of staff).

The staff structure is shown below. The numbers in brackets indicate the approximate total of employees in each section.

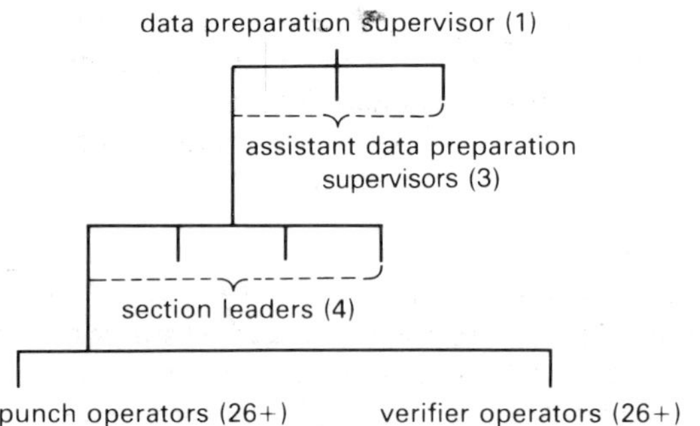

Two similar computer systems are being used in this room. Each consists of a processor, an exchangeable disc system, a magnetic tape unit and several visual display terminals.

In the left-hand photograph on the opposite page you can see a group of operators using the terminals, and in the background are the processor, disc system and racks of magnetic tapes.

All input documents are coded on forms designed by the systems analyst. **One of the jobs of the supervisor is to agree the layout of these forms with the analyst. It is of course very important that any documents are easily read.**

ENTRY TO KEY EDIT — FORM 604

SYSTEM REF: — DATE

DATA TAPE FILE NAME (PEEL ONLY): W A 1 4 6 3 8 0 2

OPENING BATCH I.D.: W A 1 / 4 6 3 8 0 2 0 0 0

PARAMETER DETAILS – INCLUDE IN PEEL

W A 0 1 [2 [4 6 4/4 ⌗ 7/7 ⌗

ACTION TO BE TAKEN ON BATCHES SPECIFIED BELOW	1	2	3	4	5	6
A. LIST						
B. CORRECT AND PEEL						
C. PEEL						

TAPE NUMBERS
1
2
3
4

CLOSING BATCH I.D.: W A 1 / 4 6 3 8 0 2 9 9 9

RUN TRAILER DETAILS: # E N D ⌗ ⌗

*	1	2	3	4	5	6
CONTROLLERS INITIALS						
DATE & TIME SUBMITTED						
A.D.P.S. INITIALS						
DATE & TIME COMPLETED						
TIME REQD. FROM K.E.						

* 1–6 SIGNIFY EACH TIME THE SHEET IS USED FOR ONE SET OF BATCHES

Sample of an input document

Operators using terminals

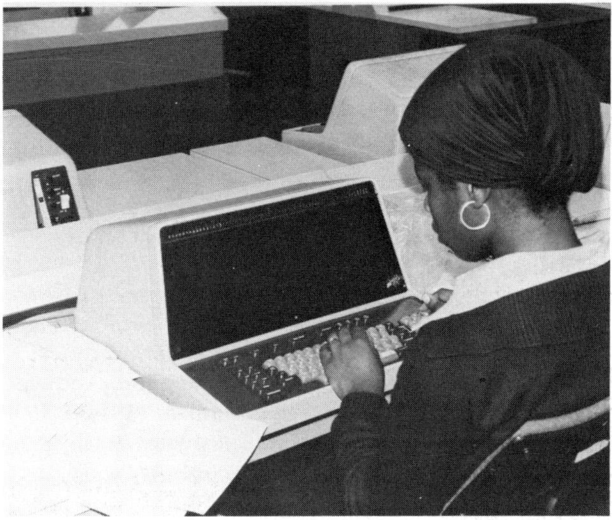

Punch operator

Control clerks

The documents are received by the control clerks, who batch them to a manageable size (for instance, in groups of fifty forms). They write a total at the head of each batch and then check to see if there is any special information for the job, e.g. the date and number of runs required. The batched documents are then taken to the Key to Disc to Tape room.

Punch operators

The supervisor sorts the batches according to their priority or the amount of work needed on them. Some jobs involve a large volume of typing, so the supervisor may give this task to a punch operator who can type quickly. Other jobs may be quite complicated but involve less typing, so the supervisor would look for a typist who is more able to deal with complicated forms.

Typing speeds of punch operators average about 12 000 key depressions an hour, but some may achieve rates of 20 000.

Having been given their batches to work on, the punch operators key in the details held on the source documents. As you can see from the photograph, a punch operator uses a visual display terminal, which enables her to see what she has typed. However, there is little data validation at this stage. Checks are made on certain fields to see that letters do not appear where numbers should be, and the output on the VDU gives a visual check.

As each record is typed in it is transferred to magnetic disc. When a batch is complete the original forms are passed to a verifier operator. Verification involves typing the data again and if what is retyped does not match the data already held on disc, the terminal locks. The operator checks the cause of the error and corrects it. The correct version is then held on the disc.

The librarian

As each job is completed it is 'peeled off' the disc on to magnetic tape, so freeing space on the disc for more data. The tape is taken to the computer room for processing. As you might imagine, a very large number of files is held on backing store. It is the job of the librarian to organize these tapes and discs. The librarian must keep details of all the generations of files and know the numbers of the reels and disc packs associated with them. Some of the files in the library are very important and so the librarian will keep copies of them in a fire-proof safe, and in another building.

Development staff

The development team investigates new tasks for which the computer could be used, develops new systems and improves and updates existing ones. The development team consists of project leaders, systems analysts and programmers.

The project leaders, as their name suggests, are responsible for organizing the various schemes undertaken by the authority.

Each project leader has the help of a team of systems analysts. Systems analysts are responsible for developing new systems. They examine the existing system, analyse their findings and produce a more efficient and practical computer system. They also try to ensure that all hardware and software are used in the best possible way. All interested parties (like the data preparation supervisor) are consulted, and when the new system is put into operation the analysts must make sure that it is maintained properly.

Chief programmers are in charge of programming teams, and programmers code the instructions necessary to make the systems analyst's specifications work on the computer.

There are about twenty analysts and thirty programmers in the development team.

In this particular organization the programmers and analysts work separately. In some other computer centres each project leader may have his own team of programmers and analysts working together as the diagram illustrates.

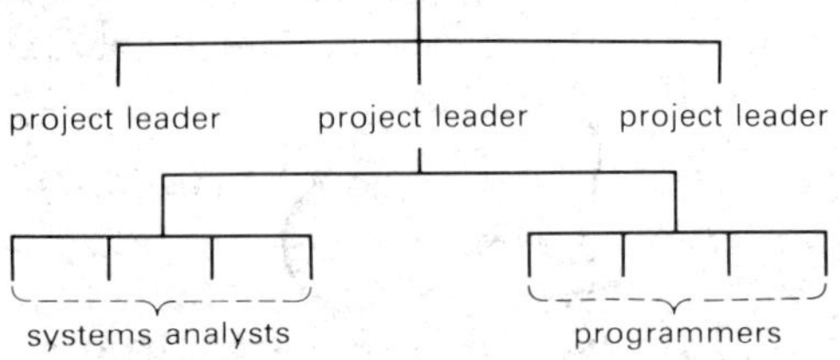

One of the problems tackled by the development team in this authority was the storage of historical documents. Documents are very bulky and are often in poor condition because of their age. Many documents need to be kept for a long time. One of the project leaders had as one of his tasks the development of a system for recording such documents on microfiche.

Microfiche consists of about 300 very small transparency photographs of documents on one sheet of film about the size of a post card. If the cellars of your County Hall are filled with very old important papers, the same information on microfiche would take up one-thousandth of the space.

The photograph shows a microfiche viewer displaying a small section of its contents. The microfiche is placed in the tray under the screen and can be positioned to show individual frames.

This process is known as computer output on microfilm, or COM.

Microfiche viewer

The next time you visit a computer centre, see how many of the staff there you can recognize by the jobs that they do. As a final reminder, the complete staff structure is shown opposite.

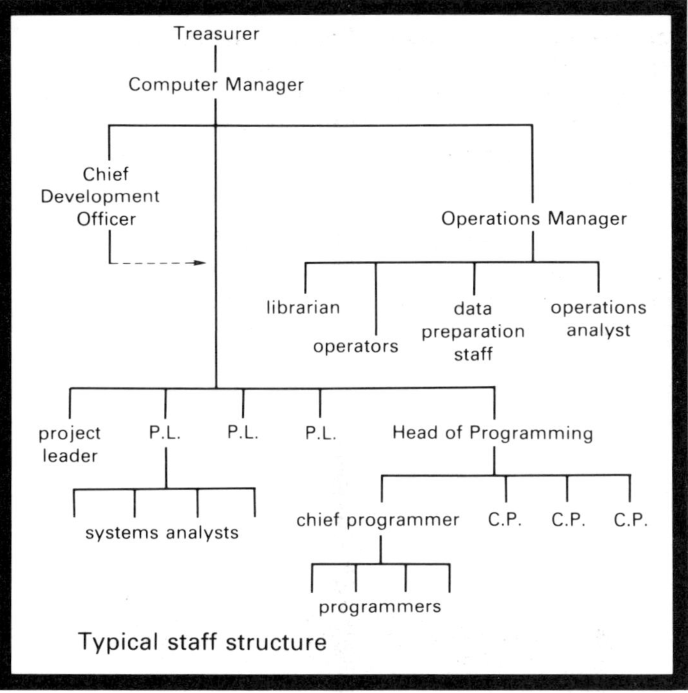

Typical staff structure

Questions

1. Which of the staff listed below is responsible for loading discs and tapes?
   (a) librarian, (b) programmer, (c) systems analyst, (d) computer operator.
2. Which of the staff listed below investigates whether it is possible to use a computer for a particular job?
   (a) librarian, (b) programmer, (c) systems analyst, (d) computer operator.
3. Which of the staff listed below is responsible for the computer centre?
   (a) chief programmer, (b) Computer Manager, (c) data preparation supervisor, (d) systems analyst.
4. Describe the job of a punch (KDT) operator.
5. Why is there a need for the careful design of input documents?
6. What is meant by COM and what are its advantages?

Vocabulary

Chief Development Officer
Chief Programmer
Computer Manager
computer operator
computer output on microfilm (COM)
control clerks
KDT operators
key to disc to tape
librarian
Operations Manager
operator's console
operator's log
programmer
project leader
systems analyst
verifier

20 Further Computer Applications

Computers in the supermarket

Tesco have for many years used computer facilities to enable warehouse deliveries, central stock control and branch ordering to run more efficiently.

A major concern of this supermarket chain is to keep stock levels to a minimum (to avoid too much capital being tied up) while at the same time providing a good supply of all items for the customer.

An experiment at the Wellingborough branch seeks to improve these matters and also to improve the efficiency of the checkouts.

Normally every item is marked individually with its price, and the cash point operator keys in the price of the goods and handles the change. There are some disadvantages in this. First, the price of an item is not always clearly marked, and this leads to delays or mischarging. Secondly, the operator may enter the wrong amounts. Thirdly, the bill printed by the cash till does not itemize goods, and fourthly, the only way of knowing that particular items have been sold is to count the stock on the shelves, and in the store warehouse.

Number coding

Special point-of-sale terminals have been installed which enable operators to enter a code for each item sold. The EPOS (electronic point-of-sale) terminal and the computer provide a much better service to both the customer and the supermarket. For example, when you buy a can of orange crush, the price is marked on the can with the code. The price is also given on the shelf by the item.
The shelf label opposite clearly shows the price and the code.

At the cash point the operator types in the code, which is sent to the computer, held elsewhere in the supermarket. The code is checked to see if it is valid.

The last number of the code is a check digit calculated in the following manner:

4 4 2 5 ×1 ×3 ×1 ×3 4 +12 +2 +15 = 33	**Multiply numbers by 1 or 3**
33 ÷ 10 = 3 remainder 3	**The total on division by 10 gives a remainder of 3.**
10 − 3 = 7	**This subtracted from 10 produces the check digit of 7.**
4 4 2 5 7	**This is placed at the end of the code.**

The computer checks the code and if an error is found (the operator may have mistyped the code) then the terminal 'bleeps' and the code must be re-entered.

The correct code gives access to the name of the commodity and its price, information which is held on backing store. The computer then transmits this information to the EPOS terminal. A visual display indicates to the customer the goods bought.

The sales receipt is printed with the type of item and its price. Meanwhile the sale has been recorded on disc for stock-taking purposes and for sales analysis. Your purchases are totalled by the terminal and printed on a sales receipt along with the money you offer in payment and the change due.

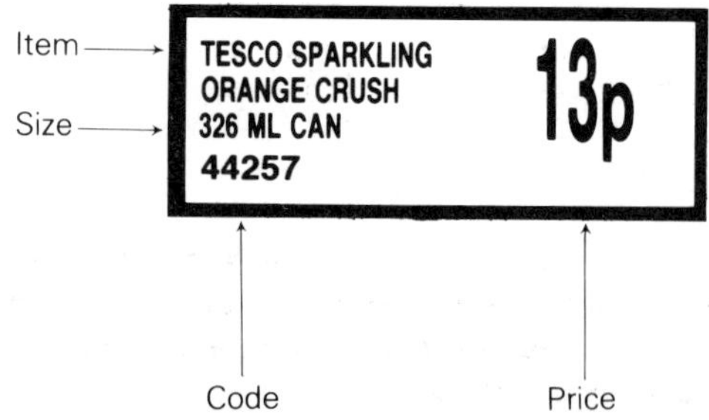

EPOS keyboard

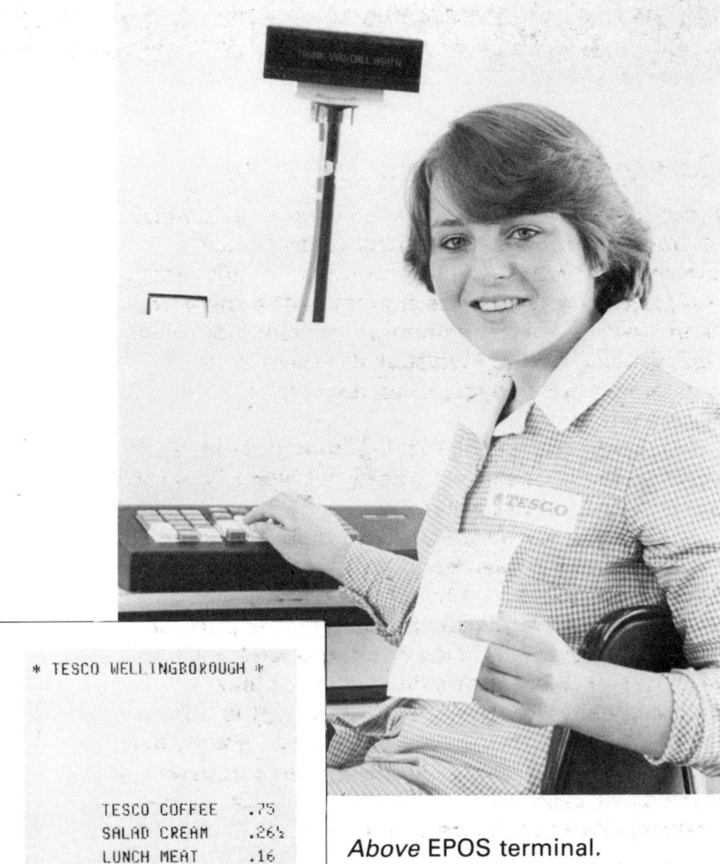

Above EPOS terminal.
The visual display unit for the customer is visible at the top of the photograph; the sales assistant is holding the customer's sales receipt

```
* TESCO WELLINGBOROUGH *

TESCO COFFEE      .75
SALAD CREAM       .26½
LUNCH MEAT        .16
PUDDING MIX       .11½
TRIFLE            .29½
HEINZ SOUP        .16½
PROCESS PEAS      .18
MEAT ROLL         .23
CAN SAUSAGES      .37
PILCHARDS         .33
QUICK-JEL         .09½
PKT CAKE MIX      .26½
SUGAR STRNDS      .17
TOTAL            3.39

CSH TEND         3.50
CHG DUE           .11

17/06/78 10:37  3368/ 3
*CHECK OUT TESCO PRICES*
```

Left Typical sales receipt

The thousand best-selling items are given a 'velocity code' of three digits along with a check digit. This means that goods with the fastest turn-over can be easily recognized and with a code of only four digits they can be typed on the terminal more quickly. The label below shows that this size of ginger ale is the 273rd best-seller in the store.

SCHWEPPES ORG DRY GINGER ALE 241 ML BOTTLE **2738**	**10½p**

The 10-megabyte fixed disc at the Wellingborough store is updated from the main Tesco computer in Cheshunt. This happens whenever there is a price change.

To serve · Empty entire contents into a saucepan and heat gently until thoroughly hot. Do not boil.

Ingredients · Processed Peas, Water, Sugar, Salt, Colour And Flavouring.

Net Weight 284 g 10 oz

Packed in England by Batchelors Foods Ltd. Sheffield.

5 000113 001449

Batchelors

BIGGA Processed Peas

Marrowfat processed peas in water: sugar and salt added

Batchelors

BIGGA Processed

The checkout, showing the bar-code reader

Bar-coding

If the experiment at Wellingborough is successful, it may lead to the bar-coding **of goods at Tesco supermarkets. If this system is introduced, the EPOS operator will not type in item codes, but will use a** bar-code reader **which automatically reads the codes printed on the labels of goods. These codes will be in the form of a bar code as shown on the label above.**

The bar code, as you can see, is made up of light and dark lines or bars. All the operator has to do is to pass the bar code over a small opening in the counter. Beneath this is a small laser beam which shines towards the label. The dark lines in the code absorb the light while the light areas reflect the beam downwards. The reflected light can then be detected and the patterns of light and dark bars can be read.

The code for 'Batchelors processed peas' (50 00113 00144 9) is thus sent to the central processor in the supermarket. On receiving the code the computer does two different jobs: first, the code is checked to see if it is valid, and matched with the data held on magnetic disc. Then the name of the goods bought, along with the price, is sent back to the EPOS terminal. The price and name are then visually displayed and printed on the sales receipt.

Secondly, the stock level is automatically updated, i.e. one tin of peas is subtracted from the stock number.

How to understand the bar code

Carefully examine the label on the peas again. Notice first of all that the code can be read directly by both the machine and man.

50	00113	00144	9
Country of origin (UK)	Manufacturer	Product	Check digit

The bar code contains a binary code for the digits 0 to 9. It should be noted that the code is not the binary *equivalent* (in which case 5 would be 101) but a real code, as may be seen below.

To make the codes more easily readable by the computer the following system has been designed:

1. **Each digit consists of two light and two dark bars.**
2. **The beginning, middle and end sections are marked by two longer dark bars separated by a light bar.**
3. **The binary codes on the left-hand side are complements of the codes on the right-hand side.**
4. **Different thicknesses of bars show 1, 2, 3 and 4 dark lines together:**

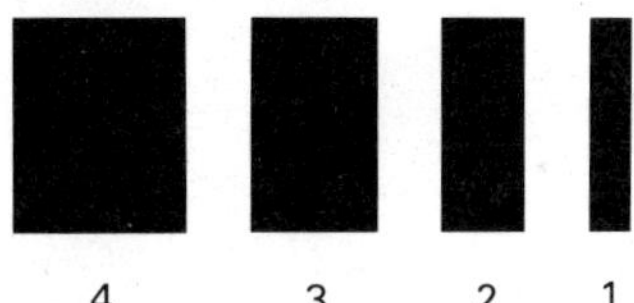

5. **The actual binary codes are given below.**

Left-hand side		*Right-hand side*	
0	0001101	0	1110010
1	0011001	1	1100110
2	0010011	2	1101100
3	0111101	3	1000010
4	0100011	4	1011100
5	0110001	5	1001110
6	0101111	6	1010000
7	0111011	7	1000100
8	0110111	8	1001000
9	0001011	9	1110100

Now check the code on the peas label and see if you can decode it successfully.

Advantages and disadvantages

Finally, let us consider the value of such an application of computers.

Advantages

1. **The checkout queue moves much faster (you do not have to wait when the cash till operator does not know the price of an item).**
2. **Errors in charging customers are reduced by at least 75 per cent.**
3. **The customer receives a clearer and more detailed sales receipt.**
4. **Prices may be changed immediately from a terminal in the manager's office.**
5. **The manager has an improved system for obtaining sales information.**
6. **Prices do not need to be stamped on to goods, which saves the time of supermarket staff.**

Disadvantages

1. **Because individual items are not priced, the customer may not know the cost of an item until it is printed on the sales bill.**
2. **The manager may increase prices from his own terminal without letting customers know, except from the sales bill. (This practice is not approved of by the Tesco Head Office.)**
3. **The cost of point-of-sale terminals is very high. The effect may be to transfer business from smaller to larger stores.**
4. **There may be a trend towards pre-packed goods. (There are, however, scales available which automatically produce bar-coded labels for perishable goods.)**
5. **Improved computer records will reveal customers' buying habits in great detail. This may encourage the manager not to stock items that do not sell very well, thus reducing the range of items available.**

Computers in design

From the earliest days of computing, designers (particularly engineering designers) realized the benefits of using computers to help them. At first computers were used to carry out the complex and time-consuming calculations necessary in designing components, especially in the aerospace and motor industries.

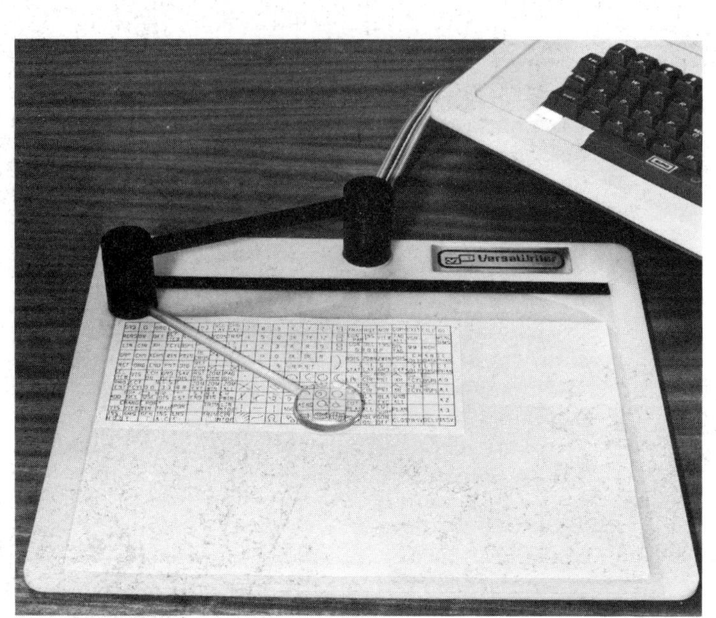

Graphics pad

More recently computer systems have been developed that allow designs to be drawn using a graphics terminal. **The complete system consists of a graphics screen on which lines and curves can be input, using a normal VDU keyboard or a** graphics pad **and a** light pen.

The light pen is used to identify an instruction (e.g. draw a circle) from a menu **on the graphics pad and then point to the graphics screen at the position where the circle is wanted.**

A hard copy of the design on the graphics screen can be obtained by pressing a button on the terminal. The hard copier **will then give an accurate paper copy.**

A flat bed plotter **will produce full-size drawings. Any ordinary drawing can be stored in the computer system by recording the position of each item by the use of a** digitizer. **As the drawing is traced electronically, binary information is stored and can then be recalled on the graphics terminal as the complete drawing.**

Menu on the graphics pad

GRD	G	ORG	ECH LAY	A)	N)	SEL LAY	CHG LAY	7	8	9	X	Y	Z		TRAN	ROT	MIR	COPY	EXIT	FILE	GO
RGRD	ON	OFF	DEF VIEW	SEL	VALL	VCON	TRAP	4	5	6	IX	IY	IZ		CON PART	INS	VIEW	TAG ALL	VER.		MENU DIMS
LIN	CIR	XH	TCYL	BSPL	DPTH :	DPTH	1 7 2 3	1	2	3	A	R	D		CON GROUP	DEL	ERS	DIS TAG	MM	INCH	
GRP	CHN	XCHN	WIN	PWIN	IN CROS					0	IA	IR	N		RDIS	ZDWN	ZWIN	PDIS	CHANGE SOLID	DASH	PHAN
REF	ORG	END	PNT	DIG	REF END						RPNT				LIST STAT	LAY	GRD	EXT	SELECT SOLID	DASH	PHAN
SEL VIEW	VIS	ECH ON	GRD OFF	SAV DIS	RST DIS	ZOM DWN	PAG DIS								ERASE LIN	CIR	PNT	XH	TCYL	BSPL	A 0
PROJECT ENT	TCYL	MESH 0 0	3 3	8 8	ZOM EXT	ZOM WIN	ZOM ALL				R		R		BLANK LIN	CIR	PNT	XH	TCYL	BSPL	A 1
PORT ADD	DEL	USE	DIS	LST	ST END	RE WIN	CH PWIN			D	D		D		ERS .	BLA ALL :	BLA EXC	UNB ALL			A 2
VIS	CHANGE PORT VIEW	WIN	TRAN	APORT		TRIM :	LIN INTOF				AGO	AEND			CUT PLAN	ALL :	CUT SURF	PLAN			A 3
INS HOLE	ERS	GEN FACE	INS	ERS		TRIM :	CIR INTOF								POLY	POLY ON	GON OFF	CLOS	TRNV	DELV	INSV

Graphics terminal

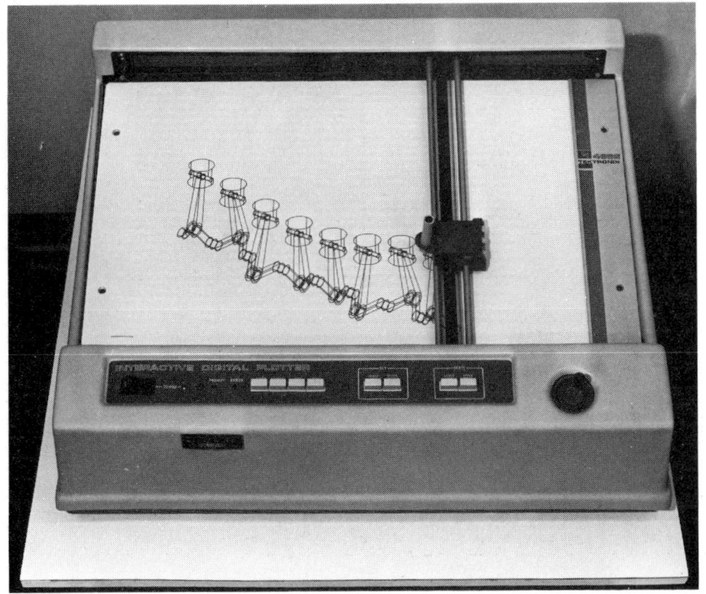

Flat bed plotter

Digitizer

CAD allows the original drawing to be shown in many different ways. Hidden lines can be dotted or removed, close-ups of sections can be shown, three-dimensional views from any angle can be drawn – in fact all the conventional types of representation that a draughtsman might use in ordinary geometric drawings are available, and more besides.

Any drawing or design can be stored in the computer so that it can be retrieved either for amendment or for a permanent drawing. Permanent drawings are produced on the flat bed plotter.

Another form of this device is the graph plotter.

A graph plotter has a pen which moves from side to side while the paper moves backwards and forwards. The flat bed plotter's pen moves vertically and horizontally, while the paper is kept still.

Design data is stored on magnetic discs and these are usually large disc packs, holding as much as 90 million characters of data. The advantage of using discs is that design data can be retrieved rapidly for both the designer operating the graphics terminal and the plotter retrieving data for permanent drawings.

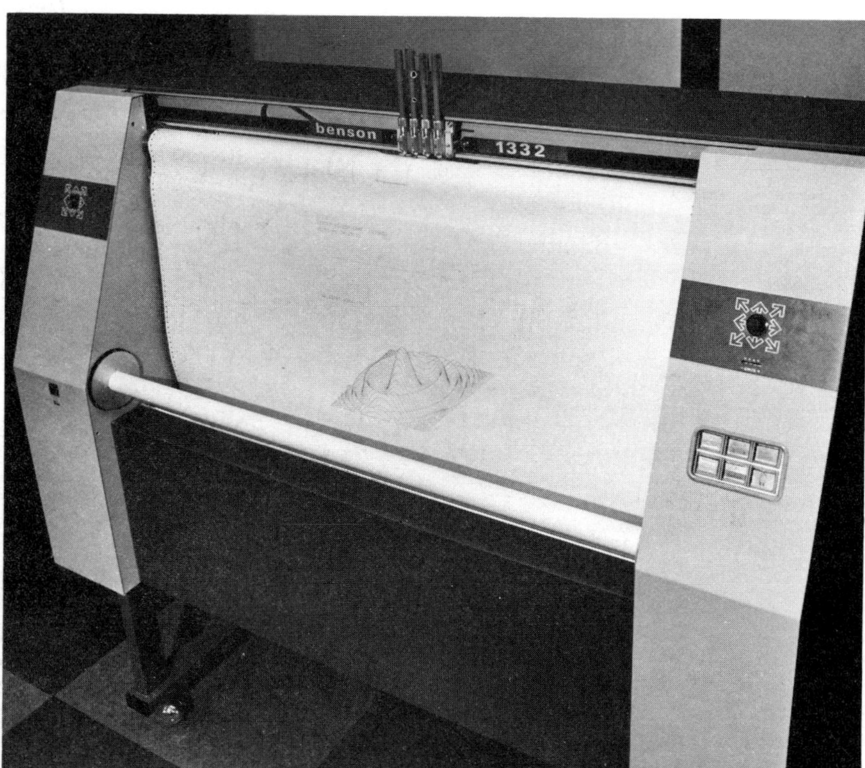

Drum plotter

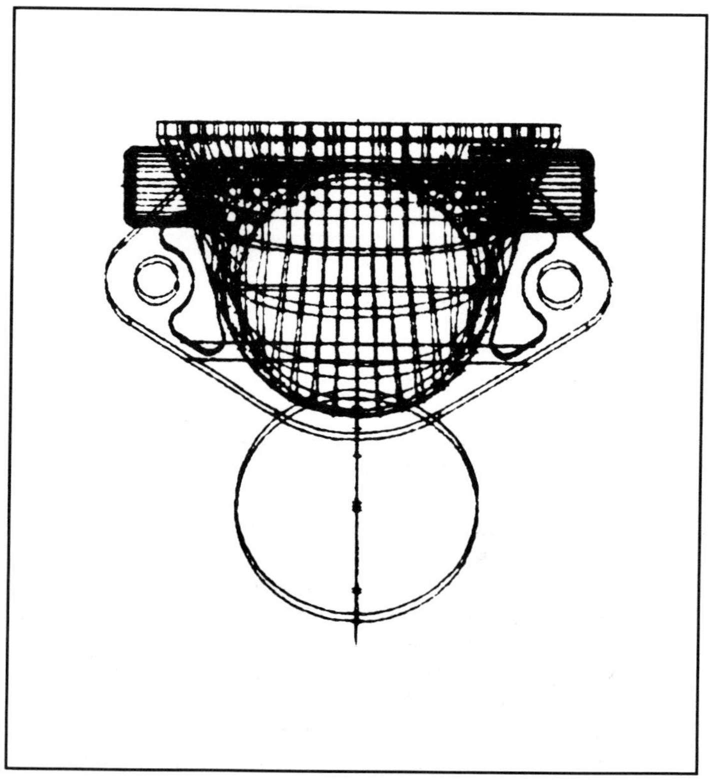

Right
Computer-drawn diagram of a carburettor elbow

British Leyland are using CAD in electric circuit and component design. The design drawing of a component that connects the air filter in a car engine to the carburettor is shown below.

The designer received all the details required for this part (sizes, shapes, hole positions, etc.) and constructed the drawing on the graphics terminal, making use of the graphics pad, the light pen and the VDU. He instructed the computer to calculate such things as surface area, weight and cross-sections.

British Leyland wanted to fit a valve inside this component, so the designer then called up various enlarged cross-sections of the drawing, and was able to calculate on the computer system the exact shape of the valve. This is shown on the hard copy below.

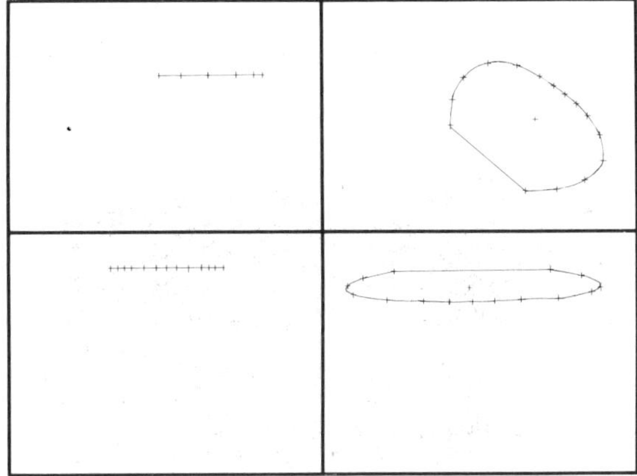

Previously a mould of the part would have been needed in order to manufacture the actual component.

To calculate the exact size of the valve, various cross-sections would have had to be cut from this actual part, so that internal measurements could be taken. All of these measurements would then have been used by the designer to produce another drawing of the valve. The valve would have been manufactured and then placed inside the carburettor part to see whether it did fit exactly.

However, with the use of the computer design system all of these jobs could be done on the graphics terminal in order to produce an exact design of the valve.

The flowcharts on the right illustrate the differences between normal methods of designing the valve and the computer-aided design.

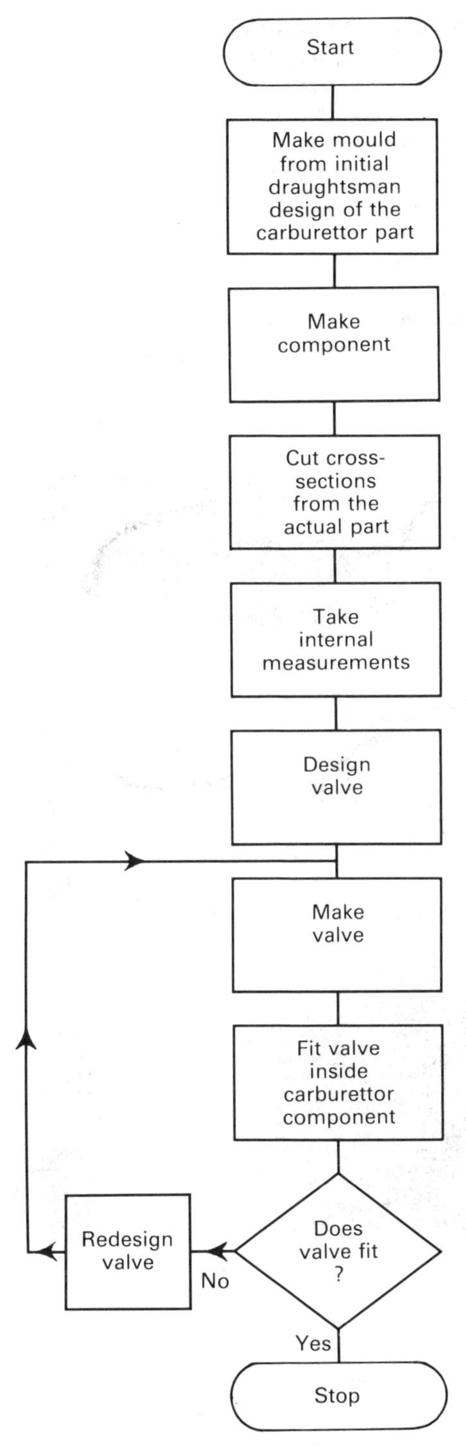

Left
Normal method of designing a valve

Below
CAD method of designing a valve

Start

Design parts and calculate valve sizes then draw the valve using graphics terminal, VDU, graphics pad, light pen, hard copier and flat bed plotter, along with mini-computer and backing store

Stop

The CAD system also allows 'exploded views' of components to be drawn for use in manuals.
A computer-produced human model can be moved about on the graphics screen to see whether such things as gear levers and seats are in the correct and most comfortable positions.

In order to produce designs for electronic circuits the menu on the graphics pad would be changed, so that other characters would be made available for the designer when using the light pen.

Computer drawings of a human model driving a car

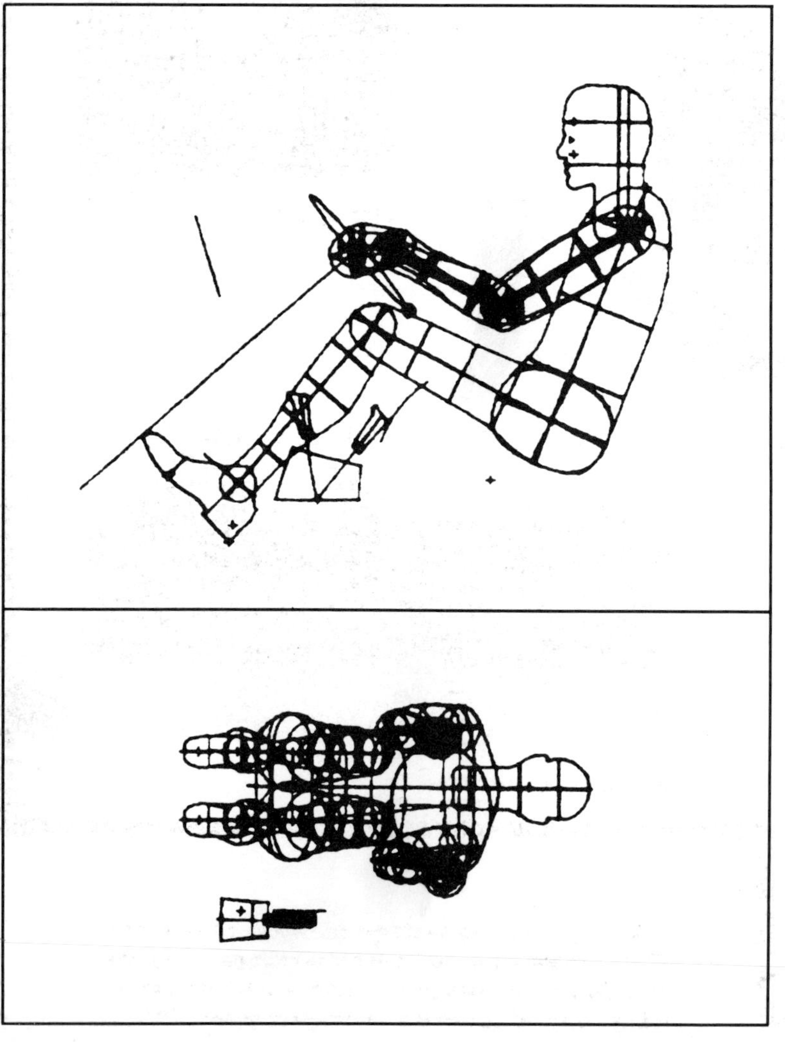

Exploded diagram

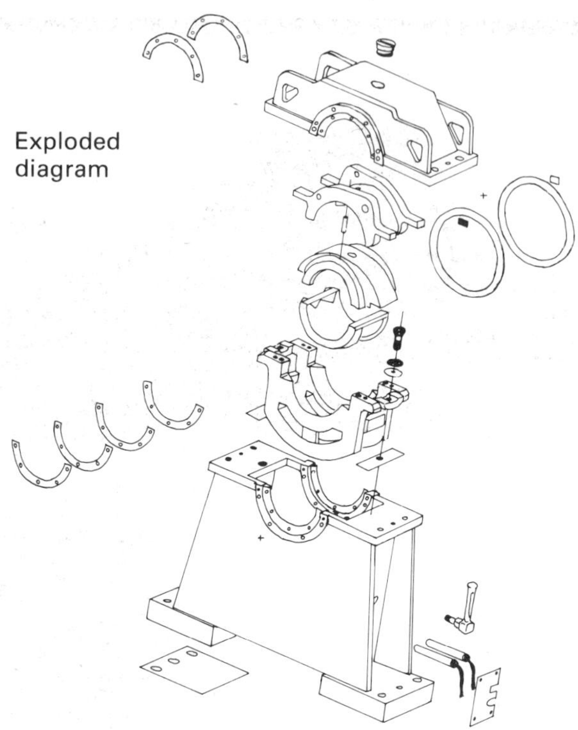

Computers in the office

In recent years, small computer systems based on micro-processor chips have become a common sight in offices.

These computers are used for many office jobs but particularly for word processing. Word processing is a system which enables the input, storage and retrieval of text in any form. The sort of information that can be stored includes letters, names, addresses, product names and prices. These systems allow data to be edited (that is, altered), deleted or inserted. For example, a letter containing a misspelt word can be corrected simply by changing the offending word, without retyping the whole letter.

The main power of a word processor lies in its ability to output text in almost any format. Many copies of a standard letter can be printed, each with a different name and address. Letters can also be constructed using a combination of standard paragraphs, and listings of stored data can be output in any chosen format.

OFFICE WORD-PROCESSING SYSTEM

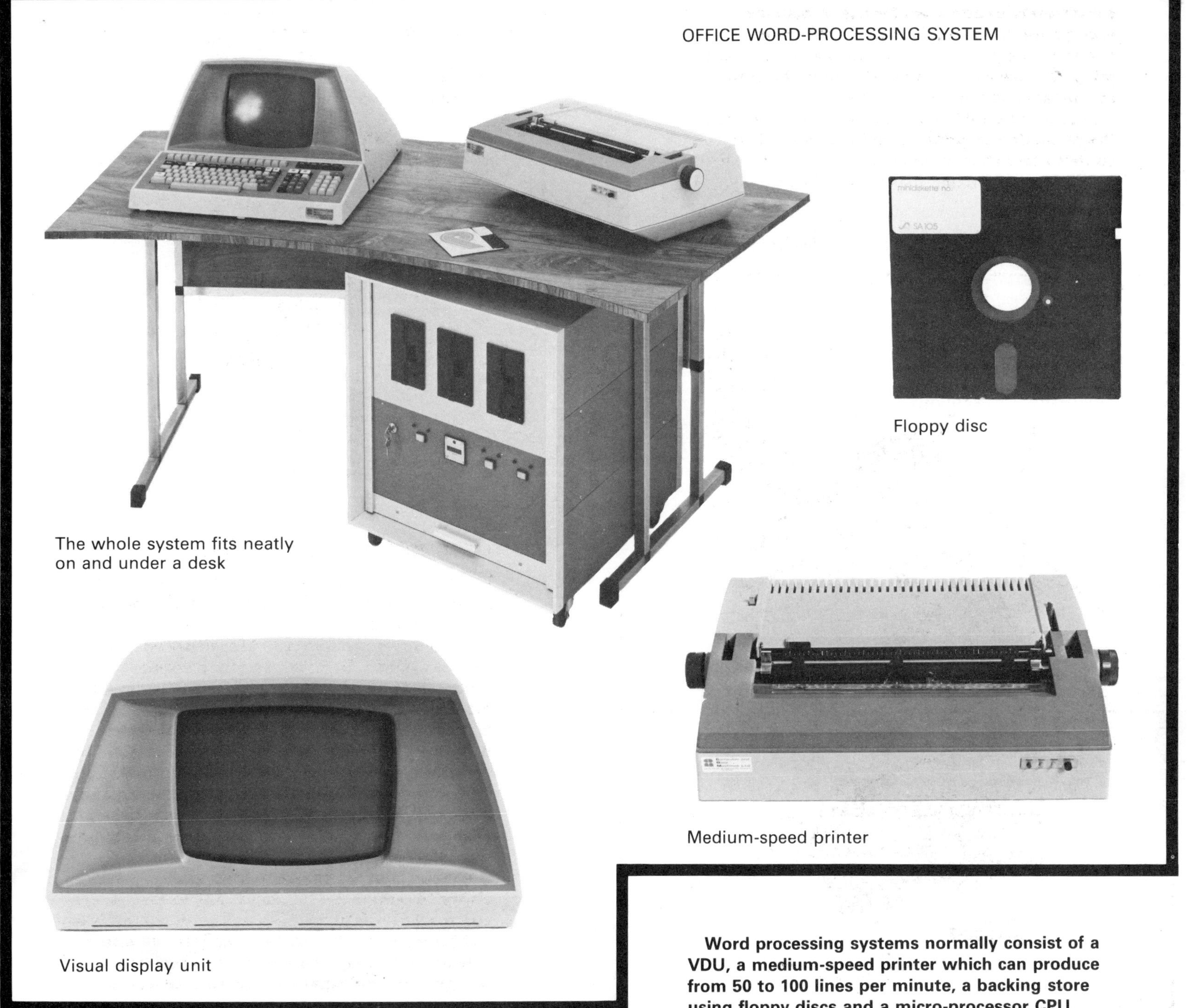

The whole system fits neatly on and under a desk

Floppy disc

Medium-speed printer

Visual display unit

Word processing systems normally consist of a VDU, a medium-speed printer which can produce from 50 to 100 lines per minute, a backing store using floppy discs and a micro-processor CPU.

Floppy discs have become popular because they are cheap and easy to use, and operators can quickly build up a library of data discs. The discs are made of flexible plastic coated with a ferric oxide, and they can have data recorded on them in the same way as on larger discs. Standard floppy discs can hold 290K characters of data. The software used in word processors needs to be efficient and compact and so it is written in assembly code.

Typical micro-computer

Modern micro-computers are cheap and relatively small, and therefore they are being used increasingly by small businesses. The complete system fits easily on a desk.

Business system with VDU, micro-computer and twin floppy disc unit

Such systems can be used for many standard data processing jobs including payroll, stock control and order processing. These kinds of job have been done for many years on main-frame computers and mini-computers. Now small organizations are using their micro-computers to do such jobs, instead of hiring time on other firms' machines.

Schools are also realizing that small computer systems are now within their budget. Systems can be purchased for about £1000 that will allow pupils to run their own programs in several different languages. Programs may be stored on ordinary cassette-recorders and displayed on a VDU.

Micro-computer system with cassette used as storage

Such systems are also useful in schools for things like pupil records and timetabling, and many programs are being written for use in other lessons besides computer studies. The ability of these systems to provide graphics on the VDU makes the micro-computer in school a very useful visual aid.

The systems are also very versatile, and once a small system has been bought it can easily be adapted to increase its store capacity and use floppy disc backing store.

Questions

1. Why is data held on disc backing store in the supermarket?
2. What items of data are likely to be held on disc?
3. What are the advantages of bar-coding in supermarkets for
   (a) the store manager,
   (b) the customer?
4. What disadvantages of bar-coding might there be to the customer?
5. Which of the following is not necessary when using bar codes in supermarkets?
   (a) a price on the goods,
   (b) an electronic point-of-sale terminal,
   (c) a check digit on the bar code,
   (d) a price on the shelf.
6. How is the bar code read and what does the computer do when the code has been accepted?
7. How does a flat bed plotter differ from a graph plotter?
8. Which of the following can a graphics terminal do?
   (a) enlarge a drawing,
   (b) construct a drawing,
   (c) choose the best drawing,
   (d) present a drawing from several different views.
9. Name the peripherals likely to be found in a computer-aided design system and state briefly why they are specifically required.
10. Describe the advantages of a CAD system over more normal, manual methods. Use the example of the carburettor component to help you with your answer.
11. Micro-computers have become increasingly popular in schools, offices and small businesses for which of the following reasons?
    (a) They are cheap to buy.
    (b) They are easy to operate.
    (c) They can do all the jobs that large main-frame computers can do.
    (d) They do not need a lot of people to operate them.
12. Describe the jobs that a word processor can do.
13. Why is it now possible for small businesses to install computers?
14. Describe a micro-computer system that may be used by schools.

Vocabulary

bar code
bar-code reader
check digit
computer-aided design (CAD)
digitizer
electronic point-of-sale terminal (EPOS)
flat bed plotter
graphics pad
graphics terminal
graph plotter
hard copier
light pen
menu
word processing

21 Social Implications

All the questions set in this chapter are taken from press cuttings that have appeared in the *Birmingham Post* and *Birmingham Mail* in the last two or three years.

1. These first two cuttings appear to contradict each other. Make a list of the arguments for and against computers causing redundancies.

Beware, a computer could give you the sack

DON'T annoy the computer or it may sack you, Britain's secretaries have been warned.

For 1984 has already arrived in some offices where machines can measure a typist's performance against an employer's target — and issue disciplinary warnings if it is not up to scratch. They can even time tea breaks!

White-collar union leader Mr. Roy Grantham said that this was only one short step away from letting computers fire people who did not comply with their warnings.

"There can be no appeal against the judgment of a machine," he said.

Mr. Grantham, general secretary of the Association of Professional, Executive, Clerical and Computer Staff, was speaking after a report by his union on the effects of new technology, which warns that 250,000 jobs could be lost by 1983 unless workers protect themselves by strong union organisation.

It says office workers should not try to ignore new technology, but should press for the wealth created to be used to open up new types of jobs.

It also urges unions not to oppose the productivity increases which will be made possible by new technology.

'Low mentality' robots are no threat to jobs

SCIENTISTS say no one should lose a job to the present generation of robots.

"The robots we are currently using in America are simple, low-mentality devices — but they are highly productive," said U.S. Robot Institute president John Wallace.

"While they can't replace a man, they can do many of the things that a man can do."

He was speaking in Washington where a collection of industrial robots performed various tasks — painting, lifting, drilling — at the ninth international symposium and exposition on industrial robots.

The group met to exchange information on robots and the complexities of their future role in society.

Scientists from Britain, West Germany, Japan, and the United States and representatives of industry said robots would not deprive humans of jobs.

"The present generation of robots are pretty moronic devices," said Prof. W. B. Heginbotham of Nottingham University.

"Most of our robot users emphasise improving the quality of working life," said Yukio Hosegawa, a Tokyo scientist.

2. **The police use computers to help store and retrieve information. Do you believe that they are justified in keeping all information because they are responsible for law and order, or do you see any possible dangers?**

Police computer plan 'is threat to freedom'

Evening Mail Reporter

A MAJOR row has blown up over a Midland police force's plan to spend £120,000 on extending its crime-busting computer.

West Mercia Police is planning the expansion to the computer, based at its headquarters at Hindlip Hall, near Worcester.

If the spending is approved by the authority it will mean that unproven evidence and hearsay allegations which could never be used in court will be stored in the computer. They will be made available to police forces throughout the country who have their own computers.

The scheme has been bitterly attacked by the National Council for Civil Liberties which says that the scheme represents a threat to personal freedom.

The Chief Constable of West Mercia, Mr. Alan Rennie, said that the computer extensions, if approved, would be used to store items of criminal intelligence as well as legitimate criminal records.

Danger

He said: "We already keep this information on paper and having it on computer will save time. It is not as though we shall be gathering new information that we do not keep already."

But Pat Hewitt, general secretary of the N.C.C.L., said: "These computer extensions will inevitably increase the amount of information available on people who may well be innocent.

"With the growth in electronics and computer frauds there is a danger that people who are not supposed to know may be able to find a way to get hold of this information."

Sign of the times

AS YOU KNOW, I love computers. And today, not a million miles from where I sit at my desk, I came across a sign that, for me, must herald the beginning of yet another big romance.

It said: "Our computer doesn't actually DO anything. We just blame it for everything."

I do, too.

3. **Read the cuttings below and overleaf concerning errors caused by computers. Is it true that computers make mistakes, or do you believe that all the errors were due to human failure? Give reasons for your answer.**

Why Donald Duck got £50,000 a year

From LANCE MORGAN
Mail Correspondent in Washington

FOR ONE day, not too long ago, Donald Duck was the highest-paid Federal employee in America.

Not even President Carter would get the single £50,000 cheque given to the cartoon character by a payroll computer at the Department of Housing and Urban Development.

In what is being called the "Walt Disney affair," the computer also approved cheques made out to Mickey and Minnie Mouse and 27 other fictitious characters who are not, to the best of anyone's knowledge, Federal workers.

Deliberately misleading information was fed into the computer by the Government Accounting Office (GAO) to see if the computer would spot the patently absurd payments. It didn't.

Now the watchdog GAO is accusing the government of shoddy and inadequate pay controls.

The GAO also was angered by discovery that one £6,500 a year government worker more than doubled his salary in overtime payments and that when a government-operated laundry room needed seven overtime workers one weekend, 21 were assigned for "morale reasons."

The revelations come at a time when the government is already under sharp attack for the unfolding bribery, theft and mismanagement scandal at the General Services Administration.

Recent investigations have uncovered widespread purchasing abuses, bribery and inefficiency that costs U.S. taxpayers an estimated £50 million a year.

Computer gives away millions

Evening Mail Reporter

MULTI - MILLION pound discrepancies have been shown up in an auditor's report on the finances of the West Midland Regional Health Authority.

It was revealed that the authority's computer in Birmingham has been issuing duplicate cheques —which could have been cashed without discovery.

And, in general accounting, the Government auditors complained of a giant "imbalance" of £2,517,235.

This was caused by the "incorrect treatment" of transactions between area health authorities and regional headquarters in Birmingham.

Mr. Kenneth Bales, regional administrator, said today: "No money has, in fact, gone adrift.

"What happened was that our old computer had a stopping device when it ran out of paper. The new ICL 1904 machines has no such attachment. It just goes on printing the last cheque."

He said the £2,500,000-plus discrepancy was over a method of book-keeping at regional headquarters which the "auditors did not like."

'Computer jam' on £13m road

Mercury Staff Reporter

BIRMINGHAM'S £13 million Aston Expressway, with the most sophisticated traffic controls in the country still relies on the policeman's waving arm to prevent accident snarl-ups—the same as any country lane.

The traffic could be diverted by the gantry signals which are controlled by a computer that is supposed to deal with "every contingency and emergency likely to occur."

But three years after the £7 million-a-mile super road opened, the computer has not been programmed to do the job.

Puncture

And, following a two-hour chaos in January when a lorry had a puncture the police have decided that the old-fashioned "bobby and cone" technique is the only emergency procedure they can apply.

A senior police spokesman revealed last night that the electronic signalling is stuck virtually in one position. They cannot change the "no entry" signs to divert the traffic automatically.

The police have asked for the computer to be re-programmed and tomorrow a re-think of the control system will be urged at a meeting of the West Midland highways and transportation committee.

The computer system, which is said to be the most advanced in the country, was designed to complement the controversial "red reversible" centre lane system, which has never been used.

Many people are worried about the effect that computers will have on their lives. Others see the development of the use of computers as a step forward that will bring many benefits.

When computers first came into use, some people thought that because these machines were able to do jobs previously done by humans, half the working population would become unemployed, or that there would be a twenty-hour working week before long. Few foresaw the number of jobs that would be created by the new industries of manufacturing, maintaining, installing and programming computers.

The computer has taken on the more mundane and repetitive jobs in the office and on the production line, which has resulted in changes in staffing. The government has recognized the need for retraining people for employment in new industries, and several retraining schemes have been established. However, it is not only the unskilled worker who has been affected, for the computer has also taken on much of the statistical analysis of sales and costs previously done by management.

The overall effect is not a significant reduction in the *number* of jobs, but a change in the *type* of job available. Fewer unskilled workers are needed and there is an increased emphasis on education and training. The trades unions have been concerned about the introduction of 'silicon-chip technology' and have insisted that they are kept informed of all developments, particularly when there is a possibility of redundancies, or retraining or regrading of staff.

Another problem concerns the vast amount of information held in computer data banks. Throughout our lives data is being assembled about us by organizations such as the Department of Education and Science, the Department of Health and Social Security, banks, the Post Office, insurance companies, tax offices, mail-order companies, trades unions, gas and electricity companies, hire-purchase companies, the Ministry of Transport and the police: the list is immense. There have, of course, always been manual files kept by such organizations, but the computer allows files to be kept more conveniently, with vastly improved means of accessing, storing and maintaining data.

The worry is that an individual often does not know that the files exist or what information is on them. If personal information is made available to other organizations it can have a damaging effect on individuals, and so stringent efforts are made by those who control data banks to ensure that the information in them is safe.

Computer files are probably more secure than old manual files, and designers of computers do take great care to make access to data available only to authorized users. Governments have not yet legislated on the matter of personal data files but it has been suggested that a Data Protection Authority should be set up.

Micro-computers have made computer applications more varied because of their low cost and small size. It is possible that many more changes in our lives will occur, and more jobs will be taken over by machines. Personal computers may well become part of every home just like a television set.

One important consideration is that we may need to accept far more leisure time and a shorter working day or week. This would of course produce additional problems. Do we have enough facilities for leisure? Should schools in the future be concerned to educate young people to enjoy and benefit from increased leisure time?

The computer and the technology associated with it have changed our lives and will continue to do so. *We as individuals, and our governments, must take care to see that these changes are for the better.* This can be done, of course, only if future generations are educated in the ways of computers: their benefits and abuses.

Appendix

Subtraction using complements in decimal

If you wanted to do the subtraction

$73 - 46 = 27$

you would probably exchange a ten. We shall try a different method.

First we subtract 46 from 99:

$99 - 46 = 53$

The answer (53) is called the nine's complement **of 46. Instead of subtracting 46 from 73, we next *add* 53 (the nine's complement of 46) to 73:**

$73 + 53 = 126$

Finally, we knock off the 1 at the left of 126 and add it to the units digit:

$126 \rightarrow 26 + 1 = 27$

This gives 27, which is the answer we get by subtracting in the normal way.

Here is another example:

Example Subtract 387 from 572

Since the numbers in this sum have three digits, we find the nine's complement of 387 by subtracting 387 from 999:

nine's complement of 387 $= 999 - 387 = 612$

Next we add this to 572:

$572 + 612 = 1184$

Finally, we knock off the 1 at the left and add it to the units digit:

$1184 \rightarrow 184 + 1 = 185$

So the answer is 185.

Check that the answer is the same if the normal method of subtracting is used.

Why does this method work?

The method uses the fact that

$100 = 99 + 1, \quad 1000 = 999 + 1,$ and so on.

Let's look again at how we did the first example above (73 − 46). First we found the nine's complement of 46:

nine's complement of 46 $= 99 - 46 \quad (= 53)$

Then we added this to 73 to get

$73 + 99 - 46 \quad (= 126)$

Next we subtracted 100 (by knocking off the 1 at the left) and added 1 to the units digit to get

$73 + 99 - 46 - 100 + 1 \quad (= 27)$

and found that this gave us the right answer to 73 − 46 (= 27).

We can see why by rearranging:

$73 + 99 - 46 - 100 + 1 = 73 - 46 + \underline{99 + 1 - 100}$

Since 100 = 99 + 1, the numbers underlined give zero, so

$73 + 99 - 46 - 100 + 1 = 73 - 46$

Therefore, working out

$73 + 99 - 46 - 100 + 1$ **gives the same answer as working out 73 − 46 directly.**

The method works in the same way for the second example (572 − 387). First we found the nine's complement of 387:

nine's complement of 387 $= 999 - 387 \quad (= 612)$

Then we added this to 572 to get

$572 + 999 - 387 \quad (= 1184)$

Next we subtracted 1000 and added 1 to get

$572 + 999 - 387 - 1000 + 1 \quad (= 185)$

Rearranging this gives

$572 + 999 - 387 - 1000 + 1 =$
$572 - 387 + \underline{999 + 1 - 1000}$

Here the numbers underlined give zero because 1000 = 999 + 1, so we are left with

$572 + 999 - 387 - 1000 + 1 = 572 - 387$

Therefore our indirect method again gives the same answer as subtracting 387 from 572 in the normal way.

Let's see how we can use the method to solve 653 − 27. First we must make the number of digits in the two numbers in the sum the same. We do this by replacing 27 by 027. The value remains the same:

027 = 27

From this point the method is exactly the same as before.

The numbers in the sum now both have three digits so we find the nine's complement of 027 by subtracting it from 999:

nine's complement of 027 = 999 − 027 = 972

Next we add this to 653:

653 + 972 = 1625

Finally we knock off the 1 at the left and add it to the units digit:

1625 → 625 + 1 = 626

Check that 626 is the right answer by doing the subtraction in the normal way.

Index

Addenda

Translating BASIC

The language called BASIC is used in most schools. Unlike many other high-level languages, which use a compiler (see p. 101), BASIC can be translated using an interpreter.

An interpreter allows each separate BASIC statement in a program to be executed as it is read from the computer store. This means that any errors can be diagnosed straight away. The programmer can then immediately change the offending piece of BASIC code. Also, errors may be detected as soon as the line of BASIC is entered through a keyboard.

In this way programs may be easily debugged (checked for errors). A program that uses an interpreter will run until an error is signalled.

If a compiler is used to translate BASIC, no errors are signalled until the complete program has been translated into a compiled form. The source program is then corrected as necessary and the whole program translated again.

Thus use of a compiler can make program writing very time consuming. However, when correct, the object program will run far more quickly in compiled form than it would if an interpreter was used.

The main advantage of an interpreter is that it allows interaction between the user and the computer in diagnosis of errors.